Richard Holloway Steele

Historical Discourse Delivered at the Celebration of the 150th Anniversary of the First Reformed Dutch Church

Richard Holloway Steele

Historical Discourse Delivered at the Celebration of the 150th Anniversary of the First Reformed Dutch Church

ISBN/EAN: 9783744752732

Printed in Europe, USA, Canada, Australia, Japan

Cover: Foto ©ninafisch / pixelio.de

More available books at **www.hansebooks.com**

HISTORICAL DISCOURSE

DELIVERED AT THE

CELEBRATION

OF THE

One Hundred and Fiftieth Anniversary

OF THE

FIRST REFORMED DUTCH CHURCH,

NEW-BRUNSWICK, N. J.,

OCTOBER 1, 1867.

BY

RICHARD H. STEELE, D.D.,

PASTOR OF THE CHURCH.

NEW-BRUNSWICK, N. J.:
PUBLISHED BY THE CONSISTORY.
1867.

JOHN A. GRAY & GREEN, PRINTERS, 16 AND 18 JACOB STREET, NEW-YORK.

PREFACE.

The First Reformed Dutch Church of New-Brunswick, N. J., completed her One Hundred and Fiftieth year, April 12th, 1867. The precise date of organization was not ascertained until quite recently. No written history of the church has ever been published. The task would have been one of comparative ease fifty years ago. Then the children of the early settlers were still living; records were in existence which have since perished with the disuse of the Dutch language; and important documents which would have been of great value in forming our narrative have been lost or destroyed. The recovery of our early book of records, incomplete as it is, has been of incalculable benefit. But I have searched in vain for publications of Rev. Mr. Leydt, Jacobus Schureman, Hendrick Fisher, and papers relating to the controversies during the times of Rev. T. J. Frelinghuysen, which are known to have been in existence at the beginning of the century.

We have endeavored to produce a history during a long period when there were no records of consistory kept, and have gathered many of our facts from traditions which yet remain with some distinctness among the people. Our work is not complete, but that we have given to it no small amount of labor will be understood by those who have undertaken similar productions. It will be found to present many facts extending beyond our particular church, and embrace materials relating to the town of interest to all our citizens.

The pastor would express his particular acknowledgments to his own people who have kindly assisted him in his investigations, and have directed him to sources of important information. He has found the volumes of William A. Whitehead, Esq., and the Historical Discourse of Rev. Mr. Corwin, of great value in compiling the early part of his narrative. He is indebted to the publications of Dr. Messler and Rev. William Demarest, in writing his history of the life and ministry of Rev. Mr. Frelinghuysen. Dr. W. B. Sprague has kindly given him access to his unpublished volume of the biographies of ministers of the Reformed Dutch Church, which we hope will soon be issued from the press. His thanks are due to Rev. Mr. Demarest, for translations from the Dutch of letters of Jufvrow Hardenbergh, and for extracts from her journal; to Mrs. Hanson, for important information in reference to her father, Dr. Condict; to Hon. Ralph Voorhees, for papers relating to his ancestor, Minne Van Voorhees, and for the draft prepared by himself and Mr. N. W. Parsells, from which was produced the accurate sketch, by Mr. Thomas N. Doughty, of the "Old Stone Church" erected in 1767, and which gave such interest to our Anniversary; to Mr. John W. Warnshuise, for his assistance in translating our early Dutch records; and to the surviving pastors especially for their information and encouragement in preparing the history.

The Historical Discourse, which comprises the main body of this volume, owes its publication to the following action of Consistory, communicated through a committee appointed for that purpose:

"NEW-BRUNSWICK, October 8, 1867.
"REV. RICHARD H. STEELE, DD.:

"DEAR SIR: By the unanimous resolution of Consistory, we hereby thank you for the valuable and interesting Historical Discourse delivered October 1st, 1867, on the occasion of the One Hundred and Fiftieth Anniversary of the founding of our church, and request you to furnish a copy for publication, with suitable notes and appendices, together with the sermon preached on the succeeding Sabbath.

"Very sincerely yours,
LEWIS APPLEGATE,
JOHNSON LETSON."

The Anniversary was celebrated on the day mentioned in the above note, with suitable commemorative exercises. Invitations had been extended to former members of the congregation and their descendants, to unite with us in the services connected with this interesting occasion. On the morning of that day the following Discourse was in part delivered; but as the material which had been gathered was deemed too important to be lost, it is now committed to the press as it was originally prepared.

The account of the celebration, with the addresses delivered on the occasion, forming the second part of this volume, was prepared under the direction of the committee, and will be found a correct transcript of an Anniversary long to be remembered.

The pastor sends forth this volume among his people and the friends of the church, with the prayer that this humble effort to produce the history of one of the most important congregations of our denomination, may be the means of awakening within us a new sense of our responsibility to the Lord Jesus Christ, and serve to advance the interests of the Redeemer's kingdom.

PARSONAGE HOUSE, No. 106 GEORGE STREET,
NEW-BRUNSWICK, N. J., December 1, 1867.

One Hundred and Fiftieth Anniversary

OF THE

FIRST REFORMED DUTCH CHURCH,

NEW-BRUNSWICK, OCTOBER 1, 1867.

———•••———

The following was the Order of Exercises:

Invocation and Reading the Scriptures.
REV. GABRIEL LUDLOW, D.D.

Prayer.
REV. ISAAC FERRIS, D.D.

Singing.
Celebration Hymn, Written by REV. PETER STRYKER, D.D.

Historical Discourse.
REV. RICHARD H. STEELE, D.D.

Singing.
Ode, Written by PROF. DAVID MURRAY.

Benediction.
REV. THOMAS DE WITT, D.D.

———◆———

AFTERNOON.

Anthem.
BY THE CHOIR.

Addresses.
REV. THOMAS DE WITT, D.D.
REV. S. M. WOODBRIDGE, D.D.
REV. CHARLES S. HAGEMAN, D.D.
REV. WILLIAM H. CAMPBELL, D.D.
REV. P. D. VAN CLEEF, D.D.
REV. DAVID D. DEMAREST, D.D.

Poem.
PROF. DAVID MURRAY.

Prayer.
REV. P. D. OAKEY.

Doxology. *Benediction.*

———◆———

EVENING.

Reading the Scriptures and Prayer.
REV. PROF. JOSEPH F. BERG, D.D.

Singing.
The Third Jubilee, Written by REV. JOHN B. STEELE.

Address.
By Senior Ex-Pastor REV. ISAAC FERRIS, D.D.

Doxology. *Benediction.*

Part First.

SUCCESSION OF PASTORS,

AND

HISTORICAL DISCOURSE,

BY

RICHARD H. STEELE D.D.

SUCCESSION OF PASTORS

OF THE

FIRST REFORMED DUTCH CHURCH,

NEW-BRUNSWICK.

1. THEODORUS JACOBUS FRELINGHUYSEN,   1720 to 1748.
2. JOHANNES LEYDT,   1748 " 1783.
3. JACOB RUTSEN HARDENBERGH, D.D.,   1786 " 1790.
4. IRA CONDICT, D.D.,   1793 " 1811.
5. JOHN SCHUREMAN, D.D.,   1812 " 1813.
6. JESSE FONDA,   1813 " 1817.
7. JOHN LUDLOW, D.D.,   1817 " 1819.
8. ISAAC FERRIS, D.D.,   1821 " 1824.
9. JAMES B. HARDENBERGH, D.D.,   1825 " 1829.
10. JACOB J. JANEWAY, D.D.,   1830 " 1831.
11. SAMUEL B. HOW, D.D.,   1832 " 1861.
12. RICHARD H. STEELE, D.D.,   1863.

HISTORICAL DISCOURSE.

The Scottish Pilgrim, it is said, in a spirit of pious veneration, visited the graves of those who had died martyrs of religion. His purpose was to refresh his own mind, and revive in the hearts of his countrymen the record of their noble lives, their heroic endurances, and their triumphant deaths. With engraver's chisel, he went from churchyard to churchyard over that land of martyrs, and on the fading stone he reproduced the record of their names, their sufferings, and their renown. Our undertaking this morning will resemble that of "Old Mortality;" for we are to recall the names and revive the record of a noble race of men, who, more than one hundred and fifty years ago, laid the foundation of our civil and religious institutions, and whose early sacrifices and toils, and earnest piety and devotion, should be held by us in sacred remembrance.

I am to give you a sketch of the history of the origin, the progress, the struggles, and the triumphs of the Reformed Protestant Dutch Church of New-Brunswick. This is the oldest religious organization in this city, reliable authorities fixing its origin in the early part of the last century, and making it coeval with the first settlement of this locality. The period itself is remote and interesting. The most wonderful movements of Divine Providence in the civil and ecclesiastical history of the world were centring around this period, giving an impulse to emigration, and marking out the distinctive character of the early settlers. In England, the nation had not yet subsided from that mighty civil commotion which had elevated William, Prince of Orange, to the throne, and reasserted the supremacy of those fundamental laws of the land which had so long and tyrannically been disregarded by the reigning power. The revocation of the Edict of Nantes, under Louis XIV., had driven into exile more than five hundred thousand of the most industrious and learned citizens of France, who carried with them the higher type of civilization and religion in which the Protestants greatly excelled, into those countries which they selected as their homes. The Dutch Republic, though shorn of its maritime strength, had obtained a supremacy in literature and religion, as well as in its system of civil toleration, which rendered it the model government of the world.

Matthew Henry had not yet completed his Exposition of the Bible. James Saurin had only recently commenced the labors of the ministry at the Hague. John Wesley had not yet been raised up to stem the prevailing tide of formalism. In Holland, her divines were justly celebrated for their extensive learning and deep piety, while her universities and schools attracted students from all parts of the world. The celebrated Marck, in his theological chair at Leyden, made this university one of the most renowned on the continent of Europe. Vitringa, noted for his accurate interpretations of the Bible and his eloquence as a preacher, gave celebrity to the institution at Francker. At Utrecht, some of the most brilliant lights shone from the chairs of theology and literature. And in the pulpit we find the names of such distinguished divines as Brakel, Vanderkemp, and Hellenbrook, whose sound views of truth and deep learning still shine conspicuously in their voluminous theological writings. The first English copy of the Bible had just been published in the American Colonies. The third college had just been founded at New-Haven; one newspaper, published on a half-sheet of foolscap, was regularly issued at Boston; the largest city was New-York, a hamlet of about six thousand inhabitants; and the total population of the colonies had not yet reached five hundred thousand. There were a few towns located in the Province of New-Jersey, and only two ministers of our denomination in the State.*

In compiling the history of this church, I have labored under the difficulty experienced in other quarters, of the imperfection of early Consistorial records and the loss of important documents. By diligent search I have recovered possession of a volume in the Dutch language, which had been lost for upward of thirty years, containing much valuable information. Some important facts are stated in reference to the origin of this church, as also that of Six Mile Run. It contains the names of the first Consistory, a complete list of the original members, a register of the additions to the church at each communion, and a full record of baptisms. The first entry in this volume bears the date of April 12th, 1717, and we are celebrating the one hundred and fiftieth anniversary of the founding of the Reformed Dutch Church of New-Brunswick. It is to be regretted that the proceedings of Consistory were not more carefully

---

* Rev. Guilliam Bertholf was the minister of the church at Hackensack and Aquackononck from 1694 to 1724; and Rev. Joseph Morgan was settled at Freehold and Middletown from 1709 to 1731.

recorded and preserved, in the absence of which we shall have to depend upon such facts as we can glean from the published minutes of ecclesiastical bodies, the historical incidents found in early records, and the traditions of the people.

Previous to commencing the history of the church, I will be expected to give a succinct sketch of the settlement and development of the civil history of this city and country adjacent. My labor will consist in arranging materials already in existence, and in bringing to light some facts which are concealed in civil and ecclesiastical documents.

The earliest instrument fixing the boundary of the State of New-Jersey is a deed or conveyance granted by the Duke of York, June 23d, 1664, to two proprietors, Sir James Berkley and Sir George Carteret. In the following year, Philip Carteret, brother of Sir George, came over as governor of this province, and devised liberal plans for the encouragement of emigration. His plans were successful, and many families from New-England, enticed by the liberal constitution which he had framed, took up lands, and made this their home. These settlements were principally made in that portion of the territory which was most convenient of access from New-York. The south side of the Raritan river was not settled until about twenty years after a large emigration from New-England had purchased lands and located in the towns of Bergen, Woodbridge, Piscataway, and Elizabethtown. About this time a small colony located at Shrewsbury, and several families from Long Island settled at Middletown, in the county of Monmouth. These were the principal settlements up to this date in this section of the State.

On the death of Sir George Carteret, in 1679, the

whole of East-Jersey passed into the hands of his executors, who continued to carry forward the government for the benefit of his estate, until a sale of the property should be accomplished according to the provisions of his will. This sale was effected in 1682, to a company of twelve proprietors, for the sum of £3400. In order to divide up their interests, and spread information respecting their possessions, twelve additional partners were received into the company, to which board as now constituted the Duke of York made a new grant, March 14th, 1682. Previous to this new arrangement, and while East New-Jersey was still in the possession of the executors of Sir George Carteret, a portion of the territory on which the city of New-Brunswick now stands, and above us on the south side of the Raritan, was surveyed and laid out into lots. It is to the credit of the early proprietors of our State that the land was purchased of the Indians by honorable and voluntary transactions, and thus the settlers were saved from the jealousies and dangers which other portions of the American Colonies experienced. Such a purchase was made in June, 1681, by John Inians & Co., for the benefit of Lady Elizabeth Carteret, "the present lady proprietrix of the province," of a tract of land embracing about ten thousand acres, called by the Indians Ahanderhamock.* This tract of land is described in the Indian deed as lying on the south side of the Raritan river, and opposite the town of Piscataway, under-

* The purchase was made of the Indians Quaramark, Sacamaker, and Camacamo, representing the Queramacks and Camacoms. The amount paid was 200 fathoms of white wampum, 10 blankets, 20 Duffield coats, 10 guns, 10 kettles—two of them eight gallons—26 yards stroud waters (?), 25 axes, 20 pairs of stockings, 20 shirts, 5 made coats, 4 pistols, 60 bars of lead, ½ barrel powder, 25 pairs tobacco tongs, 2 ankers of rum, 2 half-fatts of beer, ½ anker of molasses, 1 tramel, 60 knives, 20 tobacco boxes, 25 shot, ½ cwt. of bread.— *See Records of Proprietors, Amboy*, vol. ii. lib. i. p. 152.

stood to commence at what is now called Lawrence brook, and running along the river to near Boundbrook. A portion of this territory was shortly after surveyed and sold to different parties, and were subsequently known as the Raritan lots.

November 10th, 1681, John Inians,* one of this company, and a merchant of New-York, purchased a portion of this tract containing twelve hundred and eighty acres, bounded on the north-east by the Raritan river, on the west by Andrew Bowne, south-east and south-west by land not yet surveyed.† This was the first purchase of land in what is now the city of New-Brunswick, the line of which is still preserved in some of our ancient deeds. The starting-point was a white oak-tree standing at the foot of Albany street, opposite the Bell tavern; thence up the river one mile to a point near the residence of J. Warren Scott, Esq.; thence in a south-westerly direction for two miles, or near the property known as the Brunson tavern; thence one mile south-easterly to a point intersecting the Trenton turn-pike; thence two miles north-easterly, entering the city along Livingston avenue, to the starting-point at the foot of Albany street. The ten lots immediately north of Inians's patent contained each five hundred acres.‡

---

* John Inians, of Raritan river, was appointed a member of Governor Hamilton's Council on September 14th, 1692. (*Whitehead's East-Jersey*, p. 134.) Nothing is known of his place of residence or his history; but that he was a very extensive purchaser of lands, and a man of great wealth for the times, is inferred from his large transactions found on the Records of Proprietors at Amboy, and volumes of deeds at Trenton.

† It is described as beginning at a white oak-tree, from thence running as the river runs eighty chains, thence running south-west one hundred and sixty chains, thence south-east eighty chains, thence two miles to the tree from whence it first began. The land extending west of the Raritan lots, embracing nearly all the original territory of the Three Mile Run, New-Brunswick, and Six Mile Run congregations, was laid out into four large plots, for a description of which see Appendix I., furnished by Rev. Mr. Corwin.

‡ They were owned by Andrew Bowne, Richard Jones, George Foreman, Joseph Snelling, Andrew Gibb, Gershom Browne, Jeremiah Tothill, Joseph

South of the city, Thomas Lawrence owned three thousand acres, embracing the stream which since his purchase has been called Lawrence brook. This tract of land subsequently came into the possession of Cornelius Longfield* and Governor Barclay, while that of Inians was purchased by Philip French,† under whose supervision farms were surveyed, streets laid out, and building-lots sold.

The government of the twenty-four proprietors was so liberal, and contrasted so favorably with the adjoining province of New-York, that settlers began to pour in from every direction, and for the next twenty years the population increased with great rapidity. The landholders used every effort to induce emigration by the liberal terms they offered, the glowing accounts they sent abroad of the salubrity of the climate, the productiveness of the soil, and the peaceful character of the natives. The original settlers in our immediate vicinity were Dutch ‡ and French Protestants, or Hu-

Benbrigge, Thomas Mathew, and Edmond Gibbon. The map of Mr. Corwin, giving the Raritan lots, was compiled from Reed's map, 1685, four years after the original purchase, and indicates the rapid changes which were now taking place, as they had nearly all passed into new hands.

* This land, constituting a part of the lower section of the city, Longfield purchased June 6th, 1689, described as lying on the Raritan river, opposite a meadow or marsh belonging to Charles Gilman; about one chain and a half below where a small run of water or brook falls into said river, from thence running south to a brook called Lawrence brook, and by the Indians Piscopock, from thence running down said Lawrence brook to the Raritan river, and along the Raritan to the place of beginning. John Ryder bought one hundred and fifty-four acres of Longfield, March 11th, 1741, which farm is still owned by his descendants.—*Parchment Deed of*—— *Ryder*.

† He owned a large tract opposite the city and in the vicinity. Instead of selling the property he ordinarily leased it, in some instances for two thousand years. Through reverses during the Revolutionary War he became involved, and assigned his estate to James Parker, whose son, Hon. James Parker, Jr., of Amboy, gave to the trustees of Queen's College the lot on which the present buildings stand.

‡ In a letter to the proprietors, March, 1684, Gawen Lowrie represents the Dutch settlers as very numerous, and speaks of a number who are desiring to take up land and settle in the province.— *Whitehead's East-Jersey*, p. 289.

Several Dutch families are known to have settled on the Raritan very

guenots,* and we can fix the date of their occupancy of this territory as early as 1684. The country back of us, covering the rich farming lands of Three Mile Run, Middlebush, Six Mile Run, and onward to the Millstone, and both above and below us on the Raritan, was filled up when the central portion of our town was only known after the name of its proprietor as "Prigmore's Swamp." Early residents, in writing to their friends at home, represent the Dutch settlers along the Raritan as quite numerous and industrious. They were principally from Long Island and places adjacent. The prevailing cause of their emigration was the discontent that existed among them in consequence of the oppressive measures pursued by the civil authorities, in vexing them in reference to their religious preference and belief. These harsh measures drove out of Long Island and the vicinity of New-York a large population, who found in this territory, under the more judicious toleration of the proprietors, perfect religious freedom, and room for their love of honest industry.

There were other inducements inviting into our State the Hollanders from New-York. Their motive in emigration from the fatherland was different from that which prevailed with the Puritans of New-England, and the Scotch and Irish Presbyterians who settled in other localities. The latter were driven out of their country by persecution, and sought in the New World freedom in religious worship. The former had enjoyed

early. Hendrick Vroome, at the landing on the farm of the late Mr. Mundy; George Anderson, on the property recently Dr. McClintock's; the brothers Christopher and Jacob Probasco, on what is now the residence of Mr. Livingston.

* In our early records we find the names of several French emigrants, among them many undoubtedly of the proscribed Huguenot race, who had been expelled from the kingdom on account of their Protestant principles. De Peyster, Rappleyea, Van Duyn, La Montes, Le Queer, La Montague, and others.

ample toleration in their own little republic, and came across the water to "better their condition," and "build up another university that should rival Leyden, and another city that should outshine Amsterdam."* Their youth had been spent in a land which had been rescued from the encroachments of the sea by artificial embankments, and they had learned the art of industry long before they had encountered the hardships of this new land. Coming over the water with such intentions, they naturally sought the best soil and climate, and situations where they could build up their institutions with less fear of molestation. All these advantages the Province of New-Jersey afforded, and its very location reminded them of their former Belgian homes, while the facilities afforded them for sending their produce to the growing markets of Amboy† and New-York by river communication, urged a new motive for their emigration. Proverbially fond of water-courses, and of the flat country which reminded them of their old homes in Holland, they bought farms running down to the Raritan as they had opportunity, and showed their Dutch caution by not getting too far inland.

The earliest reference we have to the particular locality where New-Brunswick now stands is in the

---

* See "Oration on the Conquest of New-Netherland," before the New-York Historical Society, by the historian, J. Romeyn Brodhead. He says with great force: "It was for the true interest of America that New-York was founded by the Batavian race. That founding produced our own magnanimous and cosmopolitan State, the influence of which on our nation has always been so happy and so healthful."

† The design of the settlers was to make Amboy the first city of New-Jersey—the "London of America." A city charter was granted August 24th, 1718, by Governor Robert Hunter. Its fine harbor, eligible situation, and healthy locality would seem to indicate a rapid growth. But, as the historian Smith remarks in 1765, by a fatality it never became a place of extensive trade. Samuel Groom, the surveyor-general at its first settlement in 1683, with an eye to its future history, laments, "If no help comes, it will be long ere Amboy be built as London is."—*Whitehead's Amboy*, pp. 2, 6, 50, 54.

account of a traveler by the name of William Edmundson,* a minister of the society of Friends in England, who passed through the State with an Indian guide in 1677, on what was then an Indian path, afterward erected into a public highway. After crossing the ford at this place at low water, and penetrating inland about ten miles, he lost his way in the wilderness, and was a whole day in retracing his path to the Raritan river. At night he encamped in the woods, kindling a fire for protection from the wild animals. This Indian path was afterward erected into an important road, passing through the State from Elizabethtown Point to a spot on the Delaware river in the vicinity of Trenton. The travel on this route became a matter of so much importance that a grant was given to John Inians and his wife, December 2d, 1697, to ferry passengers across the river, for which privilege he was to pay the annual rent of five shillings sterling.† The place was called "Inians's Ferry" or "The River" for about eighteen years.

Probably about this date (1697) a few buildings began to spring up around this centre, wharves were built at the foot of Albany street, and vessels from Amboy and New-York began to make their regular trips. Mechanics set up their places of business for the accommodation of their neighbors, and enterprising shopkeepers erected their stores and exposed their wares to the farmers who came down to the river for barter or

---

* See *Whitehead's East-Jersey*, p. 95.
† The ferry at first provided only for pedestrians and horsemen. Even in 1716, in the rates allowed by the Assembly, mention only is made of "horse and man" and "single persons." The facilities for traveling did not develop very rapidly. In 1704, the New-York paper complains that in the "pleasant month of May, the last storm put our Pennsylvania mail a *week behind, and is not yet com'd in.*"—*Whitehead's Amboy*, pp. 269, 273; *East-Jersey*, 162.

news. This was the beginning of our town. The name of "Prigmore's Swamp" had been exchanged for that of "Inians's Ferry" about the year 1697, and now the accession of the House of Brunswick to the British throne in 1714, induced the loyal Dutch inhabitants to dignify the village with the name of the reigning family, New-Brunswick.

Robert Hunter, the royal governor of the province, residing at Perth Amboy from 1709 to 1719, frequently visited this place, and eleven years after his return to Europe wrote to his agent, Mr. Alexander, for information in respect to the value of property around Inians's Ferry, desiring to purchase five or six hundred acres, if in his judgment it would prove a profitable investment. Mr. Alexander was very enthusiastic in his description of the place, stating that, during his residence of fifteen years, New-Brunswick had grown very rapidly, for the reason that the country back of this had improved quite fast. The farmers principally raised wheat, and the facilities of the large mills in the vicinity rendered this an important flouring mart. "As New-Brunswick," he adds, "is the nearest landing, it necessarily makes this the store-house for all the produce that they send to market, which has drawn a considerable number of people to settle there, *insomuch that a lot of ground is here grown to near as great a price as so much ground in the heart of New-York.*"*

About this time (1730) several families emigrated from Albany, N. Y.; and the tradition is, that they brought with them their building materials, according

---

* *Whitehead's Amboy*, p. 155: "In a previous letter, dated in January, Mr. Alexander says that 'plantations north of the Raritan had risen *extravagantly* high, even to three, four, and five pounds per acre, and for a tract of five hundred acres, unimproved land, belonging to Hunter, south of the Raritan, he had refused twelve hundred pounds.'"

to the Dutch custom, and located along the public road, which they called, after their former home, Albany street. Among these settlers we find the names of Dirck Schuyler, Hendrick Van Deursen, Dirck Van Veghten, Abraham Schuyler, John Ten Brock, Nicholas Van Dyke, and Dirck Van Alen. These were men of considerable property and enterprise, and their arrival gave a fresh impulse to trade. The city was now a growing town of much activity. The principal streets were Burnet, Water, and Albany, with perhaps a few buildings on Church street. The inhabitants lived along the river as far south as Sonman's Hill, extending north for about one mile, or a short distance above the ferry. A few of the ancient buildings are still standing, but these will soon give place to more modern structures, and every relic of the olden time will have passed away. The old house recently standing in Burnet street, near Lyle's brook, known as the property of Dr. Lewis Dunham, was built by Hendrick Van Deursen, one of the Albany settlers, who owned several acres of land in the vicinity.* John Van Nuise, of Flatlands, L. I.,† bought a farm of one hundred acres of Enoch Freland, April 28th, 1727, having its front on Neilson street, its northern line along Liberty street, its southern along New street, extending west as far as the Mile Run. For this property, in connection with five acres of "salt meadow at the mouth of South river,"

---

* He was offered about forty acres of land lying below Morris street, and having George street for its western, and the rear of the lots on Burnet street for its eastern boundary, for $256. Judge Morris owned a large farm on both sides of Commercial avenue. Abeel and Hassert owned twenty or thirty acres above Van Deursen's.

† The ancestor of the Van Nuise family in this country is Aucke Jansen Van Nuyse, who, with his wife, Magdalen Pieterse, and children, emigrated from Holland in 1651, and settled in New-York. His place of birth is supposed to have been Nuise in Groningen, hence the surname Van Nuise. He was a carpenter by trade, and built the first church of Midwout, (now Flatbush,) completed in 1660.—*Bergen Family*, p. 157.

he paid the sum of £800.* In the summer of that year he erected a large farm-house on what is now Neilson street, between Schureman and Liberty, and surrounded it with suitable out-buildings. This house was used as the headquarters of the Hessian commander during the occupation of this town by the British army in the Revolutionary War, and is still remembered by nearly every middle-aged man. Some of our citizens will remember the Appleby House, a stone edifice with gable roof and broad hall, on the corner of Church and Peace streets, now Van Pelt's drug-store; the Gibbs House, an antique stone mansion built by Hendrick Voorhees, standing between Burnet street and the river, near Miller's brook, crossing the street below Town lane; the French property in George street in front of the hotel near the depot; and the large apple orchard on the hill, where now stand the buildings of Rutgers College. Perhaps a few may remember the old barracks standing in the rear of our present parsonage on George street, which were burned in the year 1794.†

We shall have occasion to call up some reminiscences of the past, and will leave this rapid sketch of the city, while we proceed in our narrative of the church proper, to which we now turn our attention.

There was throughout this section, as in all new settlements, great destitution of religious privileges. The inhabitants, in writing back to their friends, urged

---

* He was bounded by lands owned by Gose Vandenbergh, Court Voorhees, Roelef Voorhees, Laurence Williamses, Stephen Philips, and Siba, Mart and Cornelius Solems.—*Deed in possession of Mrs. James Van Nuise.*

† The well in Spring alley is still known as the Barrack Spring. After the destruction of the building, the stones were employed in the construction of the "old jail" in Bayard street; and the same stones now form a part of the foundation of the public school occupying the same ground.—*Dr. Davidson's Historical Sketch.*

them to encourage ministers to come and settle among them, holding out the inducement of a large field to occupy, and of the ability of the people to give them a competent support. The principal town in the county of Middlesex was Woodbridge, which obtained a charter June 1st, 1669, and deeds of land were granted that and the following years to about forty families who had emigrated from New-England. They were mostly from the parish of Rev. John Woodbridge, of Newbery, Mass., after whom they named their town. Efforts were made immediately to settle a pastor, but without success until eleven years after, when Rev. John Allen settled among them to the great joy of the people. This was the first religious organization and first minister in our county.*

As ministers of our denomination were obtained only from Holland, our churches experienced even greater difficulties in procuring pastors than other organizations, and only succeeded after long delays and frequent correspondence with the Classis of Amsterdam. But our Dutch ancestors could not long remain without the privileges of the Church. And although a pastor was not obtained until many years afterward, yet these early settlers had their house of worship, in which they statedly met to hear the Scriptures read by the *Voorleezer*, and where the Lord's Supper was administered perhaps not oftener than once a year.

The first building erected within the bounds of our congregation for religious purposes, was about one mile and a half beyond the limits of the present corporation of New-Brunswick, on the lot at the east of the burying-ground, near the residence of Abraham J. Voorhees. Our

---

* A small church building was erected in 1674, the first in our county, thirty feet square.—*Whitehead's Amboy*, p. 382.

knowledge of this organization is quite limited, and derived mostly from the traditions in the neighborhood. There are no records of Consistory known to be in existence, and no allusions to it in ancient deeds and conveyances. The remnants of its foundation were still remaining within the recollection of a few who are yet living, and it is described as a building quite moderate in its dimensions, exceedingly plain in its construction, and never completed. The date of its organization is not known, nor has the name of the minister who officiated on the occasion been transmitted to us. There is in existence a subscription paper, recently discovered, bearing the date of 1703, on which the sum of £10 16s. 6d. is provided to defray the expenses of a minister of the Dutch Reformed Church, to be procured from Holland.* This church may have existed some years before that period, and was probably the first religious organization along the Raritan; for the great highway following the Indian path, as it is called in ancient deeds, from Inians's Ferry to the falls of the Delaware, was the first point occupied by the Dutch settlers in this section of the State. The families represented in this list resided on both banks of the Raritan, from near Boundbrook to New-Brunswick, and along the route of travel to Rocky Hill.

This congregation was known as the church of Three Mile Run. Its prominent elders seem to have been Frederick Van Liew and Hendrick Vroom. The build-

* The names of the following persons are attached to the subscription: Dollius Hageman, Teunis Quick, Hend. Emens, Thos. Cort, Jac. Probasco, Neelas Wyckoff, Mic. L. Moor, John Schedemeun, Nec. Van Dyke, John Van Houten, Wil. Bennet, Folkert Van Nostrand, Jac. Bennet, Hend. Fanger, Ab. Bennet, Cor. Peterson, Philip Folkerson,—avi. L. Draver, George Anderson, Stobel Probasco, Isaac Le Priere, Simon Van Wicklen, Cobas Benat, Garret Cotman, Lucas Covert, Brogun Covert, Wil. Van Duyn, Dennis Van Duyn, John Folkerson, Jost Banat.—*Hon. Ralph Voorhees, Middlebush.*

ing stood for upward of fifty years, and was used for neighborhood services long after the project of making it a separate congregation had been abandoned. This church never enjoyed the services of a settled pastor, although two efforts are known to have been made to procure one from Holland. The first attempt in 1703, already referred to; the second in 1729, when a more extensive plan was formed to revive the church and build up a second congregation within our bounds.

In the mean time, the town around Inians's Ferry had grown into considerable importance, and, as it was the centre of traffic and commerce for all this region of country, it was soon felt that there was a demand for church accommodations in this place. Accordingly, instead of completing their building at Three Mile Run, with great prudence they removed to this locality, and erected an edifice of larger dimensions for the accommodation of this increasing population. This was the first religious organization in the town, and owes its existence to the enterprise and foresight of that portion of the original congregation residing at this point, and occupying farms along the Raritan river. The building was erected, according to an early map of the city, "previous to the year 1717, but how long before is not known." There are reasons for believing that it was built as early as the year 1714, at which time the place was beginning to assume some importance, and gave promise of considerable activity. It stood on the corner of Burnet and Schureman, then called Dutch Church street, and at that date it was called the church of the "River and Lawrence Brook." The building fronted the river, and occupied the corner lot, subsequently and for many years in the possession of Dr. William Van Deursen. The structure was of wood, and, like most of the early churches, its breadth was greater than its depth. Its dimensions, according to a plan in the volume of records previously referred to, was fifty feet broad and forty feet deep. There were seven pews on each side of the pulpit, and eight along the middle aisle. The total number of pews in the building was fifty, and the church accommodations was three hundred. It was not completed until several years afterward, and stood upward of fifty years, giving place in 1767 to our second church edifice, erected on the site of the one we now occupy.

The project of forming a church in this town did not proceed without some opposition. The old congregation at Three Mile Run were reluctant to part with any of their numbers, and those families living still further back in Franklin township urged the importance of all continuing in one organization. Several meetings of the church seem to have been held, and the matter discussed; and on the 12th day of April, 1717, " in order to prevent disturbance and contention, and thereby to establish peace in the church," the following plan was harmoniously adopted: "That the church built near Abraham Bennet shall be considered as belonging to the church of Lawrence Brook and on the River; and that the members of the congregation residing in the neighborhood of Six and Ten Mile Run shall also build a church for themselves at either of these places, or at some point intervening, as they may agree." It was also determined that the church at this place and at Three Mile Run should each have a consistory, who should coöperate with each other; and, " notwithstanding these two places of worship, the two congregations shall form one church; and in matters of great importance the two consistories shall meet as one body, and transact such business as may come before them for the establishment of the Christian church." The arrangement was not intended to be permanent, and seems to have been entered into out of respect to the older members of the church, who could not but feel an attachment to the first house of worship and the original organization. In a very short time this relation probably ceased, and all the services were held in the church of New-Brunswick.

In the old book of records, from which the above facts are taken, there is a decision that Roelef Seebring be the elder for the new congregation, and Hendrick Bries and Roelef Lucas the deacons. This number was soon after increased to three elders and three deacons, and the names of the following persons are recorded as constituting the first full Board of Consistory: Aart Aartsen, Izack Van Dyk, Roelef Seebring, elders; Johannes Folkersen, Hendrick Bries, and Roelef Lucas, (Van Voorhees,) deacons. Thus was organized the Reformed Dutch Church of New-Brunswick, one hundred and fifty years ago.* There is also a decision in the same minutes that Pieter Kinner be appointed elder, and Elbert Stoothof, deacon, for that part of the congregation at Six Mile Run. We have a complete list of the original membership of the church, numbering seventy-three persons, and it is pleasant to notice how many of their descendants are still found among our congregation.

Our register of baptisms begins on the 14th of August, when three children were baptized: Elizabeth,

---

* As this church is a continuation of the Three Mile Run congregation, which had an existence as early as 1703, there is a propriety in the statements made in public documents, that we trace our origin as a religious society to near the commencement of the last century, although we did not have a distinct organization until April 12th, 1717. The Consistory was sometimes ordained at Three Mile Run; at least, this is known to have been the case in one or two instances.

daughter of Johannes Stoothof; Cornelius, son of Martin Salem; and Jan, son of Jacobus Ouke. During the three years of vacancy twenty-nine baptisms are recorded, but who occupied the pulpit during this period we have no information.

We know that Rev. Bernardus Freeman, of Long Island, took a deep interest in this church, and through him early efforts were made to obtain a minister from Holland, in connection with three other churches already organized, namely, Raritan,* Six Mile Run, and North-Branch, now Readington.

As the result of this combined movement, there came to this country, commissioned by the Classis of Amsterdam as the first pastor of this church, January 1st, 1720,

REV. THEODORUS JACOBUS FRELINGHUYSEN.

His name is one of the most honorable in the State of New-Jersey, and the influence that he exerted among the early churches has given to this whole region the name of the "Garden of the Dutch Church." The field of his pastoral charge was very extensive, embracing all the churches in Somerset and Middlesex counties. Very little information in reference to this pioneer of the gospel ministry in this section has been transmitted to us, which is the more surprising from the fact that his descendants have always lived in this vicinity, and have exerted a great influence in the political and educational interests of the State. Short biographical sketches have been published at different times, giving the few items of history which have been

---

* The church of Raritan was organized March 9th, 1699. Their first house of worship was not erected until about the year 1730. The Readington church (then called North-Branch) was organized in 1719.

gathered from the personal allusions in the sermons which he printed during his ministry, and from the traditional knowledge of the inhabitants covering his extensive pastoral charge. To Dr. Abraham Messeler and Rev. William Demarest the church is indebted for the valuable information which has been preserved of this most remarkable man.

The residence of Dominie Frelinghuysen was within the bounds of this congregation, his grave is with us to this day, and as this was the centre of his charge, his history properly belongs to the sketch we are giving.

He was born in the year 1691, at Lingen, in East-Friesland, now a province in the kingdom of Hanover, and was educated at his native place under the instruction of Rev. Otto Verbrugge, Professor of Theology and Oriental Literature. He was ordained to the ministry by Rev. Johannes Brunius at the age of twenty-six, and for about two years was the pastor of a church at Embden in his native country. While thus engaged he received the call from the churches in New-Jersey to labor in this destitute field. The circumstance of his selection by the Classis of Amsterdam for this important mission, as related by Dr. Thomas De Witt, indicates the hand of God in the gift of the first minister of this church. A pious elder entertained a young traveler, on his way through the town to Embden to assume the charge of an academy in that place. During the evening he was so well pleased with the spirituality of his conversation, and his eminent gifts, especially in prayer during family devotions, that he immediately informed his pastor, Sicco Tjadde, that he had "found a man to go to America." In answer to this call he made his arrangements to emigrate to this country, and arrived in the city of New-York about the 1st of January, 1720, and on the 17th of that month he occupied the pulpit of Dominie Boel, immediately after which he came to New-Brunswick and commenced his pastoral work.

He brought with him from Holland, according to the custom of the church, a school-master, holding also the position of chorister and "Voorleeser," Jacobus Schureman by name, the ancestor of this family in our State. He was a well-educated gentleman, and noted for his piety. He had the gift of poetry, and wrote several pieces which are said to have displayed considerable genius as well as literary taste and cultivation. They were spoken of about fifty years ago as doing "honor to his memory." None of them are known to have been translated into the English language, and with the disuse of the Dutch they have probably long since perished. There is a tradition that he used this gift in a very effectual way against the enemies of Mr. Frelinghuysen, who commenced very early working their mischievous arts, in consequence of which he incurred their great displeasure. He was a warm friend of the Dominie, supporting him in all his plans; in consequence of which there sprang up between them an intimacy which awakened some opposition on the part of the people, who complained of the influence which he exerted over the minister. They were both unmarried, and resided in the family of Hendrik Reyniersz, in the neighborhood of Three Mile Run. He had been promised in his call five acres of land, which was increased to fifty acres on his arrival, with the use of a parsonage. Quite early in his ministry he was married to Eva Terhune, of Long Island, after which he resided at or near the residence of the late John Brunson. About the same time Schureman became his brother-in-law by marrying the sister of his wife, Autje Terhune, and resided near the farm which is known as the Schureman property.

At the time when Mr. Frelinghuysen commenced his ministry, the churches under his care were in a most deplorable state. They had been entirely destitute of the stated ministry of the Gospel since the first settlement of the country; and although church organizations existed and houses of worship had been erected, yet, as the natural result of the absence of pastoral supervision, there must have been a great departure from serious and vital piety. Indeed, this was the characteristic of the times, and was the prevailing mark among all the churches. When we consider that, for a period of at least thirty years, the early settlers in this section of the State had only enjoyed such services as could be rendered by neighboring ministers, we are surprised that there should be such a respect for the ordinances of God's house, as we have indicated by the regular administration of the sacraments, and the increase of membership to the church.

The physical aspect of the country very much resembled the morals of the people. It was wild and uncultivated. Dense forests surrounded New-Brunswick; the streams were unbridged; the settlements were widely scattered; the roads, with the exception of the main thoroughfare from New-York to Philadelphia, were little more than paths through the wilderness; and it had all the appearance of a new country.

This was the state of things when Dominie Frelinghuysen came here in 1720. But he was a man equal to the times, of great energy of character, of large attainments in knowledge and grace, and with a certain fearlessness of spirit that enabled him to go immediately at the hearts of the people. From the sermons which have been preserved, we gather that he was a warm, earnest preacher, dwelling principally upon the necessity of the new birth, and having a dreadful antipathy to all manner of formalism. He preached the doctrines of grace with so much spirituality and directness that the people, who had never had their hopes questioned, began almost immediately to raise against him a loud opposition. He was charged by his enemies with preaching doctrines contrary to the standards of the Church, and subversive to the whole spirit of the Gospel. When he insisted on the necessity of experimental evidences as a qualification for the Lord's Supper, he is represented as introducing customs contrary to the principles of the Reformed Church. A very elaborate pamphlet was published by his enemies in the year 1723, setting forth their grievances, and making an appeal to public opinion against the course he was pursuing. The complaint is issued under the sanction of Simon Wyckoff, a deacon of the church of Six Mile Run, Peter Dumont, an elder at Raritan, and Hendrick Vroom, a former deacon at Three Mile Run. In addition to these names, the signatures of sixty-four heads of families are appended, from all the congregations to which he ministered, with the exception of New-Brunswick. The controversy seems to have been quite bitter, and was continued several years. Indeed, it seems to have disturbed the peace of the church in some portions of his field during his entire ministry. Mr. Frelinghuysen states in one of his sermons, that the violence of the opposition to him had been so great that on one occasion the door of the church was shut against him, and he was not permitted to administer the ordinances. As late as the year 1729, a party existed of sufficient strength to make an attempt to bring over from Holland a pastor more after their own mind. A paper* was accordingly circulated with an idea of gathering together all the malcontents† in the old church at Three Mile Run, which is represented to be in a somewhat dilapidated condition, and, if the enterprise succeeded, they were to repair the old edifice or build a new one in the vicinity of John Pittenger. But the plan failed, and the scheme was abandoned. The church at New-Brunswick did not join in this controversy with their pastor, but, so far as documentary and traditional evidence goes, zealously supported him, and the result was witnessed in the great prosperity which this church enjoyed.

Dominic Frelinghuysen met all this opposition in the spirit of a true gospel minister. He continued at his post, preaching, visiting, and catechising, laboring for the conversion of souls and the edification of the church. "I had rather die a thousand deaths," he says in one of his sermons, "than not preach the Gospel." And his ministry was eminently successful. Sound in his doctrinal views, searching in his reproofs, and fervent

---

* The subscribers were: A. Booram, Simon Wyckoff, Dennis Van Duyn, Leonard Smock, Cor. Peterson, George Anderson, William Van Duyn, Jac. Boise, Hen. Smock, Chris. Probasco, William Kouenhoven, Jac. Bennet, Pet. Bodine, Gid. Marlat, William Bennet, Paul Le Boyton, Francis Harrison, Ab. Bennet, Isaac La Queer, Jac. Bennet, Nic. Dafley, Ad. Hardenbrook, Luke Covert, and Jac. Probasco. The committee to procure a minister was Hendrik Vroom and Frederick Van Liew. This subscription paper, as also that of 1703, were found at Mr. Abraham J. Voorhees, at Three Mile Run, and are now in the possession of Hon. Ralph Voorhees; they had been preserved in the Van Liew family, and are all that we have of the old church.

† Rev. Vicentius Antonides, from Long Island, encouraged the disaffected party, and as late as May 9th, 1734, he ordained a Consistory for the Three Mile Run church, composed of Simon Wyckoff and Hendrick Vroom, elders; Simon Van Wicklen and Dennis Van Duyn, deacons; also for North-Branch, Daniel Sebring and Peter Kinney, elders; and William Rosse and Francis Waldron, deacons.—*Records Harlingen Consistory.*

in his appeals, he won many souls to Christ, and laid foundations which have not yet passed away. Throughout his whole field of labor, he enjoyed as the fruit of his ministry several revivals of religion. At Raritan, he was eminently successful in the ingathering of the people and the establishment of the church. Our own records are incomplete, but the evidence of our history is, that he was instrumental in gathering together a large congregation.

About six years after Mr. Frelinghuysen's settlement in New-Brunswick, namely, in 1726, Rev. Gilbert Tennent arrived in this place, and was installed the first pastor of the Presbyterian church. He remained in this city about seventeen years, and was regarded as a man of very eminent abilities, especially distinguished for his pulpit talents. The first church edifice of this denomination was erected in 1727, and stood on the same street with the Dutch church below Lyle's brook, on the ground now occupied by houses No. 142 and 144 Burnet street. Mr. Tennent's residence was at No. 168 of the same street, since taken down, in which his brother William had the remarkable trance, on his recovery from which it was found that he had lost all recollection of previous events, and even had forgotten the name of the Bible.

These two New-Brunswick pastors lived on terms of great friendship, and indeed of intimacy. They found in each other congenial dispositions; and, judging from their published discourses, they were men of similar characteristics. They were both earnest and forcible in delivery, and pungent in their application of the truth. In a letter of Mr. Tennent to Rev. Mr. Prince, a historian of Boston, in 1744, one year after he had left this city, he gives this testimony: "The labors of Rev. Mr.

Frelinghuysen, a Dutch Calvinist minister, were much blessed to the people of New-Brunswick and places adjacent, especially about the time of his coming among them, which was about twenty-four years ago. When I came there, which was about seven years after, I had the pleasure of seeing much of the fruits of his ministry; divers of his hearers with whom I had the opportunity of conversing appeared to be converted persons, by their soundness in principle, Christian experience, and pious practice; and these persons declared that the ministrations of the aforesaid gentleman were the means thereof. This, together with a kind letter which he sent me, respecting the dividing the word aright, and giving to every man his portion in due season, through the divine blessing excited me to greater earnestness in ministerial labors."

The eminent evangelist, George Whitefield, paid frequent visits to this city, and preached to large congregations gathered from this whole section of country. He frequently speaks of New-Brunswick, in his journal, and of the pleasure he enjoyed in the society of Mr. Frelinghuysen. He is very earnest in his praise, and represents him as a sound, fearless, and highly successful minister. Mr. Whitefield, under date of November 20th, 1739, writes in his journal: "Preached about noon, for near two hours, in Mr. Tennent's meeting-house, to a large assembly gathered from all parts." On the 26th of April, 1740, he again passed through New-Brunswick, reaching the town about four in the afternoon, "and preached to about two thousand," he writes, "in the evening." "The next day," he adds, "preached morning and evening to near seven or eight thousand people; and God's power was so much amongst us in the afternoon service, that, had I proceeded, the cries and groans of the people, I believe, would have drowned my voice." It was upon this occasion, according to the statement of Rev. Dr. Cannon, received from persons who were present, that Mr. Whitefield preached in front of the Dutch church in Burnet street, standing on a wagon, and the immense audience were spread over a meadow sloping down to the river, listening to the sermon.

Dominie Frelinghuysen was a member of the convention which met in the city of New-York in April, 1738, with the elder from this church, Hendrick Fisher, who formed a plan to establish an ecclesiastical judicatory, with more enlarged powers than had been enjoyed by the Reformed Dutch Church in this country, out of which grew the great conflict in reference to the separation from the Classis of Amsterdam. Although he did not live to take a very active part in this controversy, yet, as he was one of the originators of the movement, and as it continued to agitate the church for about thirty years, even threatening its very existence, a brief sketch of the two principles in conflict will here be necessary as a link in the chain of history.

Our church, in this country, was not an independent organization, but merely a branch of the Reformed Church of Holland, and subject to its jurisdiction. Cases of discipline had to be referred for decision to the old country. Candidates who desired to preach the Gospel were obliged to cross the ocean in order to obtain ordination; and only such ministers as had been examined and commissioned by the Classis of Amsterdam were ·permitted to preach in our pulpits. The result was long and vexatious delays in procuring pastors, great inconvenience in obtaining the decision of the supreme judicatory, and an outlay of time and expense which greatly retarded the growth of our church. In this year (1738) a plan was matured to form a "Coetus," or an assembly of ministers and elders, who should exercise jurisdiction over the churches in this country, subject to the supervision of the Synod of North-Holland.

This was the entering-wedge of separation, and in a short time grew into a demand for an independent Classis, with all the powers belonging to the highest ecclesiastical court. But this innovation was most strenuously resisted. The church in Europe opposed the measure as subversive of authority, and some of the older ministers, with their elders, formed an assembly opposed to the Coetus, to which they gave the name of "Conferentie." This was the commencement of a strife which has hardly been surpassed in the history of ecclesiastical disputes, and was not finally adjusted until Dr. John H. Livingston matured a plan of union in 1772, which met the cordial approbation of all who sought the peace of Zion.

Mr. Frelinghuysen exerted a great influence in connection with this most important measure. Indeed, he was a thorough representative of the Coetus party, while the early controversies through which he had passed prepared him to be a leader on the side of reform. He was evangelical in his sentiments and progressive in his spirit, and he saw that the interests of the church demanded an independent organization, with all the facilities of school, college, and seminary to provide a well-educated ministry. Although he did not live to see this result, yet he is justly honored as one of the originators of a system which at first greatly agitated but finally prevailed to the establishment and enlargement of the church. There were a few in this congregation who sympathized with the Conferentie party, but they never attained any considerable strength, though in other parts of the old charge of Mr. Frelinghuysen the strife was carried on with a violence which it is almost impossible for us to understand.*

The Dutch population in the town of New-Brunswick received quite an accession between the years 1730 and 1734, by the emigration of several families from Albany, previously referred to in our narrative. Their ancestors had removed to that place immediately from Holland, and their names are found on the register of church-members as early as 1683. They are uniformly represented to have been an intelligent and pious class of people, who added very greatly to the strength of the church. Families also continued to arrive from Long Island, and settled on the farms along the Raritan, both above and below New-Brunswick, and on both sides of the river. From these causes and the increasing prosperity of the congregation, the completion and enlargement of the church edifice was demanded, and in 1735 we find that the object was accomplished under the direction of a committee of which Dirck Schuyler was chairman. The amount expended in reseating the church was about £200.

---

* Harlingen especially seems to have been an important point in the Coetus and Conferentie difficulties. The original house of worship at the cemetery and the church records fell into the hands of the Conferentie. The Coetus party, therefore, who could not be limited and restrained by the formalities of the other, erected a new church in 1749 near the present site, and kept a distinct record of their own. Both records have come down to the present time. On May 9th, 1734, Dominie Antonides met some Conferentie friends at the house of Ryner Veghte, and ordained a new Consistory, in opposition to Frelinghuysen's Consistory, namely, Koert Voorhees and Daniel Polhemus, elders. This new Consistory secured possession of the church-books, and hence Frelinghuysen was obliged to begin a new book of records in 1737. In this is noted the arrival of his son John in 1750, who preached his first sermon in that locality, August 19th of that year, in the house of Simon Van Arsdalen. His first sermon was preached in the church December 2d.—*Rev. E. T. Corwin.*

At this date the pews were sold under an article of agreement to which the signatures of the heads of families are affixed. We have a plan of the building thus remodeled, a complete list of the families in the congregation,* and the original disposition of the pews.

Among the names I find recorded that of James Hude,† one of the prominent citizens of New-Brunswick, and held in very high esteem. His father was a Scotch Presbyterian, and fled from the religious oppressions of the Old World to enjoy the freedom promised in the New. Mr. Hude filled all the civil offices in the city, and spent most of his life in the service of the government. He was one of the judges of the pleas for eleven years, a member of assembly in 1738, one of the council of Governor Morris, and for several terms mayor of the city. He was a man of great benevolence, and on his death, November 1st, 1762, the New-York *Mercury*, in an obituary notice, speaks of him as a "gentleman of great probity, justice, affability, moral and political virtues." His residence was in Albany street, in the house known as the Bell tavern, the original part of which is one of the oldest buildings in the town. Though he does not seem to have been a communicant in the church, yet I find his name on the list of families in the congregation, and his children were all baptized by Mr. Frelinghuysen, and appear on our register.

On the same list I find also the name of Philip French, who came into possession of Inians's patent, and was a man of great liberality and distinction. One of the streets of our city still bears his name.

---

* For a list of the heads of families at this date, see Appendix II.

† *Whitehead's Amboy*, p. 374. His daughter Catherine married Cornelius Lowe, and a daughter of theirs married a son of Rev. Mr. Hardenbergh, the Hon. J. R. Hardenbergh.

The name of Jacob Ouke is found on the catalogue, one of the original members of the congregation, a prominent elder in the church; at several times a mayor of the city, and holding an office which had been created by Mr. Frelinghuysen to meet the growing demands of his large charge. In addition to these names, there were others who shone with equal eminence, the Schuylers, the Van Deursens, the Van Derbelts, the Van Voorhees, the Schencks, and the Van Harlingens. The list embraces the names of about one hundred heads of families, showing that at this date (1735) there was here a large congregation built up under the ministry of Mr. Frelinghuysen.

Perhaps no name is more prominent in our early records than that of the distinguished Elder Minne Van Voorhees, one of the ancestors of the large family of this name in this section of the State. He came to this vicinity from Long Island about the year 1715, and two years after, on the organization of this church, we find his name on our list of communicants. He resided at first on the property now known as the College farm, and was the proprietor of a large tract of land in that vicinity, including the mills below the city; subsequently he removed to New-Brunswick, and resided here until his death, which must have occurred about the year 1734. He was a man of great prominence in the church, elected to the office of elder when quite a young man, and a ruling spirit in the congregation. In the controversies which Mr. Frelinghuysen sustained in the early part of his ministry, he found in Minne Van Voorhees a staunch and intelligent supporter. From the fact of his coöperation with his pastor, the inference is natural that he was of a kindred spirit. Tradition reports him to have been very gifted in prayer and exhortation. His memory was so retentive that he was able to repeat nearly the entire sermon after hearing it preached. When Mr. Frelinghuysen was exhausted with his excessive labors, he would frequently call upon Minne to take the evening lecture in one of the neighborhoods, and he would conduct the services with great edification. His name was very precious in the church for several generations, and he has left behind him even unto this day a savor of great piety. His descendants were connected with some of the most distinguished families of the city, the Pools, Neilsons, Abeels, Bennets, Schuylers, Van Deursens, and Hasserts.*

In order to meet the growing wants of his extensive charge, Mr. Frelinghuysen resorted to various expedients. The plan of a colleague was discussed at a joint meeting of the four Consistories, held at Raritan in 1737, and finally adopted. An address is sent to that Reverend Father in God Schuyhenburg and Jan Stockers to send over from Holland a young man, who should act as an assistant to the minister. The call is prepared by Mr. Frelinghuysen, and in his characteristic way he asks for a man of good health, who will be able to endure a large amount of labor, and a willing worker; but above all, for one who shall be filled with the love of Christ and God's kingdom. He is to preach under

---

* The ancestor of the family of Voorhees in this section of country is Steven Coerte, or Koers, who emigrated from Holland in 1660, on the ship Bontekoe, (Spotted Cow,) and settled in Flatlands, Long Island. Having no surname, they subscribed themselves "Van Voorhees," or "from before Hees." Stephen Coerte married Willempic Roelefse, and died about 1684. His son, Lucas Stevense, married on Long Island, and six of his children emigrated to New-Brunswick and vicinity, and were members of this church at its organization. Hans (Jan) Lucas married Neeltije Nevius; Catryntje Lucas married Roelof Nevius; Roelof Lucas married Helena Stoothof; Minne Lucas married Antje Wyckoff; Wilmetje Lucas married Martin Nevius; Albert Lucas married Catryntje Cornell.—*See Genealogy of Bergen Family*, p. 61.

the direction of the senior pastor, catechise the children and youth, and perform pastoral visitation. He is promised a parsonage with fifty acres of land, a horse with necessary accompaniments, and £80 a year, one half of which shall be paid as soon as he shall be installed. This excellent arrangement did not succeed, the right kind of a man not being found ready to emigrate to America.

On the failure of this effort to secure an assistant, Dominie Frelinghuysen resorted to the expedient of appointing "helpers," after the plan of the apostles. (1 Cor. 12:28.) Men who were gifted in exhortation and prayer, and who had commended themselves by their godly lives to the people, were selected under the sanction of the Consistory, to hold neighborhood services, to visit the sick, to direct the inquiring, and to be generally useful in the congregation. Indeed, this plan was matured previous to sending the call to Holland; for we find in our minutes that, in 1736, a joint meeting of the four Consistories was convened for the purpose of consulting upon the subject, and that appointments were actually made of such extraordinary officers in the church. At this meeting the following selection was made: For North-Branch, Symon Van Arsdalen; for Raritan, Hendrick Bries and Teunis Post; for Six Mile Run, Elbert Stoothof; and for New-Brunswick, Hendrick Fisher, Roelof Nevius, and Abraham Ouke. The tradition is, that these men were eminently useful; and while the measure was a novelty in the Dutch Church, and, so far as we have learned, was confined only to the pastoral charge of Mr. Frelinghuysen, yet it was eminently successful, and tended greatly to the prosperity of the church. These men held the office during life, and one of them, as we shall presently see, became a lay preacher and catechist.

On examining the records of our church, I find that there was received into its membership, during Mr. Frelinghuysen's ministry, about sixty persons. Many names are undoubtedly omitted from the list, as some are not found on the catalogue who are known to have been in communion with the church. The largest number received in any one year was in 1741, when there was the addition of twenty-two persons, a most cheering evidence of the divine favor, and a great encouragement to that noble minister who had now triumphed over all opposition, and whose work was thus crowned with God's approbation. Although the whole number does not seem to be large, yet it is a fair representation of growth, considering the sparseness of the population, the agitations of the times, and the fact that he received into the communion only those who gave the clearest evidence of conversion.

Concerning the events that transpired during the latter part of Mr. Frelinghuysen's life, no record has been preserved, nor is the time of his death or the place of his burial definitely known. In the summer of 1744, he bought of Daniel Hendrickson, of this city, a farm of 200 acres, for which he paid £550. This property is located at Three Mile Run,* and is a part of the land occupied by the late John Brunson. Here he built a spacious house, a part of the foundation of which was

---

* It is described as being bounded on the south-east by the land of Daniel Hendrickson, north-east by the "pretended line of the heirs or assigns of Peter Sonmans," north-west by David Sequire, south-west and north-west by Cornelius Bennet.—*Trenton Deeds.*

He lived at one time in Burnet street, as I find a reference to his "residence" in an old deed in my possession, but the precise location I have not ascertained. He spent his whole ministerial life within the bounds of this congregation, and his family made this church their religious home.

used in the construction of the edifice now standing. At this place he probably resided at the time of his death, which must have occurred about the commencement of the year 1748, when he had not yet reached his fifty-seventh year. He is buried, according to all the evidence we can gather, in the old yard of the Six Mile Run church, and a spot is still pointed out as his last resting-place.* His monument should stand in the ground adjoining our church, and his name should be preserved among the greatest lights of our Zion. The character of his mind is sufficiently indicated by his published sermons; his fidelity, by the fearlessness with which he preached the Gospel in its purity and pungency; his success, by the ingatherings which he enjoyed, the foundations which he laid, and the seed which he planted; and his piety, by the savor which yet breathes from his memory.

When he came to this field, he found it spiritually destitute and uncultivated. A church had here grown up in this new settlement without a pastor, and, bearing in mind the type of the religion of that age, we are not surprised that there was so much of the formal element in the churches. When he was called away, he left behind him a strong body of Christians, who had been brought into the church under a searching Gospel, and who gave every evidence of real godliness. That he was blessed by God in his work is the unqualified

* The first house of worship of the Six Mile Run church was built in this yard, and remains of the foundation were visible until quite recently. The second building was erected before 1766, for in the survey of the county line, made at that date, it was called the "new church." The tradition is, that Mr. Frelinghuysen's grave was under a tree near the centre of the ground. The aged remember that their parents pointed to the spot as the resting-place of a "great man." Is it not a striking fact that the minister who first broke ground for the Gospel in this new territory lies in an unknown grave? Let us cherish his memory, and show him honor by loving, as he did, the pure doctrine of the Gospel.

testimony of our history; and when such eminent men as Gilbert Tennent, George Whitefield, and Jonathan Edwards speak of him as one of the great lights of the American church, we freely accord to him the distinguished position which he occupies. To their testimony I may add that of Dr. A. Alexander, of Princeton, who says: "If you wish to find a community characterized by an intelligent piety, a love of order, and all that tends to make society what it should be, seek it among the people of Somerset and Middlesex. And their present character," he adds, " is owing very much, under God, to the faithful preaching of the Gospel under old Dominie Frelinghuysen."

The name of his wife has been recently recovered, but no traditions are preserved in respect to her character. But the piety of the household is clearly indicated by the character of her children. All of her sons entered the ministry, and her two daughters became the wives of pastors in our church. We attribute this fact mainly to the piety and religious instruction of the mother, Eva Terhune. They were baptized in this church, and their names appear upon our register. Theodore was settled in Albany, from 1745 to 1759. He is represented to have been frank and popular in his manners, earnest and eloquent in the pulpit, and blameless in his life. He sailed for Holland in the year 1759, with the expectation of returning to his field of labor. The date and circumstances of his death are not known.* His memory was very precious in the church of Albany, meriting the tribute paid to him of "the apostolic and much beloved Frelinghuysen." His

---

* "A letter has been found, written at New-York on the 10th of October, 1759, which establishes the fact that he sailed on that day, and that gossip and predictions of a fatal voyage were rife, which led to the tradition of his

second son, John, succeeded his father at Raritan in August, 1750, and died very suddenly while on a visit to Long Island, attending a meeting of the Coetus, in 1754. The third and fourth sons, Jacobus and Ferdinand, died on their return passage from Holland, of the small-pox, in 1753, and were buried at sea. They were promising young men, and had both received calls, the one at Marbletown, the other at Kinderhook, N. Y. The fifth son, Hendricus, pursued his studies in this country, and was licensed by the Coetus, and in 1756 settled over the church of Wawarsing, in Ulster county, N. Y.; but in a short time he also died from an attack of small-pox, and was buried at Napanock. Thus rapidly did these young ministers close their work, just at a time when the whole church was needing the labors of such devoted and godly men. One of his daughters, Anna, was married to Rev. William Jackson, who for thirty years was the pastor of the church in Bergen; she died at the age of seventy-two, in May, 1810. And Margaret became the wife of Rev. Thomas Romeyn, whose only son, Theodore Frelinghuysen Romeyn, was the pastor of Raritan in the same charge of his grandfather and uncle, whose short and promising ministry of only eighteen months was brought to a close by his sudden death at an early age, amid the lamentations of a bereaved people.

On the death of Mr. Frelinghuysen, the churches under his charge had so far increased in strength that they immediately resolved to settle two pastors. Raritan, North-Branch, and Millstone, now Harlingen, settled Rev. John Frelinghuysen, whose short ministry of only

loss at sea, and which is nowhere authenticated except by the garrulous Mrs. Grant. The tradition seems to have grown out of the ominous breaking down of the bench in the pulpit of a new church in which he preached on the Sabbath previous to his departure."—*Munsel's Annals of Albany.*

four years was eminently successful. While he was possessed of much of his father's bold, evangelical spirit, he seems to have been of a more pleasing disposition, although he did not have to encounter difficulties which disturbed the early ministry of his honored parent. He was much interested in the education of young men for the ministry; and there is still standing in Somerville a house built by him of bricks brought from Holland, where Hardenbergh, Jackson, and others pursued their theological studies. Although party spirit raged very high in his charge, yet his ministry was remarkably blessed by the outpouring of the Spirit, and at his death there was great lamentation. The churches of New-Brunswick and Six Mile Run, very conveniently located, and both of considerable strength, formed an ecclesiastical connection for the settlement of a minister who should devote himself entirely to this field. The choice of the people immediately fell with great unanimity upon a young man who had just completed his studies, and in September, 1748, there was called, as the second pastor of this church,

Rev. Johannes Leydt.

Our knowledge of Mr. Leydt is quite limited, though he labored in this field for thirty-five years. In respect to his early history, I have only been able to learn that he was a Hollander by birth, and was educated at one of her universities—which one is not certain—and that he came to this country with an elder brother, settling at first in Dutchess county, in the neighborhood of Fishkill. He was born in the year 1718. The time of his emigration to America is not known. The first notice we have of Mr. Leydt is in the minutes of the

Coetus held in New-York on the 28th of April, 1748, in these words: "The student Leydt, according to appointment, delivered a proposition upon 2 Corinthians 3 : 6–8, and gave such satisfaction that he was likewise received with Van Der Linde to be examined in the morning, after reading the church certificate, from which it appeared that they had been communicants for some years." The Elder Hendrick Fisher was a member of this assembly, and presented a letter from the Consistory of New-Brunswick, "urging the speedy examination of the student, in order that their congregation, which was vacant, might employ him as a candidate, and, if satisfied, might call him."

As permission had been previously obtained from the Classis of Amsterdam, the examination was accordingly proceeded with, and, proving satisfactory, these two young men were sent forth to preach the Gospel. September 27th, 1748, a formal call was laid before the Coetus by the Elder Hendrick Fisher; and, having passed his final examination, Mr. Leydt was set apart to the work of the ministry, and constituted the pastor of the churches of New-Brunswick and Six Mile Run. There was great joy among the people in having so soon obtained a successor to the excellent Dominie Frelinghuysen, and who, according to all accounts, was influenced by a similar spirit of entire consecration to the ministry. I have not been able to ascertain the place of his church relations, nor the circumstances of his introduction into the ministry. It is said that he was a student of Mr. Frelinghuysen, and was well known in the city.

The first act of the Consistories was to provide him a home; accordingly, they purchased a parsonage with fifty acres of land. This property was located at Three

Mile Run, and is known as the Skillman farm, now in the possession of Isaac W. Pumyea. The old house is still standing, a short distance from the road, in which Mr. Leydt lived during his entire ministry of thirty-five years.

Great changes had taken place in this town and the surrounding country since the organization of this church. The land had been cleared up and cultivated, more substantial buildings erected, farms increased in value, and the morals and intelligence of the community greatly improved. In 1717, the Dutch church was the only organization in the town; but in 1748 there was a Presbyterian church, of which Rev. Thomas Arthur was the minister; and the Episcopalian church, erected in 1743, on a lot given by Philip French, of which Rev. Mr. Wood was the missionary; and all of these congregations are represented to have lived in a spirit of great harmony and Christian coöperation.

A very interesting description of our town at this date, 1748, the year in which Mr. Leydt commenced his ministry, is given in the account of a traveler by the name of Peter Kalm, a professor in the University of Abo in Swedish Finland, who visited North-America as a naturalist, under the auspices of the Swedish Royal Academy of Science. "About noon," he writes, "we arrived in New-Brunswick, a pretty little town in a valley on the west side of the river Raritan; on account of its low situation it can not be seen coming from Pennsylvania, before coming to the top of the hill which is close up to it. The town extends north and south along the river. The town-house makes a pretty good appearance. The town has only one street lengthwise, and at its northern extremity there is a street across; both of these are of considerable length.

One of the streets is almost entirely inhabited by Dutchmen who came hither from Albany, and for that reason they call it Albany street. On the road from Trenton to New-Brunswick, I never saw any place in America, the towns excepted, so well peopled."*

Very shortly after his settlement, Mr. Leydt interested himself in procuring a charter from the royal governor for the churches originally embraced in the charge of Mr. Frelinghuysen. This instrument was obtained under the administration of Jonathan Belcher, Esq., Governor-in-Chief of the Province of New-Jersey, and was executed on the 7th day of June, and the twenty-sixth year of the reign of King George II. (1753.) The trustees under the charter were the two ministers, Rev. Johannes Leydt and Rev. John Frelinghuysen, with the several members of the Consistories of the five churches. The first meeting of the new corporation was held at Raritan, October 31st, 1753, when Hendrick Fisher, one of the elders of this church, was chosen president of the board, and arrangements made to carry out the provisions of the charter.†

The increase of population in the town, and the popularity of the minister, soon called for more enlarged church accommodations. The old building in Burnet street was full, and as early as 1754 the plan was agitated for the erection of a new and more commodious church edifice in a more central location. An

---

* In some of his statements Mr. Kalm is not accurate. In reference to his "two German churches, one of stone, the other of wood," it is certainly a mistake. The Dutch congregation had but one building, a structure of wood, in Burnet street. His error is equally apparent in the remark that "the Presbyterians were building a church of stone." They never had a stone edifice, and there was no church building going on in the town at this date. The statements of travelers in reference to local matters, unacquainted with the language of the people, and merely passing through a place, are to be taken with some degree of allowance.

† See Appendix III.

article of agreement was entered into at this time for the purchase of a lot on which to erect a new building. But the subject was postponed from time to time, in consequence of a difference of opinion in the congregation as to the proper location. One party insisted on remaining in Burnet street and enlarging the old edifice, and the other desired a removal into that part of the city which had the prospect of growth. The matter was finally adjusted by the gift of the plot of ground on which our present building is erected, by Philip French, Esq., one of the members of the congregation. The deed of conveyance is dated September 12th, 1765. The Consistory was then composed of Hendrick Fisher, Ferdinand Schureman, and Derick Van Veghten, elders; Cornelius Seebring, Ernestus Van Harlingen, and Jacobus Van Nuise, deacons. A building committee was immediately appointed, of which John Schureman, son of the school-master, was the chairman, and arrangements made for the erection of the second church edifice of our denomination in the town.

The new building was completed and occupied by the congregation in the autumn of 1767, one hundred years ago, when the old church in Burnet street was taken down, and the lot sold to John Schureman. The ground plan of this building is given in our records, the sale of pews, and a complete list of the congregation at this date. The building was of stone, nearly square, and would seat comfortably four hundred persons. The cost of construction was £1097 13s. 7d. It had a front entrance on Queen, now Neilson street, and a side-door on Prince, now Bayard street. At the south side was a long pew for the accommodation of the public officers of the city, and on the north similar pews running parallel with the walls, which, it is said, were much sought after, "as one eye could be directed toward the minister, and the other to any thing that might require attention in the other part of the house." Far off and up in a circular pulpit, supported by a pedestal, was the minister, beneath the old time-honored sounding-board. Two pillars support the roof from the centre, which went up on four sides, ending in a small steeple. A bell* was put up about the year 1775, and the sexton, in ringing, stood in the middle aisle, winding the rope during service around one of the pillars. The church was never desecrated with stoves, but in the midst of winter the good Dutchmen kept up what heat they could by an occasional stamp on the floor, and tradition says the Dominie would keep warm by an extra amount of gesture.

The city presented a far different appearance from its present aspect. The streets were unpaved; a swamp extended from Church to New street, affording a fine skating-pond for the boys in winter; there were a few buildings to the right of the edifice, and only an occasional house between this and Albany street. On the hill occupying the ground in the rear of our parsonage stood the stone barracks, a commodious building one hundred feet in length and sixty in depth, erected in the year 1758; and the farm of Jacobus Van Nuise covered all that ground now occupied by Schureman, Liberty, and New streets, extending west as far as the residence of Richard McDonald. This building stood for about forty-five years; and, unornamented as it was, it had gathered around it unusual interest. Here your fathers

---

* I have been informed that the bell was taken down at some period during the war, and buried in the orchard where now stands Rutgers College, and restored to its place after the enemy left the city.

worshiped; and from the old pulpit was preached the true Gospel of Christ. A few are left who remember the edifice well; but fifty-six years have passed since this venerable structure was taken down, and soon all recollection of it will have passed away.

We can picture to our minds the Sabbath morning, one hundred years ago, when the church was completed, and the building was set apart for the worship of God. In the absence of the precise date, we can imagine that this most beautiful season of the year, and this very month of October, was selected for the service. The day opens with a bright sunshine, and the patriarchal head of the house unclasps the huge, old-fashioned Bible, and reads a chapter for the family devotions, commenting on the verses with an ability which shows his knowledge of the Scriptures, and his strong belief in the theology of the Reformation. The day is to be an important one in the church of New-Brunswick, and earlier than usual the whole surrounding population are on their way to the house of God. All the roads leading into the city are lined with travelers, some on horseback, many on foot, and a few enjoying the luxury of a wagon-ride over the rough and winding roads.

There is no service that day at Six Mile Run, and the whole congregation are present. Every family in the surrounding country is represented in the throng. The men are attired in their best Sunday garments, low-crowned hats with very broad brims, coats of large dimensions, with plated buttons, polished brightly for the occasion, ruffled bosoms and wristbands, with silver sleeve-buttons, and the more aged in small clothes, with knee-buckles, and a linen neck-tie of perfect whiteness. The women were modestly and appropriately attired; the dress was of homespun material of fine texture, extremely short-waisted, but not entirely devoid of ornament; their bonnets were large and expansive, with crowns of sufficient size to inclose the most aspiring head-dress; a neat linen collar, with knit gloves of their own manufacture, and a stout pair of shoes completed the toilet.

Thus attired, the people gather into the sanctuary. The building is plain, and for the times ample in its proportions. It is of rough stone, brought all the way from Hurl-Gate in sloops, up the Raritan, and they are still preserved in the walls of this edifice. The pews have been sold the preceding week; and, since there is no bell in the tower, the signal of a horn announces the hour of worship, while the services are regulated by an hour-glass. The voorlezer takes his seat in front of the pulpit, and, according to the custom of the day, commences the exercises by reading the ten commandments and selections from the Scriptures, after which the psalm is read, and for the first time those walls resound with the praise of God. During the singing the minister enters the church, bowing to the right and left as he passes up the crowded aisle, pausing for a few moments with covered face in silent devotion before entering the sacred desk. He is now in his full prime, having served the congregation for about nineteen years. The hour-glass stands at the right of the minister, by the side of the Bible. While the sermon is in progress, the sand has run out; it is then turned, and the congregation know that a half-hour of the discourse is yet to come. But the people listen with grave attention, and are full of reverence. We have the names of all the heads of families. We may suppose that John Schureman, the patriot and scholar, was present that day, and had a glad time in seeing the building for which he had toiled completed; as also Philip French, who gave the lot, and Christian Van Doren, Hendrick Fisher, Derick Van Veghten, Abraham Oakey, and Jeremiah Van Derbilt, former elders of the church. Hendrick Van Deursen, with his son William, were in the assembly; so also were Jacobus and James Van Nuise, both young men. Then there were John and Matthew Sleight, and a long list of Voorhees, Roelef, Albert, Lucas, John, James, Garret, Martinus, Matthew, and Abraham; there were Edward Van Harlingen, John Ryder, Charles Borram, Peter Vredenberg, Matthew Egerton. Abraham Schuyler was also there, giving promise of the useful man which he afterward became. So also the Van Liews, Dennice, John, Hendrick, and Frederick; the Stoothoffs, Whilhelmus, Johannes, John, and Cornelius; the Suydams, Charles and Cornelius; the Outgelts, Fredrick and Johannes; the Waldrons, Leffert and John. And, while we have the familiar names of Nevius, Spader, Garretson, Van Sickle, Provost, Thompson, De Hart, Wyckoff, Van Pelt, and Cortleyou, all represented among us to-day, we have also some which are no longer known in our city, as Hyse, Hortwick, Standley, Wilton, Probasco, Hance, Kin, and Hassert. All these, with others, listened to the word of God that day. The morning service was followed by an intermission of half an hour, and then they all returned to hear another sermon. Thus the Sabbath day passed, closing with the family recitation in the catechism, and evening worship.

The services in this church were held on each alternate Sabbath, and there is the evidence of great punctuality in the administration of the ordinances. Mr. Leydt was a very laborious minister; and while he does not seem to have left any distinct impressions of his pulpit talents, he is represented to have been very faithful as a pastor. He took a very active part in all the public enterprises of the day. In connection with the organization of new churches, the calling and installation of pastors, and the healing of difficulties in congregations, we will find the name of Dominie Leydt. He was a regular member of the Coetus, a constant attendant on their meetings, and, from the frequent references to his name, he seems to have been a prominent and influential member. He took a warm interest in this long controversy, and is placed among the number of those who were chiefly instrumental in procuring the independence of the church in this country. He wrote several very excellent pamphlets on the subject, which were answered by the opponents of the measure, and are referred to in the minutes of that body. The Classis of Amsterdam, in their correspondence with the churches in this country, speak of his writings as excellent in spirit and argument.* At one time he represented the Coetus to the Conferentie party, and was chairman of the committee. In the minutes of the latter body he is represented as being very pointed in his remarks, and as saying some things so piercing that they could hardly keep silent. On the erection of the General Synod, he was associated with Dr. Livingston in conducting the principal part of their business, and at their annual meeting at New-Paltz, in 1778, he was chosen president.†

* I have this fact from Dr. Thomas De Witt, but have not seen the minute itself This valuable correspondence would have been of service, no doubt, in compiling this history. There is an admirable paper in the collection by Dr. Hardenbergh, which presents the points of controversy in a strong light. I regret very much that I could not obtain access to the book of minutes copied from the original under the direction of Synod. We are pleased to learn that all the documents are soon to be given to the public.
† See *Minutes of Synod*, Vol. I.—*Gun's Life of Livingston*, p. 143.

Mr. Leydt was one of the prominent movers in the establishment of Queen's, now Rutgers College. This was the favorite object of the Coetus, or progressive and evangelical party in the church. With them an educated ministry was the great want of our American Zion; as Mr. Leydt expresses it in a letter to Dr. Livingston, "I humbly conceive that, without a regular course of collegiate studies, we shall never make any respectable figure in church or state." The Charter of this institution was procured of Governor Franklin, March 20th, 1770. In the following year the long controversy in which the church had been engaged was finally adjusted by adopting a plan of union, drawn up by Dr. Livingston, which received the approval of the church in Holland, and which dated our separate ecclesiastical organization. The consent was based upon a condition that the Dutch Church in America should make provision in her constitution to provide herself with an educated ministry. The founding of our college was an event that gave great joy to our church. Mr. Leydt was one of the signers of the petition to Governor Franklin for the charter, and was named as a trustee; as such he attended a meeting of the board at Hackensack, when the location of the college was definitely fixed at New-Brunswick. In the letter to Dr. Livingston, from which I have quoted a sentence, he rejoices over the event in this language: "The great and glorious promise consequent upon the noble confession of Nathanael, '*Thou shalt see greater things than these,*' frequently exercising my mind upon favorable turns in Divine Providence, with acknowledgment and expectations, hath with some energy of late reverted to my mind with respect to our present situation; as a door seems to be opening, not only for a desirable union and fixed order, but also increase of knowledge and effusion of the Holy Spirit." In the same letter he apprises Dr. Livingston of a motion in the board of trustees to elect him president of the college, and of certain other plans to render the institution prosperous and efficient.*

We are brought in the course of our narrative to the commencement of the Revolutionary war, a most interesting period in the history of our country and our church. During all these exciting years of conflict Mr. Leydt was the pastor of this church, and there are indications of great interruption in the growth of the congregation. There had been a steady increase in the number of membership up to the year 1773, but during the next six years there are no records of additions to the church. The minds of the people were agitated with the din of preparation, the city during a portion of this time was in the possession of the enemy, and for more than a year the services in the church building were entirely suspended.

Mr. Leydt was a firm patriot, and took a warm interest in the conflict. He preached upon the topics of the day in such a manner as to rouse the patriotism of the people into a pitch of enthusiasm; he prayed for the success of the American cause, and counseled the young men to join the army of freedom.

New-Brunswick suffered during the war to an extent to which few towns were subjected. It lay in the path of the two armies crossing and recrossing the State, and in the varying fortunes of war was at one time in the hands of the enemy, and at another under the protec-

---

* Mr. Leydt was a member of the Board of Trustees of Princeton College, and served in that position for six years, under the presidency of Dr. Samuel Finley.

tion of friends. During the winter of 1776–77, the city was in the possession of the British army, who occupied it by a very large force. Lord Howe, the Commander-in-Chief, had his head-quarters in the Neilson house in Burnet street; the Hessian commander in the Van Nuise house in Queen street. Fortifications were thrown up on the hill beyond our Theological Seminary, and two important out-posts were erected—one at Raritan Landing, on an eminence overlooking the river; the other on Bennet's Island, two miles below the city. Many of the officers were quartered upon the inhabitants; and on the property of William Van Deursen, below New street, there was an encampment with a redoubt thrown up for their protection.

Many of the citizens were compelled to abandon their residences; all business was suspended; public worship broken up, and the whole town under the control of the enemy. The British army immediately appropriated to their own use all the public buildings of the city. The pews were taken out of our church, and it was converted first into a hospital, and afterward into a stable. The Presbyterian church was burned under the following circumstances: On the retreat of the American army from New-Brunswick, Captain Adam Hyler, with a small force, was the last to leave the town. Hotly pursued through the streets by the enemy, he defended himself for a short time behind the walls of the building; when, overcome by a superior force, he was compelled to abandon his position, and the British fired the edifice, which, being constructed of wood, was partially consumed. Colonel Taylor was in this engagement, and for about an hour was retained as a prisoner in the hands of the enemy; but by a bold charge, he was rescued from the guard, and returned to his own party.*

The British remained in possession of the city for about six months, and during this period they sent out frequent foraging expeditions into the country. During the months of January, February, and March, they were shut up in the town, being cut off from their base of supplies at Amboy. The army was short of provisions, and a fleet was sent up the Raritan to replenish their exhausted stores. Lord Cornwallis, who was the military commander of the post, was apprised of this expected relief, and watched eagerly for the approaching boats. Just as they rounded the point below the city, a battery of six cannon, which had been put into position during the preceding night, opened upon them, when five of the boats were immediately disabled and sunk, and the remainder returned in a crippled condition to Amboy. It was at this time that General Howe in person made an attempt to open communication by land; but the expedition failed, and he came near falling into the hands of the Americans.†

The farmers throughout this whole section of country were compelled to deliver over their stores into the

---

* The records of their church are supposed at this time to have been destroyed. They were in the hands of an elder, Dr. Moses Scott, who was compelled to take a sudden flight, leaving his property in their hands, and barely escaped capture. He was just sitting down to dinner when the enemy entered the town, who made a feast at the doctor's expense. He was Surgeon-General of the Army of New-Jersey, and procured a valuable supply of medicines from France, stored away in boxes, all of which fell into the enemy's hands. But they were of no advantage, for a neighbor told them that the doctor had poisoned the medicines on purpose to destroy the British, who at once emptied his boxes into the streets.—*Dr. Davidson's Historical Sketch*, pp. 17, 31, which see, as also for other facts connected with the Presbyterian church.

† See *Whitehead's Amboy*, p. 341. Also for other incidents of the Revolution in this country. Local traditions are still abundant and distinct. The city which suffered so greatly has an unwritten history which should be preserved. Would it not be well to gather together these items before they perish beyond recovery?

hands of the British.* At Three Mile Run the buildings were all plundered, and frequently fired. Barns were torn down to supply timber for the construction of a temporary bridge over the Raritan, and some of the most wanton cruelties were inflicted.

But they were not allowed to remain in the undisturbed possession of the town. Colonels Neilson and Taylor gave them constant trouble; Captain Guest was on the watch for a favorable opportunity to pounce upon the Hessians; James Schureman, who had learned something of war at the battle of Long Island, gave them no rest; while Captain Hyler, whose adventures with his whale-boats around Staten Island seem almost romantic, and who could fight on land as well as on water, kept them in constant apprehension. These officers watched every movement of the enemy, drove back their foraging parties into the city, and often skirmished with their outposts.

Deeds of personal valor were of frequent occurrence, and traditions are preserved in the families of the town of heroism unsurpassed in the whole history of the conflict. Colonel Neilson organized a secret expedition

---

* The following schedule of property taken from Mr. John Van Liew, of Three Mile Run, will illustrate the ruthless spirit of the enemy, and the hardships encountered by the inhabitants of this region during the war. The list is valuable as exhibiting the price of different articles at the commencement of the Revolution, a pound representing $2.50 of our currency. I only enumerate the more important articles taken by "the Regulars:"

	£.	s.		£.	s.
1 span horses	36	00	38 Albany boards	4	15
1 colt, two years old	12	00	700 thin Albany boards	2	09
50 bushels corn	12	10	1 house burned	80	00
28 bushels wheat	10	00	15 bushels potatoes	1	17
Riding chair and harness	15	00	300 cwt. flour	2	14
30 tons of hay	105	00	100 fowls	3	15
9 cows	51	15	8 turkeys	1	00
25 head of sheep	17	10	50 pounds of pork, 5d. per pound.		

Floors of house and barn taken up. 1 negro, 23 years old, smart and active, £105.

against the outpost of the British on Bennet's Island, now known as Island Farm. With a picked command, numbering two hundred men, he stealthily approached the works on the morning of February 18th, some time before daybreak. It was a clear, cold night, and a fresh fall of snow rendered the undertaking extremely hazardous. But they reached the works without being discovered, and Colonel Neilson was the first man to leap the stockade. Captain Farmer saved the life of his commander at this moment by aiming a well-directed blow at the sentinel, who was in the act of discharging his musket into his breast. The short engagement lasted only a few minutes, when the works were surrendered by Major Stockton, who was the acting commander of the post in the absence of Colonel Skinner. One captain, several subordinate officers, and fifty-five privates were taken prisoners, and a quantity of munitions of war were captured. The British knew nothing of the event, as only a few guns were fired, until some time during the morning, when the Americans with their prisoners and booty were far on their way toward Princeton, where General Putnam was stationed, into whose hands they delivered their spoils. Colonel Neilson and his men received from General Washington a very high compliment for the wisdom with which he had planned, and the secrecy with which he had executed, this most successful expedition.

On the 28th of May, Washington, who had spent the previous winter at Morristown, marched his army of 7500 to the heights of Middlebrook. Here he lay for two weeks watching the movements of the enemy at Brunswick, from a position which has since been called "Washington's Rock." In the mean while the route to Amboy had been opened, both by land and water, and troops had been pushed forward to this point in large numbers, until by the 12th of June an army of 17,000 British and Hessians was assembled, under those veteran commanders, Generals Howe, Cornwallis, and De Heister. Both the English and German commanders were agreed that they had never seen a more splendid army, or one so well disciplined and equipped, and in better spirits.* On the 14th, they marched out of the city in the direction of Middlebush, with the design of drawing on an engagement with Washington if they could induce him to leave the strong position which he occupied. Remains of the fortifications which they hastily threw up are still visible on the farm of Mr. John Wilson. Here the enemy remained until the 19th, when, failing in their design, they returned to Brunswick and made immediate preparation to evacuate the State. They were pursued by the Americans, and so greatly harassed on their retreat that it was not until the 1st of July that they were able to cross over from Amboy to the place of their destination on Staten Island.

After their evacuation of the city, the inhabitants returned to their homes and found every thing in a most desolate condition. The work of destruction had been carried on indiscriminately and ruthlessly. The devotion of the inhabitants to the cause of their country had exposed them to the special wrath of their enemies. We have the authority of Governor Livingston for the statement that there were very few whose sympathies

---

* "For its numbers, that army had not its equal in the world. Every soldier was eager for a battle."—Bancroft, vol. 9, p. 351. The time was eventful and critical. About the time when these two armies confronted each other, namely, June 14th, Congress adopted the flag of our country. The historian remarks: "The immovable fortitude of Washington in his camp at Middlebrook was the salvation of that beautiful flag." P. 352.

were with the royal cause. In a letter to Governor Bowdoin, of Massachusetts, on behalf of the Presbyterian church, who solicited aid from abroad to rebuild their church edifice, he writes: "With respect to the political principles of the inhabitants of New-Brunswick, it may be proper to do them the justice of adding that they have, through the whole course of the war, approved themselves firm and distinguished Whigs, and inflexibly persevered in their attachment to the cause of America in the most gloomy and perilous times of her conflict with Great Britain."

This, as we may well suppose, was a gloomy summer in the town, as well as a dark day for the country. But nothing could discourage the hearts of patriots, and they immediately addressed themselves to the work of rebuilding. Our church edifice underwent a temporary repair, and for some time was occupied on alternate Sabbaths by the Presbyterian congregation, the blackened walls of whose building were left standing below Lyle's brook.* Mr. Leydt was immediately at his post, and preached for his people two Sabbaths in the month of July, the first service which he had been able to hold in the city since the beginning of December. This long interruption had a very sad effect upon all the interests of the church, and the troubles of the times prevented the growth of the congregation.

Indeed, during the whole subsequent part of his ministry, which was brought to a close in 1783, the town was kept in a constant state of alarm. Captain

---

* The building was not entirely destroyed, but, as the congregation contemplated removing to another part of the city, instead of repairing the old edifice it was sold to Mr. Hassert, who removed it to New street and converted it into a dwelling-house. This building is still standing, and is now No. 21.

Hyler, to whose romantic exploits I have referred, made this place his rendezvous. He had under his command one gun-boat, the Defiance, and several large whale-boats, with which he would proceed down the Raritan and annoy the trading vessels, transports, and plundering parties of the enemy around Staten and Long Islands, and in the neighborhood of Sandy Hook. He selected only the bravest men, so expert in the use of the oar that, when rowing at the rate of twelve miles an hour, they could be heard only at a short distance. He had the faculty of infusing into his men his own spirit of adventure and daring. On one of his excursions he captured five vessels, two of them armed, in about fifteen minutes, within pistol-shot of the guard-ship at Sandy Hook. In another enterprise he captured an eighteen-gun cutter, which he was forced to blow up, after removing a quantity of stores and ammunition. His plan was to sally out of his berth near the upper lock, pass rapidly down the river, make his captures, and dash back again often pursued by the enemy, who made slow progress with their heavier vessels, and dared not to follow him along the tortuous channel of the Raritan.

The annoyance was so great that an expedition of three hundred men, in several boats, was fitted out to proceed to Brunswick, and destroy his whale-boats and recapture some of the ammunition. The plan was carried into effect January 4th, 1782. The river was clear of ice, and, proceeding cautiously up the Raritan, they had nearly reached the town, when at midnight Mr. Peter Wyckoff was awakened by the barking of a watch-dog; and, holding his ear to the ground, he heard the measured stroke of muffled oars, and at once concluded that an attack was to be made upon the city.

Mounting a fleet horse, he gave the alarm to Captain Guest, and spread the word from house to house, warning the inhabitants of danger. A scene of great excitement now ensued. Lights flashed through the town, and in a short space of time all the able-bodied men were under arms. But the enemy had reached the whale-boats and set them on fire, when our men came up, and, driving them off, prevented them from accomplishing their purpose They now found that their only safety consisted in a hasty retreat. The night was dark, and a running fight took place in the streets. The British endeavored to reach their boats by passing down Queen street to their rendezvous at the foot of Town lane. But they were intercepted at the Dutch church, from behind the walls of which a volley was fired as they pressed on, eager only to escape. The principal skirmish took place near Mr. Agnew's; but they succeeded in reaching the river, and made their way back to Staten Island. The enemy's loss in this encounter was four men killed and several wounded. On the side of the Americans there was the loss of six persons wounded, none proving fatal, and five or six prisoners. A ball was shot through the body of John Nafey in this skirmish, but the prompt attention of Colonel Taylor saved his life. The enemy completely failed in the object of their expedition, and Captain Hyler was on the water in a few weeks, more daring than ever. He died in this city in 1782; but, strange to relate, no one knows the place of his burial.

Some of the members of our congregation took a very active part in this contest, and their names are honorably mentioned in the history of the State. Of this number the Elder Hendrick Fisher was most devotedly interested in the cause of his country. Perhaps there was no man whose influence was greater, or counsel more sought after, during the whole progress of the war. He had been long at the head of the affairs of the church, and was the acknowledged leader in the congregation. He was born in the year 1697, emigrated to this country when quite a young man, and was received into the membership of this church in 1721, shortly after the settlement of Mr. Frelinghuysen. His election to the office of deacon was resisted by the party opposed to the minister; but their objections were overruled, and he was accordingly ordained. He was a mechanic by occupation, but a man of great intelligence, who deservedly commanded the respect and confidence of his fellow-citizens, and occupied a very prominent place in public estimation. In his private character he was irreproachable, and for nearly sixty years he was a consistent, useful, and active member of the church. The confidence which was reposed in him is indicated by his reëlection to the office of elder on several occasions, and his appointment to represent the church in all ecclesiastical courts. He was a zealous supporter of the Coetus party, a member of the first convention in 1738, and an attendant at each one of their subsequent meetings. On the adoption of the Plan of Union, in 1771, his name appears among the delegates; and, as a member of one of the important committees, he was instrumental in the inauguration of that new era of reconciliation and harmony in the church. With all his other attainments, he was thoroughly versed in the science of theology, and became a lay preacher and catechist. Some of his sermons were published and circulated among the people, and are said to have been rich in their doctrinal statements and pungent in their application of the truth.

In civil life he took a very honorable and important stand. He was elected a member of the Assembly of this State, and was serving in that capacity at the commencement of the Revolutionary war. Although he was at this time quite advanced in life, yet he entered into the contest with great warmth and decision, and is justly reputed to have contributed largely to the success of our struggle for Independence. He was a delegate to the Provincial Congress of New-Jersey, which met at Trenton in May, 1775, of which important body he was elected president, and in an opening address set forth in a forcible manner the grievances of the American Colonies. He was chairman of the Committee of Safety, exercising legislative authority during the recesses of Congress, and held other offices of honor and trust. In his public life, as in his private character, he was without a blot, and evinced in all his acts the spirit of a Christian patriot. While he made himself obnoxious to his tory neighbors on account of his uncompromising loyalty to the cause of his country, and had to go constantly armed in his journeys, yet he was a man of great courage, as well as of integrity. The scattered materials of his history should be gathered together, and his name preserved among the honorable men of our State. The residence of Hendrick Fisher was about five miles above the city, on the road to Boundbrook, and the farm which he occupied is now in the possession of Isaac Brokaw. In an obscure burial-ground, overgrown with a dense thicket, stands a plain brown slab, with the simple inscription, "In memory of Hendrick Fisher, who departed this life August 16th, 1779, in the eighty-second year of his age."

Hon. James Schureman was at this time a young man,

and was in active service during the war. He had graduated at Queen's College about the year 1773, and was an accurate scholar. Chiefly by means of his example and eloquence in pleading at public meetings, a company was formed in the town, who enlisted in the army, and served with great credit at the battle of Long Island. He had a command as captain in the early part of the war, and was offered a high position in the regular army. But he preferred to serve as a volunteer, and held himself ready to go out at a moment's warning against the enemy. In the daring expedition of Lieutenant-Colonel Simcoe, at the head of the Queen's Rangers, from Amboy to Somerville, and thence to Millstone—one of the most brilliant exploits of the war—October 25th, 1779, Captain Guest intercepted him on his return about two miles beyond Brunswick, and attacked the party. One man was killed and several wounded; Simcoe's horse received three balls, and, falling on him, wounded him severely, when a militia-man was on the point of piercing him with his bayonet, when Schureman knocked up his musket and took him prisoner. Among the pursuers of the party was a Captain Peter G. Voorhees, a grandson of the Elder Minne, and a brother-in-law of Colonel Neilson, who, in his zeal, got in advance of his men, and was assaulted by the enemy. In his effort to leap a fence at the intersection of George's road and Town lane, his horse became entangled, and the British, on coming up, with great cruelty wounded him with their swords, although he was a prisoner in their hands, and left him senseless in the road. He was brought into the city, and survived only a few hours. He was a young man very highly esteemed, a brave officer in the regular army, and the rage of the inhabitants at the brutal murder was so great that, during the night, the town was searched for Simcoe, threatening revenge on his person. He was concealed in the old stone house on the corner of Neilson and Albany streets, from whence he was removed to Burlington, where he remained a prisoner until honorably exchanged.

Mr. Schureman was taken prisoner during the war near the Mills on Lawrence Brook, and, after being confined for a few days in the guard-house near the Neilson mansion, he was removed to the notorious sugar-house, in the rear of the Middle Dutch Church, New-York, from whence he made his escape to the American army at Morristown. After the war was closed, he was elected a member of Congress, in 1789, after which he was chosen to the United States Senate for a full term, and again returned to the House of Representatives in 1812, as colleague with Richard Stockton. He served several terms as Mayor of the city, and as a citizen was held in high esteem. He was a grandson of the school-master, Jacobus Schureman, and an influential member of the church. He died January 22d, 1824, in the sixty-eighth year of his age. The confidence in which he was held by the community is attested by the offices of trust to which he was appointed, both in church and state, and, to perpetuate his name, one of the streets of the city was called after him, Schureman street.

The ministry of Mr. Leydt was brought to a close by his sudden death, June 2d, 1783, in the sixty-fifth year of his age, and thirty-fifth of his pastorate. He preached on Sabbath morning, the day preceding, and was smitten down by paralysis about noon. His funeral was attended from his residence, and he was buried in the yard at Three Mile Run.* He was the pastor of this church for thirty-five years. He left two sons, both of whom graduated from Queen's College, and subsequently entered the ministry. Matthew was pastor of a church in Bucks county, Pa., and died November 24th, 1783.† Peter was settled at Ramapo, and died at that place June 12th, 1796.‡ None of the descendants of Mr. Leydt are now living.

He is described as a short, stout man, of dark features, very quick in his movements, and in his disposition kind and affable. As a pastor he is said to have been highly esteemed, and to have had a peculiar faculty of drawing around him the young people of his charge. His dress was the clerical costume of the times, and in his manners he was a gentleman of the old school and made himself agreeable to all classes. His preaching was in the Dutch language, during the early part of his ministry, exclusively; in his latter years he preached in English one half the time. His sermons were instructive, and always delivered with a full voice and an earnestness of manner that held the attention of his hearers. He was a good man and universally beloved, and his death was a public loss. The

---

* The graveyard had no connection with the old church at this spot, as it was not used as a place of burial until some years after the building was removed. Mr. Leydt's tombstone stands immediately in front of the gate, with an inscription stating the day of his death and age. His wife, Treyntje Sleight, died December 2d, 1763, aged thirty-six, and is buried by his side. Two other stones mark the graves of his children—Elizabeth, died October 27th, 1760, aged twelve; and Anna, died June 10th, aged seven months.

† He is buried in the old ground, at a place familiarly known as "The Buck," near which stood the first church building of the congregation of North-Hampton, Pa. His tombstone bears the inscription, "In memory of the Rev. Matthew Light, who died the 24th of November, 1783, aged twenty-nine years."

‡ In the family burying-ground of Andrew Hopper, on the margin of the river Ramapo, is a plain stone, with the inscription, "In memory of Rev. Peter Light, who was born the 6th of November, 1763, and departed this life the 12th of June, 1796."

total number of additions to the membership of the church during his ministry was one hundred and twenty-four. The names of several are omitted from the record, and we have no means of ascertaining the actual number of communicants. The times were unfavorable for religious growth, and the War of Independence effectually checked the prosperity of the congregation. But during all these years he had around him a strong body of active and praying men, and a goodly company of helping women. That there were no revivals in his ministry is not a matter of surprise; that the church continued in existence during all these troublous times is owing to the grace and power of her Head.

While his time was very much occupied with the public affairs of the church and the nation, in his particular charge he was always diligent. He has left behind him the reputation of being a great peace-maker. The fact that he carried the two congregations through the perilous time of church-building in a spirit of harmony—one previous to 1766 at Six Mile Run, the other at New-Brunswick completed in 1767, in both instances selecting new sites at a considerable distance from the former localities—would go far to confirm the record.

During the period under review the property known as the old burying-ground came into the possession of the church. The southern portion, including and lying below Liberty street, which was opened through it in 1810, was deeded to the congregation about 1729 by Mr. Jan Van Nuise, and was the first public cemetery of the church. On August 1st, 1773, the lot was enlarged by the gift of about two acres from Mr. Dennis Van Liew, deeded to the trustees under the old charter, for the benefit of the Reformed Dutch Church. A clause in the deed states that "the greatest part of the said piece of ground was anciently given as a burial-place for the dead, and always has been used for that purpose."

During the vacancy that followed on the death of Mr. Leydt, the pulpit was supplied by neighboring ministers. On one of these Sabbaths the services were conducted by Rev. William Jackson, the son-in-law of Mr. Frelinghuysen. An anecdote is related of him, which, at this stage of our discourse, will seem quite appropriate. He was a great orator, according to all accounts, but addicted to the unfortunate habit of preaching long sermons. The days were short, and in the morning service he had given them a discourse of near two hours in length, and the afternoon seemed to promise quite as long. Darkness was coming on, and there were no arrangements for lighting the building; when James Schureman gave to the minister a sign that it would be agreeable to the congregation if he would bring his sermon to a close. With great vehemence of gesticulation Mr. Jackson cried out in a stentorian voice, in the Dutch language, "*Zit neer, Jacobus Schureman, ik zeg zit neer; Paulus predikte tot den midder-nacht!*"—"Sit down, James Schureman, I say sit down; Paul preached until midnight."

Sixty-six years had now elapsed since the organization of the church, and from 1720, the year of Dominie Frelinghuysen's settlement, they had enjoyed without interruption the stated administration of the ordinances. But in the summer of 1783 the situation of the church was most perplexing, and some were greatly discouraged. The excellent pastor, Mr. Leydt, had died, universally lamented, just at the close of the Revolutionary war. The church building, which had been almost destroyed by the enemy, though temporarily repaired on the evacuation of the town by the British army, still showed signs of the depredations to which it had been exposed. The people were exhausted with the long struggle through which they had passed, while the business of the city had been entirely suspended. Many of the families had removed into the country to escape the troubles of the times, and had not yet returned. The Presbyterian church experienced similar troubles. After the loss of their edifice by fire, instead of rebuilding on the old site in Burnet street, they removed to their present eligible situation, purchasing four lots at a public vendue held by the sheriff of the county, Abraham Schuyler, Esq., for the sum of £148. But the labor of building the new church did not commence until the following year, when that congregation was forced to seek aid from abroad, under a recommendation from Governor Livingston, who represents them as "greatly reduced in number, and injured in property, by the havoc of war."

This was the situation of affairs in the city on the death of Mr. Leydt. But public worship was maintained with considerable regularity, as appears from the register of baptisms, and the entries made in the almoner's book of collections for the poor. But there was a work yet for this church to do under God, who had in store for them a rich gift in their next pastor.

On the death of Mr. Leydt, Six Mile Run united with Millstone in the settlement of Rev. John M. Van Harlingen; while New-Brunswick undertook the support of a minister alone. Rev. Simon Van Arsdalen, of Readington, was called in 1784, but he could not be induced to accept the invitation, and it was not until the fall of the following year that they secured the services of the third pastor of this church.

REV. JACOB RUTSEN HARDENBERGH, D.D.

The call was sent to him in October, 1785, but he did not commence his ministry until the next spring, at the same time he assumed the Presidency of Queen's College. His father, Colonel Johannes Hardenbergh, emigrated from Prussia in the latter part of the seventeenth century, and, by purchase, became the proprietor of a tract of land in Ulster county, N. Y., known as the Hardenbergh Patent. Jacob was born at Rosendale, in 1738. His literary education was not so extensive as might be desired, enjoying only the advantages of the Academy of Kingston. His theological studies he pursued under the direction of Rev. John Frelinghuysen, of Raritan. He was licensed to preach by the Coetus, in 1757, when only twenty years of age. His preceptor dying suddenly, he was immediately called to succeed him in his pastoral charge, and in the month of May, 1758, he commenced his labors in the five united congregations of Raritan, North-Branch, Millstone, Bedminster, and New-Shannock. Of two of these congregations he was relieved in 1761. In this extensive field he labored with great fidelity during a period of twenty-five years. While at Raritan he encountered numerous difficulties. At the commencement of his ministry, the church was distracted with the long controversy, which was carried on with great warmth in his own charge, and his latter years were spent amid the din of the Revolution.*

---

* During the latter part of his ministry the congregation was destitute of a house of worship. Their church edifice was destroyed by fire in 1779, by the British forces under Colonel Simco, and was not rebuilt until

He remained at Somerville until the year 1781, when he retired to his native place and served the church at Rochester until his removal to this city in the month of April, 1786. Almost immediately on the death of Mr. Leydt, this church looked to him as his successor, and at the same time the trustees of the college desired his services as its President, electing as his associate John Taylor, the patriot of the Revolution, Professor of Natural Philosophy and Mathematics. With this two-fold charge he labored with intense zeal and devotion, and drew around him a strong congregation. Early in the year 1787, the church edifice, which had been temporarily repaired after the destruction of the war, was thoroughly remodeled. The building was reseated and painted, a fence for the first time erected around the inclosure, and burials in the ground commenced.

This was the beginning of a marked period in the history of the church. Dr. Hardenbergh had endeared himself to the people by the influence he had exerted during the struggle for Independence. He had shown a willingness to serve his country by any sacrifice or labor that he could render in her cause. He was the personal friend of Washington, whose headquarters during several months were within the bounds of his congregation at Raritan, and who uniformly attended his church, taking his seat at the head of the elders' pew. On two different occasions he was selected by our citizens to deliver the oration at the Anniversary of Independence, and among all classes he was eminently popular.

1788, seven years after Mr. Hardenbergh's resignation. The sufferings of that community were so great that it is not a matter of surprise that they were so long destitute of a sanctuary.

He was a man of slender frame, and gave early indications of pulmonary disease. His failing health interfered with his ministerial work, and he was only sustained by great firmness of purpose and a spirit of elevated devotion. Admonished by his failing health that his ministry might be short, he embraced every opportunity to make the Gospel message tell upon the hearts of his hearers. I have a letter written by him to Dr. Livingston, a short time preceding his death, breathing a beautiful spirit of Christian trust and resignation, and exhibiting the character of a true ambassador of the Lord Jesus.

His increasing indisposition led him "to take frequent reviews of a life so far spent," and he exclaims: "Oh! what abundant reasons of humiliation before God has such a poor creature as I am. Blessed be God! a Jesus is given, is living, is interceding for poor, indigent, sinful worms. I am sure, if there was not such a plan of salvation provided and irresistibly executed, my hope for a world of happiness would sink into gloomy despair. But on a review of many experiences of pardoning and supporting grace—free, infinitely free grace—my hope for a future happy world receives wings; and, on renewed views of such a suitable and glorious plan of redemption—views of my dearest Jesus—I try to mount on high, and now think I would venture with satisfaction into the world of spirits."

But in the midst of great feebleness he labored incessantly in the cause of his Master and for the upbuilding of this church. On the 30th of March, 1790, he procured for this church an act of incorporation under the general law of the State of New-Jersey, passed at Perth Amboy, November 25th, 1789, assuming the name of " the Ministers, Elders, and Deacons of the Congregation of New-Brunswick." The seal of the corporation adopted at a subsequent meeting of Consistory has the appropriate device of a burning lamp in the centre, and the words "Dutch Church of New-Brunswick" in the circumference, which was henceforth to be affixed to all legal documents. This is the present title which we hold in law, and according to which we transact all the temporal concerns of the congregation.

But his useful and laborious life was drawing to a close. In hopes that traveling and a change of climate would administer relief, he spent a few weeks in the months of April and May, 1790, in his native town; but he returned worse than when he left the city, "and was almost determined to relinquish business, and to retire to his farm during the summer season." But he could not abandon the work of the ministry, nor leave his post as the President of the college. Again he sought relief in a change of objects, and in rest at Perth Amboy, in attendance upon the Legislature then in session. And now he returns so much invigorated that he is able to preach the preparation sermon on Saturday, and administer the communion and preach twice on the Lord's Day with comparative ease. "I entertain some hopes," he writes, "that the God of all grace did not leave himself without some witness." It was his last communion season, and he enjoyed in an unusual degree the presence and support of his precious Saviour. "Oh! how sweet, how comforting the promise," is his language to Dr. Livingston, "that he will not forsake his people. Let us believe, trust, and pray for grace, to be made faithful to our God unto death." And that event for which he was so fully prepared was not far off. His work was now done, and the Master was waiting to receive him. He resigned the presidency of the college in the summer, and died quite unexpectedly on the 20th of October, 1790, in the fifty-third year of his age. His tomb stands at the east of the pulpit, and the inscription, prepared, as we understand by Dr. Livingston, though nearly erased by the action of the elements, gives a most admirable exhibition of his character.*

His call to the presidency of the college shows the estimation in which he was held as a scholar and disciplinarian, as well as a divine. His analyses of sermons speak for both the vigor of his intellect and the thoroughness of his theological education. He was a man of strong mind and extensive reading, and in his day was justly regarded as one of the pillars of the Reformed Dutch Church. On four different occasions he was chosen President of General Synod, and he was long regarded as second only to Dr. Livingston, with whom he constantly coöperated in all the interests of the church and the college. He labored for the establishment of this institution, and by personal applications from door to door, along with Dominie Leydt, procured the original funds for its endowment. Several memorials to the General Synod urging the claims of the college, written by him, are still preserved, and bear witness to the zeal with which he advocated the claims,

---

* Here lies the body of J. R. Hardenbergh, D.D., late pastor of this church, who departed this life the 30th day of October, 1790, aged fifty-two years, —— months, and —— days. He was a zealous preacher of the Gospel, and his life and conversation afforded, from his earliest days, to all who knew him, a bright example of real piety. He was a steady patriot, and in his public and private conduct he manifested himself to be the enemy of tyranny and oppression, the lover of freedom, and the friend of his country. He has gone to his Lord and Redeemer, in whose atonement he confidently trusted. He has gone to receive the fruits of his faithful labors, and the reward of a well-spent life. Reader, while you lament the loss to society and his friends, go walk in his virtuous footsteps; and when you have finished the work assigned you, you shall rest with him in eternal peace.

and the affection which he felt for an institution to which he had devoted his best energies. His last public act was a plea before the Synod, at their meeting in New-York, October 5th, 1790, that they would provide means to sustain the college and furnish the early succor so greatly needed. As its first President, he labored under the disadvantages of a small endowment, few assistants in giving instruction, and the want of proper facilities in the way of library, buildings, and apparatus. But he sent out several able scholars, and laid foundations which have made this cherished seat of learning one of the prominent institutions of our land.

As the pastor of this church he had a very successful ministry. On two different occasions there was the unusual manifestation of God's Spirit in the conversion of souls. The whole number received into the church during the four years of his pastorate was sixty-nine. At his first communion he admitted fifteen on profession of their faith, and in the year 1788 twenty-seven were added to the church. Indeed, his whole ministry seems to have been a continual revival, a most blessed close to a most useful and laborious life. He was remembered by a few of the aged inhabitants when I first settled here, and it would seem that they were not able to speak sufficiently in his praise. He was eloquent in the pulpit, and impressed every one with his tone of devotional feeling—a minister eminently beloved by all who knew him.

Dr. Hardenbergh was the last minister of this church who preached in the Dutch language. His plan was to use the Dutch at the morning service and the English in the afternoon. From this date all the records of the church are kept wholly in English, and the Dutch passed away forever.

On his settlement at Raritan he married the widow of his preceptor, Rev. John Frelinghuysen, to whose influence he was indebted, in no small degree, for his eminent usefulness. The character which she has left behind her, under the familiar name of the Jufvrow Hardenbergh, distinguishes her as one of the most remarkable women of her day. Dinah Van Berg was born in the city of Amsterdam, February 10th, 1725. Her father was a wealthy merchant, extensively engaged in the East India trade, who reared his family in the midst of all the fashion and refinement of the metroplis, but without any instruction in religion. She became the subject of divine grace in early youth, and was remarkable for her rapid attainments in godliness and unusual exercises of faith. Her naturally strong intellect was developed by her early education, and the vigor of her mind was seen even down to the period of old age. While still residing in her father's house, her attainments in the religious life were so marked and decided as to arrest attention from all who knew her. It is related that on the occasion of her prostration by sickness, though the prospect of her recovery was regarded as hopeless by the most skillful physician, yet she had such faith in God that he would raise her up, and give her a work to do in the church, that she fixed upon the very day when the progress of the disease would be arrested and her health completely restored. And almost at the hour indicated she started in a course of rapid improvement, and it was always believed by her that God had spared her life in answer to special prayer.

She became acquainted with Mr. John Frelinghuysen, then pursuing his theological studies, during this very sickness; and shortly after, though at first strongly opposed by her parents, she was united with him in marriage, and embarked for her home in America. The death of her husband, in the twenty-fifth year of his age, brought her to the decision of returning immediately to her native country. She was upon the point of embarking with her two children on the voyage to Holland, when Mr. Hardenbergh, who had not yet completed his studies, made her an offer of marriage. Her surprise was indicated by the answer, "My child, what are you thinking about?" Yielding to the solicitation, she consented to a second marriage, with this young man, who became, as we have seen, a distinguished scholar and divine, and was, no doubt, a most efficient co-worker with him in the important services he rendered to his country and the church.

She was a woman of great intelligence as well as of piety, an extensive reader and correspondent, and her influence was felt throughout the whole denomination. For a considerable period she kept an elaborate journal, still preserved, which is said to be superior for its tone of spirituality and of great intellectual vigor. Thus she commences: "It was the beginning of the year 1747; midnight had arrived and passed, and I continued in earnest supplication before the Lord, yielding myself anew to walk in his ways, to be engaged in his service, and to cleave to his people. My heart went forth in earnest desires after larger measures of the renewing grace of the Holy Ghost. Oh! that old things might be made more fully to pass away, the power of depravity be brought into subjection, and the blessed image of the Lord Jesus be more fully transferred to me, and all things become new. My soul arose in petitions to God for the dear people of the Lord, both at my own place at Amsterdam and elsewhere, that God would grant them a renewal of his loving-kindness and larger measures of faith. Oh! that the Lord would bring many of the people out of their distresses; that a formal Christianity might pass away, and the power of godliness be made again to appear. For God's ministering servants I also found in my heart to supplicate much assistance in their weighty work, that they might be more and more faithful, and firm in their attachment to the cause, truth, and people of God, and be enabled by a consistent and godly walk to be examples to the flock."

The following devout exercises on her birthday are recorded in her journal: "Friday, February 10th, 1747, I was twenty-two years old. I awoke with these words upon my mouth, 'I was cast upon Thee.' My thoughts became fixed in intent contemplation upon the wonderful dealings of God with me even from the first moments of my existence, and I was led to say, 'Many are thy wonderful works towards me.' I was led in devout meditation upon the preserving care of God over me, and the wonderful deliverance I had experienced; upon his bounty to me as to the things of this world; but especially upon the dealings of his grace that *in my youth* he was pleased to draw me out of the midst of the evil world. I now earnestly desire more entirely to consecrate myself unto God, and to yield to him the best of my time and strength." The whole journal is pervaded with a similar spirit, and exhibits a mind in direct and habitual communion with God.

Mrs. Hardenbergh has left at her first home in Raritan, as well as in New-Brunswick, a name which places her in the highest rank of female Christians. In this city she was a most efficient aid to her husband in the discharge of his various duties. She visited the sick, attended to the necessities of the poor, and was a comforter in homes of affliction. The two services on the Sabbath were held with an intermission of one hour, during which time the country members of the congregation would remain until the afternoon sermon. Jufvrow Hardenbergh employed the interval in pious conversation with the people, and, gathering around her a group of hearers, would frequently enter into an elaborate exposition of some point in Christian doctrine or passage of Scripture. She was a warm friend of the college, and on the death of her husband was anxious that a successor should be immediately appointed, and the institution fostered and built up. There is in existence a letter written to Dr. Livingston, July 2d, 1791, in which she pleads earnestly with him to accept the position of president, to which he had been elected, and remove to New-Brunswick. New-York could spare him in view of this more pressing call. She writes: "There are more hopes that that breach would be healed than the one among us. Where is there a man for us? Our Dutch ministers are young men of little experience, and have no publicity in the church, however much otherwise esteemed and loved by us. My dear sir, I have heard you say to my now departed husband that you regarded the college as the fountain of the church; why, then, be engaged with the streams, and let the fountain dry up? The Lord enable you to discern what is His holy will; and, if you can do nothing more, oh! pray for us, and by your counsel and coöperation be to us instead of eyes." She had just been permitted to partake of the Lord's Supper in this church, and she assures Dr. Livingston that the Saviour never seemed to her more precious. "This precious Lord Jesus will be our joy in heaven. Oh! the blessedness of being permitted to cast our crowns forever before him."

This remarkable woman survived her husband seventeen years, and died at the residence of her son, Hon. J. R. Hardenbergh, No. 14 Water street, March 26th, 1807. She had attained the venerable age of eighty-two years, and her death was a scene of triumph. She rests by the side of her husband, " of high attainments here in grace, now resting in glory." The following verse, of great poetic beauty, very appropriately testifies to her exalted attainments, and is engraved upon her tomb-stone:

> "Tell how she climbed the everlasting hills,
> Surveying all the realms above;
> Borne on a strong-winged faith, and on
> The fiery wheels of an immortal love."

The children of her first marriage were a daughter, Eva, who became the wife of Mr. Casper Van Nostrand, of Ulster county, N. Y., where several of her descendants are still living; and Frederick, the father of the late Hon. Theodore Frelinghuysen. All who bear this honored name in our section of country are the descendants of Frederick, the only son of Rev. John Frelinghuysen, of Raritan.

At the close of Mr. Hardenbergh's ministry, the church was in a settled, prosperous, and harmonious condition. They had enjoyed only for a short time the labors of this devoted man, but they had been years of growth and improvement in every department of church life. His ripest views of truth he had here preached, his fervent appeals and instructions had been blessed by encouraging ingatherings, and the tenderness of his spirit, disciplined by affliction, had left its impress on all hearts. It is said that the day of his funeral was one of great solemnity. He had been a man of distinction in civil life, as well as in ecclesiastical and educational interests. An active member of the convention that framed the first constitution of New-Jersey, a patriot whose life, often threatened by his tory neighbors, had compelled him to sleep with a loaded musket at his bed-side, caused the whole community to recognize in his death the loss of one of their most distinguished citizens, as well as a great divine.

As soon as the church could recover from the pain of their loss, they sought for a suitable successor, but were subjected to repeated disappointments. It was again proposed that the Consistory of the church should call as their pastor, and the trustees of the college should elect as their president, one who should discharge the duties of both offices. Under this arrangement Dr. Livingston was elected, but declined; so also did Dr. Theodoric Romeyn. In the mean while the college continued to languish, until the year 1795, when its doors were closed, not to be opened until its revival under the efficient management of the succeeding pastor of this church, in 1807. Two years were consumed in these negotiations, and now the church enters upon the work alone, and in earnest.

An effort was made to settle Rev. John Bassett in October, 1792, then pastor of the church of Albany, but without success. So urgent was the congregation that the effort was renewed, with the promise of a large addition to the salary, but with a similar result. The pulpit remained vacant until quite late in the year 1793. In the early part of the summer of that year, a man in the prime of life preached in the Presbyterian church, with whom our people were so well pleased that they invited him to remain and supply their pulpit the following Sabbath. The result was a unanimous call, August 24th, 1793, to the fourth pastor,

REV. IRA CONDICT, D.D.

He was born at Orange, Essex county, February 21st, 1764. He received his academic instruction under Dr. McWhorter, of Newark, and became a student of Princeton College. He became a subject of grace while a member of college, and immediately devoted himself to the gospel ministry. It is said that he cherished a desire for the ministry from his youth, and was accustomed to view every Providence as pointing toward the sacred office. While a member of college, he took a very high stand as a scholar, and was particularly distinguished for his accuracy in the classics. He graduated from that institution in the year 1784, under the presidency of the celebrated Dr. John Witherspoon. His theological studies he pursued under the direction of Dr. Woodhull, of Monmouth, and was licensed by the Presbytery of New-Brunswick in 1786. April 20th, 1787, he was called to the united congregations of Newtown and Hardwick, in Sussex county, and immediately entered upon the field of his labors. Here he found a wide and destitute region, demanding great energy of character and powers of endurance. Within the compass of his old pastoral charge now exist several flourishing Presbyterian churches, as also of other denominations. His ministry continued at this place for six years, and he left there the impress of his noble character. He was aided and encouraged by a most excellent wife, whom many of you will remember as "highly gifted in intellectual and spiritual graces," and whose mind retained all of its vigor in the midst of protracted sufferings.

In Dr. Condict's call it is stipulated that the services are to be conducted in the English language, and that he should preach two sermons in summer and one during the winter months. He was also to hold regular services "on the instituted feast-days of Christmas, New-Year, Easter, Whitsunday, and Ascension day, according to the custom of the church." The salary promised was £180, and a comfortable dwelling-house. The names of the following officers are attached to the call: John Schureman, John Van Neste, William Van Deursen, Garret Voorhees, elders; Fredrick Outcalt, John Thompson, Denice Vanliew, and John Bice, deacons. The original subscription-paper is still preserved, headed by the name of John Schureman, the son of the school-master. On the list we find, in a large bold hand, the signature of Dinah Hardenbergh, a ruling power in the church, as we have seen; as also that of John Neilson, a Presbyterian, whose wife, Catharine Voorhees, always retained her connection with the Dutch Church.

Dr. Condict did not commence his regular duties as the pastor of the church until the first of November. The extent of the congregation at the commencement of his ministry will give some idea of the amount of labor that he performed. In addition to the town charge, the families extended north to Boundbrook, and on the opposite side of the Raritan to New-Market, south along George's road five miles, and down to South river, and west two miles beyond the present site of the Middlebush church.

The first act of the Consistory was to procure a suitable residence for the minister. For a few months Mr. Condict lived in Neilson street, now number eight, in a house rented of William Lawson, at the rate of £37

10s. per annum. When the churches of New-Brunswick and Six Mile Run were in connection, they owned a parsonage at Three Mile Run. On the death of Mr. Leydt, this property was sold to Mr. Jacob Skillman, and the portion that fell to the share of this church, £195 8s. 4d., was appropriated to the purchase of seventeen acres of land on George's road, now in possession of Mr. Edwin Allen, at a cost of £200, and also a house and lot in Church street, now number sixty-two, of John Bray. The building was in an unfinished state, and cost, with the repairs, made under the direction of the Consistory, £475 11s. 6d. Here Dr. Condict resided until his removal, in 1798, to a farm of one hundred and thirteen acres, near Milltown, now the property of Mr. Henry H. Booram, but which is still known as the Condict farm.* The situation was distant and inconvenient; but that the church did not suffer in consequence of his residence so far from the centre is evident from its steady growth, demanding additional church accommodations, which was accomplished in 1803 by the erection of commodious galleries, and by the advance of his salary from £180 to £280, in connection with a commodious parsonage.

While there does not seem to have been any remarkable season of revival under his ministry, yet there was a gradual increase to the membership of the church,

---

* Dr. Condict purchased a property in Church street, number seventy-four, to which he removed in the spring of 1794, and resided there until the parsonage was completed. This house was sold by his widow a few years after his death. The parsonage remained in the hands of the Consistory until 1809, when it was sold to Mr. Henry Van Arsdalen. The seventeen acres in George's road were sold about the same time, and a property of four or five acres purchased on Somerset and Hamilton streets, known in subsequent transactions of Consistory as "the parsonage lot." In the speculation in city lots which prevailed in this town in the year 1814, a part of this ground was surveyed, laid out into squares, and sold at high prices; but parties who purchased failed, and very little was ever realized for a property which is now of great value.

and it is a gratifying record that no communion season passed without the addition of some new members.* Among this number there were three young men who subsequently entered the gospel ministry, and occupied distinguished positions in the church, John Schureman, John S. Vredenbergh, and Robert Bronk.

Dr. Condict was one of the most efficient pastors whom this church has enjoyed. While he was practical and earnest as a preacher, and always came into the pulpit with a well-prepared discourse, among the families of his charge he excelled. In catechising, pastoral visitation, and labors among the poor he had not his superior. He was remarkably punctual in all his engagements, and in his most distant preaching places he was found at the hour ready to commence the services. While he has left behind him a character for remarkable gravity in his deportment, 'and was subject to occasional moods of despondency, yet he was gifted with fine conversational powers, and frequently, in social intercourse with his people, he would throw off all reserve and exhibit a mind full of vivacity. As a member of church judicatories he was active, and always took a prominent part in debate. The General Synod of our church elected him their President at their meeting in Albany, in June, 1800. It is said that his assistance was greatly sought after by congregations who were vacant, and his judicious counsels often led to the amicable adjustment of difficulties which were beginning to assume formidable proportions.

He gained a very just popularity for his learning, and while he was laborious as a pastor he did not neglect his study. The minute of Classis, referred to by Mr.

---

*For a list of church members made at the commencement of his ministry, see Appendix IV.

Corwin, in reference to the necessary suspension of the strict examination of students on the removal of Dr. Condict by death, while "not very complimentary to the survivors," at the same time exhibits the estimation in which he was held as a scholar.

Intimately connected with the history of our church, at the period now under review, are connected the removal of the Theological Seminary to this city and the reorganization of the College. In addition to his labors as the pastor of the church, Dr. Condict took a deep interest in these institutions, and, as a trustee of Queen's College, by his personal exertions was mainly instrumental in its partial revival in 1807. An endowment of twenty thousand dollars was secured, and when it again went into operation, after having been suspended for twelve years, he was chosen Vice-President and Professor of Moral Philosophy. The building in which the exercises were held stood near the site of the Second Presbyterian Church, afterward removed to Schureman street, and is now known as the Lancasterian School. The college owned two acres of land lying west of our old burying-ground, which property was afterward sold and the funds invested in the erection of the present edifice, the foundation of which was laid in 1809. Dr. Condict had removed about the year 1805 from Milltown, and resided during the remainder of his pastorate at No. 32 Water street. The number of students was very encouraging, and for the measure of success which this institution then enjoyed it is indebted largely to the personal labor and sacrifice of the pastor of this church. When the history of this institution shall be written, it will be found that to him more than to any other man is she indebted for this noble building, standing in its beautiful location as an ornament to our city. He was mainly instrumental in securing from Mr. James Parker, by gift, the lot on which it stands. The first subscription paper for the edifice was drawn up by his own hand, and by great perseverance he overcame all the obstacles thrown in his way, and some time before his death he had the satisfaction of seeing the building rise in its fine proportions, and his efforts crowned with complete success. The first commencement, under this new impulse, was held in October, 1809, in the old stone church; and in the class of five graduates three were young men of this congregation—Cornelius L. Hardenbergh, the grandson of the former pastor, J. M. Van Harlingen, and the valedictorian of the day, Dr. William Van Deursen, who is present with us on this occasion with a memory reaching back to the college scenes of fifty-eight years ago.

Connected with the revival of the College, and as a part of the plan, was the removal of the Theological Seminary to this city, in the year 1810, at which time that distinguished professor, Dr. John H. Livingston, took up his residence here, assuming at the same time the Presidency of the College. It is to the honor of our denomination that she organized the first Theological Institution in our land, Dr. Livingston receiving his appointment as early as 1784. But it was not until the year 1810 that the Seminary, on its permanent establishment in this city, started on a career of prosperity which has made it a fountain of life for the church and the world. The institution prospered greatly under the labors of that venerable man, whom the church delighted to honor. One hundred and twenty young men enjoyed the benefit of his instructions in their preparation for the ministry. And it would hardly be possible to set boundaries to the sphere of his influence. The Seminary in his day had its discouragements and trials; but it has passed through them all, and with the advance of years it is more than ever imbedded in the affections of the whole church.

Dr. Condict was greatly favored during the whole period of his ministry in the character of those who labored with him in the Gospel, both in the city and surrounding country. In the Presbyterian church he was associated with Dr. Joseph Clark, (1797 to 1813,) a man of eminent ability, remarkably dignified in his appearance, and greatly esteemed by the people. His sudden death created a great sensation through the town. The text for his Sabbath morning discourse was, "The time is short," and on the following Tuesday, retiring to rest with ordinary health, he was arrested by the hand of death some time before the dawn of morning. In the Episcopal church we find the Rev. John Croes, (1801 to 1832,) afterward the Bishop of New-Jersey, characterized as "the watchful pastor, the instructive preacher, the thoughtful writer, the sound, well-read divine." Of the ministers of our own denomination, in the churches surrounding New-Brunswick, we have, at Six Mile Run and Hillsborough, (1796 to 1807,) a young man of great promise, and afterward of great distinction, Rev. James S. Cannon. At the old church of Mr. Frelinghuysen, at North-Branch, Rev. Dr. Peter Studiford (1787 to 1826) labored with all his strength until God called him home. At Raritan we have Rev. John S. Vredenbergh, (1800 to 1821,) one of the gifted young men of our own church, the son of a prominent elder, whom Dr. Condict had himself received into her communion, and whom he rejoiced over as his spiritual offspring. And Rev. William

R. Smith, (1794 to 1817,) with his colleague, Rev. Henry Polhemus, at Neshanic and Harlingen, fills up the catalogue of those who labored with him in the Gospel throughout this region.

Under the efficient labors of Dr. Condict the church steadily increased in strength, and with the growth of the population enlarged accommodations were again demanded. For two years the question was agitated of enlarging the old building, or of constructing a new edifice. After discussing various plans, the project of a new building was finally adopted with great harmony. An efficient building committee was appointed March 11th, 1811, consisting of Matthew Egerton, Staats Van Deursen, John Clark, John D. Van Liew, and Michael Garrish. The arrangements were all completed, contracts were entered into with builders, and the work was going forward in a spirit of harmony which seldom marks such undertakings, when a sudden cloud rested upon the whole enterprise in the unexpected death of the beloved Condict.

The old stone church in which your fathers worshiped for nearly fifty years, and which, though unadorned, had connected with it so many precious associations, was to be occupied for the last time on Sabbath, May 20th. On the following morning the work of demolition was to commence preparatory to rebuilding. In the Providence of God this was also to be the last sermon which Dr. Condict was to preach previous to his departure. As if in anticipation of what was to take place, he took for his text this striking passage of Scripture from Deut. 4: 22, 23: "But I must die in this land, I must not go over Jordan: but ye shall go over, and possess that good land. Take heed unto yourselves, lest ye forget the covenant of the Lord your

God, which he made with you, and make you a graven image, or the likeness of any thing, which the Lord thy God hath forbidden thee." He dwelt with particular emphasis upon keeping God's covenant, and the touching allusions which he made to the old sanctuary made the house a scene of weeping.

On Monday the workmen commenced; the bell was taken down from the tower and the pews removed, when on Friday the word was circulated that Dr. Condict was confined to his house by sickness. The Sabbath came, and he was unable to meet his people. During the early part of the week there were hopes of his recovery, but all expectation was removed as early as Wednesday, when the announcement was made that he would not probably recover. Dr. Thomas De Witt, who was residing in his family pursuing his studies in the Seminary, has left us in manuscript a record of the closing scene.

The disease which terminated in his death was very violent from its commencement, and Dr. Condict himself thought that it would prove fatal. While he manifested the greatest resignation during the whole of his sickness, toward the close his faith amounted to rapture. Dr. Livingston visited him daily, and these two godly men, the one on the bed of death, the other in the ripe experience of age, held such conversation as we may suppose that the saints in glory enjoy. In the early stages of the disease, he was exposed to great spiritual conflicts and distress. To the venerable professor he remarked: "I have been much harassed and disturbed; still I hope." When the reply was made that it was a precious exercise of faith simply to wait upon the Lord and leave the event with him, he answered: "It is so, but Jesus must give the grace." And that grace the

REFORMED DUTCH CHURCH, NEW-BRUNSWICK, N. J.
Erected 1767. Taken down 1811.

THE NEW YORK
PUBLIC LIBRARY

ASTOR, LENOX AND
TILDEN FOUNDATIONS.

Saviour did bestow. On Wednesday, (he died on Saturday after suffering great bodily pain,) he said: "How good is the Lord to me in the midst of affliction. I can say, I have waited for thy salvation, O Lord; it is a precious salvation."

On Thursday evening, as if in profound meditation, he used this language: "I know Christ died for, I know he can keep, and will keep what I have committed to him. *It is done, it is all sealed.*" Observing some one at his bed-side, he added: "Ah! I am talking."

During the whole of Friday night his death was anticipated at any moment. At one o'clock he arose in his bed and spoke in these words: "The main question with us all is, whether we are willing and ready to die. It is now ascertained to a certainty that I must die. I trust that I am sincerely willing to die. Heavenly Father! into thy hands I commit my spirit, and I pray for that grace for which I have often prayed to support me in the trials and agonies which now await me." After a few minutes of rest, he called around him his family for the farewell blessing. The scene was like that of Jacob parting with his children. To his son Harrison, a young man of great promise who soon followed his father, he said: "My son, I must leave you. Hitherto I have been your teacher, at best an imperfect one. You shall no more have my instructions; but there is the word of God, which has an abundance of knowledge and grace. The Lord has given to you reason, and the capacity for knowing and loving him. Let that word be your instructor, and you will experience riches of grace." "Fear not," he said to his wife; "*you have special promises.* As for our children, you know I have often committed them to God." To one of the elders of the church he spoke words of counsel and encouragement, and sent to his flock a message of great tenderness, pointing them to the heavenly Shepherd now as they were to be left destitute. He is now at the closing moment; his work is done, and he is waiting for the Lord to call him.

Just before his departure occurred a most remarkable scene, equaling any thing in the experience of God's people. Dr. Thomas De Witt has given us this record: "When to all appearance he was near his end, to our wonder and satisfaction he arose in his bed, observed the great necessity of prayer, and that finding the house of death a solemn one, requested those who were present to join with him. He then made a most powerful, solemn, and connected prayer of about four minutes. What appeared surprising was that in his feeble condition he was enabled to speak so long without interruption. It appeared as if the Lord had given him special strength."

He died on Saturday, June 1st, 1811, at eleven o'clock. Thus departed, in the triumph of faith, the beloved Condict. The next Sabbath was a gloomy one in the city. Many of the people from the country came, expecting to hear him preach, and were startled with the intelligence of his death. His funeral was attended from his residence in Water street, Dr. Livingston making the address, and the clergy of the city acting as pall-bearers. The bell of the Episcopal church was tolled during the services, and all the places of business in the city were closed. When arrived at the grave, it seemed as if the whole population of New-Brunswick and surrounding country was crowded into the inclosure. A few words were again spoken by the venerable Professor to the weeping people, and beneath the walls of the old church in which he had preached for seventeen years, now in process of demolition, he was buried. To the left of the pulpit, not far from the grave of his predecessor, Dr. Jacob R. Hardenbergh, will be seen the monument erected by the congregation to the memory of one of their most devoted ministers.

He is represented to have been a tall, muscular man, with black hair, of prominent features, very grave in his deportment, and a man of undoubted piety. It is not probable that in the whole list of pastors there was one more affectionately regarded than the man whom every one esteemed as the "beloved Condict." He seemed to walk these streets as a stranger, and any one who saw him would be impressed with his striking countenance and demeanor. Some of you will remember his sedateness of appearance, and not one who ever heard him in prayer will forget the unction and spirituality of his devotions. In social intercourse he was affable, cheerful, and gave to every one the impression that he had a warm and affectionate heart. He was honored and welcomed beyond the limits of his own extensive charge. Other societies recognized in him a true-hearted minister of Christ, and among the people in city and country he had hosts of friends. With Dr. Clark he was on terms of particular intimacy, frequently exchanging pulpits and visits, and forming united plans for systematic labor. In his arrangements he was exact, and had for every department of labor a fixed time and method. No man could have accomplished more than he did, and the secret of his efficiency lay in the wisdom of his plans. Public institutions honored themselves by placing his name on their catalogues. The corporation of Princeton College elected him a member of their board in 1804, having previously bestowed upon him the title of Doctor of Divinity.

As a preacher he was always excellent, dwelling with particular emphasis upon God's covenant. Indeed, this was his life-work, for he felt that God had set him apart in order that he might preach the Gospel. Although the hand of death has removed almost the entire number of those who sat under his ministry, yet I am happy to have rescued sufficient facts to recall, in part at least, a just portrait of the man. He wore in the pulpit the gown and cassock, and his very appearance was dignified and solemn; not a solemnity that repelled, but which was becoming in a minister of the Gospel. He distrusted very much his own abilities, and was occasionally depressed in mind to such a degree that he felt scarcely fitted to enter the pulpit. He would often stop, on his way up the aisle of the church, at the pew of Jufvrow Hardenbergh, for a word of comfort or encouragement, which she was always sure to have ready for him. It would not be correct to affirm of him that he was gifted with the power of oratory, for this he did not possess; nor with any singular originality of thought or forms of expression, for this he did not cultivate or covet; nor with any brilliancy of imagination and vivid paintings of truth, for he was too intent upon the single purpose of preaching Christ to be led away by any outward display. His strength lay rather in his powerful conviction of the truth which he preached; in his intense earnestness of soul, driving him on as if he had a great work to do for his Master; in his deep sympathy with his hearers, which wrought within all souls the conviction that he sought their good; in a life so consistent that he had not to overcome any unfavorable prejudice, for they felt that he was speaking out of an honest heart; and in a singleness of aim which held him in close contact with the cross. The death of a lovely daughter, Ruth, in the opening flower of her beauty, struck all hearts with great surprise and sorrow, affected him very deeply, and it is said that he went into the pulpit on the following Sabbath and delivered a most tender, earnest, and powerful message from God to the young, and ever afterward his soul more than ever seemed to be given to the cause of Christ.

He had a great aversion to appear in print, and although he was frequently requested to give his sermons to the Consistory for publication, yet he uniformly declined so doing. The only production of his pen that I have seen is a sermon preached before our citizens on the occasion of the death of George Washington, by the invitation of the Mayor and Common Council, and published under their direction. If this is a specimen of his pulpit abilities, we can readily account for his extensive popularity. I am pleased to add a few sentences from the short obituary notice which appeared in the *Guardian, or New-Brunswick Advertiser*, the week succeeding his death: "He was learned and pious, with a discriminating mind and sound judgment. He believed the doctrines of grace, and preached them with precision and zeal. Amiable in his temper, humble, prudent, and without guile in his conversation, he gained the love and possessed the confidence of all who knew him. His time and talents were devoted to the cause of the Divine Redeemer, and his exertions in preaching, visiting, and catechising, throughout his extensive parochial districts, were arduous and unremitted. Dr. Condict was also Vice-President of Queen's College, and had, besides other academical duties, the principal charge of the senior class. The labors attached to this station, in addition to his ministerial cares, proved too severe; they gradually exhausted his strength, and a severe attack of pneumonia terminated in the death of one of the first characters in the church." He died in the forty-eighth year of his age, and in the twenty-fifth of his ministry, seventeen of which had been given to this congregation. His son, Daniel Harrison, whom he addressed so affectionately on his death-bed, soon followed his father, dying August 28th, and was buried by the side of his honored parent. His beloved wife, after surviving her husband many years, a woman of sweet and amiable temper, and of an intelligent piety, was brought from the residence of her daughter in Newark, and "laid in the sepulchre in the full exercise of a holy faith that she would rise again."

The church had now been in existence ninety-four years, and Dr. Condict was the fourth pastor. They had all died while ministers of this church, and their graves are with us unto this day, a beautiful exhibition of the permanence of the pastoral relation, and of the affection existing between minister and people.

The church at this date was very much disheartened; with the loss of their pastor in the midst of rebuilding their church edifice, they felt that all was gone. But Dr. Livingston, by his counsel and encouragement, gave them new strength. He visited the sick, occupied the pulpit of the Presbyterian church at the service of this congregation in the afternoon, and stood in the place of a pastor for nearly two years. In the mean time the work of building went on, the principal amount of the labor falling upon two members of the committee, John Clark and Staats Van Deursen. The corner-stone was laid with appropriate ceremonies July 6th, 1811. The building was completed and occupied for the first time September 27th, 1812. The dedication sermon was preached by Dr. Livingston, from Ezekiel 43 : 12 : "This is the law of the house: Upon the top of the mountain the whole limit thereof round about shall be most holy. Behold, this is the law of the house." The pews were sold on the fifth of the following January. So satisfactory was the whole arrangement, and with such care were the funds managed, that, on the final report of the committee to Consistory, they gave over the building into their hands free of debt, and, out of compliment, were presented with one of the square pews. The cost of the building was $16,415. The edifice was at that time one of the largest in the State, and is now the most commodious house of worship in the city. Its dimensions are ninety-four feet in length, including the tower, which projects four feet, and sixty-six feet in breadth, and will comfortably seat eleven hundred worshipers. This building will always attract attention, on account of its noble proportions and commanding situation, as well as from the interesting associations which it awakens. Since its erection, all the Presidents of our College have here been inaugurated, and the Professors of our Seminary, with only a single exception, have here been inducted into office. Until recently all the commencement exercises have been held in this edifice, and hundreds of young men have looked upon it as the scene of their collegiate honors. It has stood for more than half a century in its massive proportions, testifying to the integrity of the builders and the watchfulness of the committee. It has been twice remodeled—in 1847, by lowering the galleries, and erecting a new pulpit, and in 1862 by reseating and furnishing the entire edifice.

But, while the work of building was going on, the Consistory was not negligent of the great want of the church—a pastor. Negotiations were carried on with the trustees for two years to settle two ministers, who should hold the joint pastorate of the church and professorships in the College. But the plan was finally abandoned, and on May 25th, 1812, an urgent call was extended to the fifth pastor,

REV. JOHN SCHUREMAN, D.D.

This was a happy selection, and very pleasing to the whole congregation. He was one of their own sons, a great favorite, and universally esteemed. His ancestors had been active members of this church for more than ninety years, and were distinguished for their piety and influence. His father was Hon. James Schureman, the patriot of the Revolution, and at this time was a prominent member of the congregation; and his mother was a descendant of the Schuyler family, who came to this town from Albany at its early settlement. His grandfather was Hon. John Schureman, after whom he was named, a merchant of this city, and frequently representing this district in the State Legislature—who was the son of Jacobus Schureman, the schoolmaster, who came from Holland with Mr. Frelinghuysen in 1720, with whom he diligently coöperated in the good work of building up the interests of the Redeemer's kingdom in this favored section of the church.

Dr. Schureman was born October 19th, 1778, near New-Brunswick, to which place his parents had resorted during the occupation of the city by the British army during the Revolutionary war. His religious exercises commenced in very early life, and when a mere youth he was often observed in the devout study of the Scriptures and prayer. In consequence of the absence of his father in the public service of the country, his education devolved principally upon his aged grandfather, to whom he was much indebted for a sound religious training. Young Schureman displayed quite early those traits of character which shone so brightly through his whole life. He was cheerful and amiable in his disposition, affectionate and dutiful to his superiors, kind in his intercourse with his companions, and beloved by all who knew him. He was received into the membership of this church on profession of his faith, under the ministry of Dr. Condict, at the communion in April, 1797. That he was apt to learn may be inferred from the fact of his completing his literary course before he had finished his seventeenth year, graduating from Queen's College September 30th, 1795. After studying theology with Dr. Livingston he was licensed in 1800. His first sermon was preached in the old church for Dr. Condict, and he at once gave promise of the solid, judicious minister which his subsequent life confirmed. His successive fields of labor were at Bedminster for six years, at Millstone for two and a half years, and in the Collegiate Church of New-York for two years. In the latter charge his health soon failed, and he came to New-Brunswick, succeeding Dr. Condict as Vice-President of the College. But this institution was in a very depressed condition, and, in consequence of the exhausted state of its funds and other unfavorable circumstances, with all his diligence and ardor he was not able to restore it to its former honorable position. His love for the pulpit, and his recovered health, secured by rest from public speaking, induced him to listen to an urgent call from this church, and he was installed early in January, 1813. But the flattering prospects of usefulness which now opened before him were speedily disappointed; he soon found that his cherished wish to preach the Gospel was to be denied him, and in June of the same year he resigned his charge, and, in consequence of frequent hemorrhages of the lungs, he very seldom after this entered the pulpit.

The disappointment of the people was very great. He was a finished scholar and a Christian gentleman. That this church was attached to him may be seen in the fact that he had been unanimously called as a colleague with Dr. Condict in 1809, that he might devote more of his attention to the college, which call he declined in order to accept the invitation from New-York; and, while the actual pastor of this church, they not only relieved him of much of the burden of the ministry, but importuned him to remain in his official connection with the congregation, in hopes that a return of health would enable him to assume the full duties of a pastor. And they had reason to love him, for he was truly one of the excellent of the earth. In his subsequent intercourse with the people he was a most judicious and kind counselor, and his influence went far toward healing the unhappy division which arose during the ministry of his successor. Few men understood human nature better than he did, and no man could have been possessed of a heart more affectionate. As a preacher, he was sound in the faith, clear in his method of arrangement, simple and concise in his style, earnest and impressive in his delivery, tender in the very tones of his voice, not frequent but appropriate in his gesticulation, and would leave upon the minds of his hearers the impression that he had in his own soul a deep conviction of the truth that he uttered, and was pervaded by an earnest desire that they should receive profit under his ministrations. That he did not arrest the attention by any bold and striking figures, or move his hearers by pathetic appeals to the passions, was undoubtedly true; but he won his way to the heart by preaching Christ in a method so distinct, and with a manner so fervid, that it is no wonder that he became one of the most useful and popular ministers of his day. One of our ministers* writes: "He was my *beau ideal* of a man, a minister, and a preacher. Well do I remember how he charmed my heart by his solemnity and suavity." Another,† who knew him well, remarks: "I may be thought to exaggerate his merits, but it is difficult to hold the pencil steadily when portraying a man so uncommonly amiable. You loved him even upon a first interview, and you could not withhold your love after it was bestowed. It seems but as yesterday," he adds, "when the venerable Dr. Livingston, in an address at the funeral of the deceased junior professor, turning to the theological students, said, 'My children, *you will not, you can not forget your dear Schureman.*'"

After his resignation of the pastorate of this church he was elected, October, 1815, a Professor of Ecclesiastical History and Pastoral Theology in the Seminary, and died in that office May 15th, 1818. His grave is in the yard near that of Dr. Condict, the fifth of your deceased pastors, beneath a monument erected by General Synod. At a meeting of that body, a short time after his death, the sentiments of the whole church were expressed in the following action: "The death of the late professor, Dr. John Schureman, is an event

---

* Dr. I. N. Wyckoff. † Dr. Gabriel Ludlow.

which, however it may have been his incalculable gain, is deeply to be deplored by us. So amiable were his manners, so undoubted his piety, so acceptable his services, and so flattering were his prospects as to his usefulness in the church, that we can not but mourn that such a man is removed from our institution." It was also provided that a plain tombstone be erected over his grave, with a suitable inscription declaring the important station he occupied in the church, and the esteem which this body will long cherish for one whose praise was in all the churches.

The resignation of Dr. Schureman was followed by a short vacancy. October 2d, 1813, the church, with great unanimity, called, as the sixth pastor,

REV. JESSE FONDA.

He was born in the town of Watervliet, Albany county, N. Y., April 27th, 1786. He made a profession of his faith in the Reformed Dutch Church of the Boght, and graduated from Union College, in 1806, in the same class with Dr. C. C. Cuyler and the Hon. John C. Spencer. His theological studies were pursued under the direction of ministers of our church, and he was licensed by the North Consociation of Hartford County. His first settlement was at Nassau, N. Y., where he labored with all the enthusiasm of a young pastor, and in which place his ministry is still remembered as one of great prosperity and usefulness. He removed to this city and commenced his labors in the month of November.

This church had suffered much for the want of pastoral supervision, Dr. Schureman's feeble health having prevented him from doing much active work in the congregation. Mr. Fonda found a large amount of labor upon his hands, and, blessed with a vigorous constitution and great energy of character, he gave himself fully to this ministry. He was systematic in his labors and intensely active. About this time an unhappy controversy commenced in the church in reference to the hour for holding the afternoon service on the Sabbath, which continued to disturb the peace of the church for a number of years, and was the ultimate ground of his removal. The pastor and city portion of the charge desired a change to three o'clock, but the more distant members of the congregation were in favor of the plan which had been the established usage of the church. At one time the difficulty had grown to such proportions that the plan of a new organization was proposed. The matter in controversy was carried before Classis, who recommended, through a committee, the formation of two new churches, one to be located at Three Mile Run, the second at Milltown or on George's road. It would, no doubt, have been to the interest of the denomination had this plan been carried out, and these churches organized in a spirit of harmony and with a desire to extend the Redeemer's kingdom.

But the existence of this controversy was not so absorbing as to divert the attention from spiritual interests. During the ministry of Mr. Fonda there was a healthy growth of the church, and at one communion twenty-eight persons made a public profession of their faith. The total number of communicants received into the church was one hundred and seven.

Mr. Fonda was dismissed from this congregation July 3d, 1817, in order that he might accept a call from the Reformed Dutch Church, of Montgomery—at that time, as at present, one of the most intelligent and flourishing congregations in our body. He preached his last sermon on the 28th of the month from the text, "Casting all your care upon him, for he careth for you." By request of his numerous friends the sermon was published, and it exhibits, with great tenderness, the doctrine of "confidence in God in the day of trouble." It is inscribed to his personal friends Drs. Livingston and Schureman, and to the reverend clergy of New-Brunswick, "brethren who dwell together in unity."

Mr. Fonda continued at Montgomery in the faithful discharge of his duties until his death in 1827. Few ministers excelled him as a preacher. He had a full, sonorous voice, well modulated, and would draw attention by the pleasantness of his countenance. He prepared his sermons with great care, writing them out in full and then preaching from memory. He never paused for a word, but carried his hearers along in a train of rapid argument or pungent appeal to the close of his discourse. Dr. Livingston regarded him as one of our most finished ministers. It is said that he greatly excelled on extraordinary occasions. His ministry occupied the important period of our last war with England. The public mind in this section of the country was intensely agitated, and seizing hold of these important national occurrences he enforced with great power the lessons of religion as taught by "the signs of the times." His sermon, preached April 13th, 1815, on the occasion of the close of the conflict, entitled "Thanksgiving for Peace," produced a wonderful sensation. This large building was crowded to its utmost capacity, while he discoursed with great eloquence upon the passage, "Sing, O daughter of Zion; shout, O Israel; be glad and rejoice with all the heart, O daughter of Jerusalem. The Lord hath taken away thy judgments." (Zephaniah 3 : 14, 15.)

In 1814, Mr. Fonda was chosen a member of the Board of Trustees of Queen's College; and at the annual meeting of General Synod in Albany, June, 1823, he was chosen the President of that body. He has left, in his work on the Sacraments, a very fair reputation for authorship, which deserves to be reproduced from the press and given a wide circulation.

Mr. Fonda left here in the summer of 1817. In the graduating class of that year there was a young man, a member of this church, of fine abilities and of great promise, to whom all eyes were immediately directed. It was not necessary for him to preach as a candidate, for every one knew him, and so urgent was the Consistory that, even before he received his license, a committee waited upon him with an informal presentation of a call. This student, who became the next pastor of the church of New-Brunswick, was

REV. JOHN LUDLOW, D.D.

His calls bears the date of September 17th, 1817, fifty years ago. The first invitation he declined, but on its renewal he accepted the charge with the understanding that he was not expected to preach but once on the Sabbath during the first year, and be released from all pastoral labor. It is said that he broke through these conditions almost immediately, for he was a faithful pastor, and in the pulpit a Boanerges. Some of you remember him as he appeared when he first came among you, and the interest that was awakened in the church by having for their pastor a young man fresh from our Theological Seminary. His ministry, however, was short. Only two years after his settlement he received an appointment to a professorship in the Theological Seminary, which he felt constrained to accept, and was accordingly released from his pastoral charge.

His character and history are well understood in this community, where the last years of his life were spent in the education of young men for the ministry. After spending four years as professor under his first appointment by General Synod, he returned to the pulpit, for which he had special qualifications, and was for eleven years the pastor of the North Church of Albany, at that time, as at present, the first in position and influence in the Synod of Albany. In 1834, he accepted the position of Provost in the University of the City of Philadelphia, which office he held for eighteen years; and only resigned that he might obey the will of the General Synod in his election to the Professorship of Ecclesiastical History, Pastoral Theology, and Church History in our Seminary, succeeding the venerable Professor Cannon, which position he filled with great ability until his death, September 8th, 1857. His grave is among the group of pastors and professors in the yard at the left of the pulpit.

Dr. Ludlow, as a man, a minister, and a Christian, was universally esteemed. The confidence which was reposed in him by the church is sufficiently indicated by his election at five different periods to professorships in our institutions. In the Northern Synod no minister exerted so wide an influence. If a church building was to be dedicated, or a corner-stone laid, or an installation sermon preached, the services of Dr. Ludlow were solicited. In his early ministry in this church he developed rapidly, and soon exhibited all those traits of character which distinguished him in after-life. Says one of his early students: "We loved him as a preacher. He elucidated his texts fairly, strongly, with dignity, and as one ever under a sense of God's requirements. His subjects were rich and diversified. He loved what he used to call a good fat text, one full of Gospel truth and bearing on men's hearts and conscience." His brother remarks that "his strength as a preacher lay very much in his *manner;* in the fire of his eye; in the expression of his countenance—an expression very varied and corresponding very fully with his varied emotions; in the stentorian tones of his voice—a voice that easily filled the largest buildings; in his strong and well-placed emphasis; in his forcible gesticulation; in his positive, authoritative, confident manner." A most admirable analysis of his character was given by Dr. Bethune, who knew him well. Based on the thought that his leading quality was strength, he presents Dr. Ludlow as a man, "strong in person, strong in voice, strong in intellect, strong in will, strong in affections."

His activity in carrying forward all the great measures of our church is deserving of high praise. And the noble result of his last labors for the church he loved—the Theological Hall—stands before us to-day as a monument to his memory. All those traits of character which distinguished him in after-life he displayed at the commencement of his ministry, and while he was yet the pastor of this church. And it is not surprising that they yielded to the will of General Synod with extreme reluctance, and "a general murmur arose through the congregation not easily or soon hushed."

The resignation of Dr. Ludlow left this church vacant for the third time in the short space of six years. Rev. Gabriel Ludlow, the brother of the late pastor, was now called, but declined the invitation. The pulpit was supplied by the professors in the Seminary for about one year, during which period the attention of the Consistory was directed to another young student, who graduated from the institution in the first class under the instruction of their former minister; and on January 21st, 1821, there was called, as the eighth pastor of this church,

REV. ISAAC FERRIS, D.D.

Dr. Ferris was installed pastor of the church on the third Thursday in April, 1821. Early in May, Rev. Samuel B. How, D.D., commenced his labors in the Presbyterian church, of which he was installed the pastor the 13th of June.[*] April 13th, Rev. G. S. Webb, D.D., became the minister of the Baptist church. It is a striking coincident that these three New-Brunswick pastors, all in early manhood, entered upon their work in this city the same spring, and it is not necessary to remark that the intimate relation then formed has continued unbroken until the present. It is a pleasing feature of our anniversary that these servants of the Lord are all still living, with memories reaching back to their labors in this city. Two have their homes with us, spending the close of life among the people to whom they ministered for near a generation, and the other is in the discharge of active duties. As the

---

[*] The following have been pastors of the First Presbyterian Church: Rev. Gilbert Tennent, (1726-'43;) Rev. Thomas Arthur, (?) (1746-'51;) Rev. Israel Reed, (1768-'86;) Rev. Walter Montcith, (1786-'94;) Rev. Joseph Clark, D.D., (1797-1813;) Rev. Levi J. T. Huntington, 1815-'20; Rev. Samuel B. How, D.D., (1821-'23;) Rev. Joseph H. Jones, D.D., (1825-'38;) Rev. Robert Birch, (1839-'42;) Rev. Robert Davidson, D.D., (1843-'59;) Rev. Howard Crosby, D.D., (1861-'62;) Rev. William T. Beatty, (1863-'67,) and at present without a pastor.

senior ex-pastor of this church, with great propriety the committee have solicited from him the favor, and the congregation will enjoy the pleasure, of listening to the closing address of our anniversary from one who, forty-six years ago, was set apart to the work of the ministry within these walls by the laying on of the hands of the Presbytery.

November 10th, 1821, there was received into the membership of the church, on profession of his faith, a young man, in the seventeenth year of his age, who subsequently became one of the most devoted of our foreign missionaries—David Abeel. His father was a man of great moral integrity and of remarkable energy of character; while his mother, Jane Hassert, was a woman of uncommon amiability of temper and of devoted piety. There were beautifully blended in the character of young Abeel great firmness of purpose, a quick intellect, and an unusual development of gentleness and affection. He was one of those men who drew toward him the warmest esteem and admiration; and, when grace gave him a new heart, he was of all others the one whose soul would overflow with commiseration for the perishing heathen, and who was ready to consecrate himself to a work which demanded the most heroic sacrifices, and which he continued to prosecute with untiring devotion to the close of his life. The interest with which he was regarded by all those who knew him, as well as indicating one element of his strength, is sufficiently attested by the uniform name which he bore of "the beloved Abeel." His early death, at the age of forty-two, filled the whole Church with mourning; for well she knew that such men are rare—men of similar faith and ardor, and of entire consecration to the cause of God and man. It is an honor to have upon our church-rolls the name of such a man, and to have sent forth into the Gospel ministry and into the heathen world David Abeel.

In addition to Dr. Abeel, there were six young men from this congregation who consecrated themselves to God in the work of the ministry, and who united with the church by profession during the ministry of Dr. Ferris. The whole number of additions to the church during the period under review was seventy-eight by profession and twenty-seven by certificate, and of the whole number, one hundred and five, only seven are now in communion with us.

The pastoral relation between Dr. Ferris and this congregation was dissolved in October, 1824, when he removed to Albany and was installed over the Second Reformed Dutch Church of that city, succeeding Dr. John De Witt, who had recently assumed the Professorship of Biblical Criticism, Ecclesiastical History, and Pastoral Theology in our Seminary. The successive fields of labor occupied by Dr. Ferris were, in Albany twelve years; in the Market Street Church, of New-York, twelve years; and, since 1852, as the Chancellor of the University of New-York, in which honorable position may he long be spared to serve the cause of education and advance the interests of the Redeemer's kingdom.

Forty-three years ago, when the ministry of Dr. Ferris terminated, New-Brunswick was an ancient town. Those who were then familiar with the city would now recognize only a few things which have not passed through changes, and the inhabitants with whom he was then familiar would no longer be seen in our streets. The population, numbering about four thousand five hundred, lived between New street at the south,

Somerset street at the north, and George street at the west, with a few families on the outskirts of the town. This building, without a steeple, had stood for twelve years, and at the time of its erection it was thought that it would be too far distant from the centre of population, as at that time only a few families were living further west. About one half of the congregation were from the country, and of the city charge about fifty families resided in Burnet street, thirty in Church, in Water and Albany streets there were forty, and the balance were living in Neilson, New, Peace, and Hiram streets. All that portion of the city beyond George, New, and Somerset streets was out of town. The College was standing in an unfinished condition on quite a barren hill. The grounds now occupied by the Seminary and the beautiful residences beyond were desolate in the extreme, presenting the remains of the old fortification of the British army during the Revolution. The Presbyterian congregation was worshiping in their second edifice, fronting Paterson street, a short distance below the present site. Dr. How had preached his last sermon in this church October 5th, 1823, to accept a call in the city of Savannah, and they were now vacant. The first building of the Baptist church was standing on the spot now occupied by the depot, surrounded by a cemetery of about one acre, where they continued to worship until 1837, when the property was sold and the present edifice erected.* There was

---

* This society was connected with the church at Piscataway for several years, the pastor serving both congregations. The first church edifice was completed in 1812, and the church organized September 21st, 1816. The following have been pastors: Rev. James McLaughlin, (1812–17,) Rev. John Johnson, (1818–19,) Rev. G. S. Webb, D.D., (1821–43,) Rev. George R. Bliss, D.D., (1843–49,) Rev. Shobel S. Parker, (1850–52,) Rev. George W. Kempton, (1852–57,) Rev. Thomas R. Howlett, (1858–59,) and Rev. Mortimer S. Riddell, D.D., since 1860.

only one Methodist church, in Liberty street, built in 1811. A trip to Philadelphia was an event to be planned some weeks before the undertaking, and a journey to New-York and return consumed two days.

The successor of Dr. Ferris, and the ninth pastor, was

REV. JAMES B. HARDENBERGH, D.D.

He was called April 2d, 1825, and was the second minister of this name who held the pastoral office in this church. He was born in Ulster county, N. Y.; graduated from Union College in 1821, and from our Theological Seminary in 1824; immediately after which he was installed Pastor of the Reformed Dutch Church, of Helderberg, in the county of Albany. He was holding this position when the Consistory of this church presented him an urgent call through one of their deacons, Mr. H. H. Schenck. He remained in connection with this church until December, 1829, discharging his duties with great fidelity and success, in order that he might accept an invitation to labor in a new enterprise in Orchard street, New-York City, from whence he removed to Rhinebeck for six years, to the First Church, of Philadelphia, for four years, and thence to the North-West Church, in New-York, for fourteen years.

The property on which our church edifice stands was enlarged, in the years 1823 and 1825, by the purchase of two lots of forty-three feet front on Bayard and Paterson streets, with a depth along the alley of two hundred and forty-four feet, at a cost of $395.50. The first lecture-room owned by the congregation was erected in 1826, on the corner of the alley and Bayard street, at an expense of $1468. All the weekly services of the church were held, up to this date, in the Lancasterian school-room in Schureman street. The church edifice was still further improved by the erection of a steeple in the year 1827, under the direction of three very efficient members of the congregation, Staats Van Deursen, Matthew Egerton, and Peter Spader. The amount expended was $2725.

On our list of church members received during the ministry of Dr. Hardenbergh I find the name of that excellent missionary, Rev. Frederick B. Thompson. Through the influence of his pastor he was induced to commence a course of preparation for the gospel ministry. His missionary life commenced September 17th, 1838, when he reached Singapore, on his way to the island of Borneo, where he spent several years laboring with great industry and devotion for the cause of Christ among the benighted Dyaks. His course was soon finished. He died in the city of Berne, Switzerland, January 17th, 1848, in the thirty-ninth year of his age, "just at a time when his great usefulness became apparent, and at a peculiar crisis, when the church most needed his labors. Had he lived," adds his biographer, "to the ordinary age of man, he would, undoubtedly, have stood among the very first missionaries of his age." In a commemorative discourse, preached in this church after the news of his death had reached America, Dr. How remarked, "The life of our departed brother has been short, but it has not been in vain; and we doubt not but that, hundreds of years hence, the name of Frederick B. Thompson will be pronounced in Borneo with blessings upon it." The memory of this godly man is still precious in our church, and it was a privilege in the pastor to have received him into her communion.

Dr. Hardenbergh's resignation was not accepted until repeated efforts had been made to retain his services; but, under a conviction of duty, he was constrained to leave an established and prosperous church for a new enterprise in the city of New-York.

The last three pastors of this church, Drs. Ludlow, Ferris, and Hardenbergh, were young men, educated in our own Seminary, and called to exercise the work of the ministry at a most interesting period in the history of the church. They lived at a time when all the great benevolent institutions of the age were set in operation, and the Kingdom of Christ was organized for more efficient activity against the kingdom of darkness. They all identified themselves with the prominent schemes of Christian benevolence, and aided in carrying forward the plans of religious enterprise.

The date of the reorganization of our College occurred during this period. At a meeting of the Board of Trustees in May, 1825, a committee was appointed to increase the endowment of the institution, so that its literary department might be revived and the machinery of education set in full operation. Rev. Jesse Fonda was chairman of the committee, and Rev. J. Ludlow and an elder of this church, Jacob R. Hardenbergh, were members. The plan was successful, and so promptly was the effort responded to throughout the church that, at an adjourned meeting of General Synod, held in September following, the gratifying report was made that subscriptions for a third professorship to the amount of $26,000 had been obtained, principally within the bounds of the Synod of Albany, and arrangements were made for the revival of the College. At the same time the name of the institution was changed from Queen's to Rutgers, in honor of a noble

Revolutionary patriot, a liberal contributor to its funds, and a distinguished elder in the church. Since that period the College and Theological Seminary, which have given such distinction to our city, have increased in prosperity and usefulness, until, by the munificent endowments recently procured, they have been placed on a substantial foundation, and have obtained a position of great prominence among the institutions of our land.

January 20th, 1825, an event occurred in the congregation which clothed not only this church but the whole denomination in mourning. I refer to the death of the venerable Professor Dr. John H. Livingston. He was a resident of this city and a member of the congregation for fifteen years, and during all this period he was the honored head of our institutions and the acknowledged leader of all religious enterprises. Dr. Livingston was a man of mark in every position he occupied, the observed of all observers. Many things in this city remind us of him. The name of one of our most beautiful streets is called after him, Livingston Avenue. The seat which he always occupied in this sanctuary was at the head of the elders' pew, with a form erect even amid the infirmities of age, and an attention that never wandered for a moment. This building reminds us of him. He laid the corner-stone with an appropriate address, and, when it was completed, he preached the dedication sermon. He presided at the ordination of pastors; during the time of vacancy was chairman of meetings of Consistory, and directed the affairs of the congregation; he offered consolation to the people on the death or removal of their ministers, and stood himself in the room of a shepherd. It was regarded as a great privilege to hear him preach, and communion Sabbaths in the church of New-Brunswick always drew a large congregation; for the duty devolved upon him, by the courtesy of pastors, to take the prominent place in the services. And it is said that, while he was always excellent, on these occasions he was superior. The subject in which he most delighted was Jesus the Mediator of the Covenant, and at the Table of the Lord he would grasp the doctrine of the cross with a comprehensiveness which was peculiar to himself, and present it in a manner so adapted to his theme that all hearts would melt in the presence of Infinite Love.

Dr. Livingston's sudden death was almost like a translation. On the day preceding he had delivered an important lecture in the institution, and, retiring to rest at the usual hour, during the night he was received into the glory of the Lord, at the ripe age of seventy-nine years. His funeral was attended in this building by an immense concourse of people, and an address delivered by Dr. Milledoler. A commemorative sermon was preached on a subsequent Sabbath by Dr. John De Witt, and by request of the Consistory was published. His monument is in our churchyard, beneath which his precious dust is resting until the resurrection into life eternal.

It is forty-two years since this noble man was taken from the church, and yet the impressions left upon the minds of hundreds in our city are as vivid as if they had met him in our streets only yesterday. Indeed, not one who saw him in the pulpit could ever forget him. His clerical dress of the old style; his tall, erect, dignified form; his deliberate but elastic step; his countenance so regular, with a blended expression of benignity and intelligence; his tones of voice so full, varied, and flowing; his style animated, tender, colloquial, often sublime, would arrest the attention of the youngest hearer. I have heard descriptions of him, most accurate, from persons who at the time of his death were mere children. There must have been something peculiar about him to stamp on the mind an impression which is so permanent. "As a preacher," writes Dr. Sprague, "he was among the most prominent of his day; his sermons teemed with the richest evangelical truth, presented in the most luminous way, and in a style of delivery impressive, majestic, and yet singularly unique. He was for many years recognized as the patriarch of the Dutch Church, and his memory is embalmed in the gratitude and veneration of the whole church."

The General Synod immediately made choice of Rev. Philip Milledoler, D.D., one of the ministers of the Collegiate Church in New-York, as the successor of Dr. Livingston in the chair of Didactic Theology, and at the same time he was appointed President of Rutgers College. This position he filled for fifteen years, during which time he was a constant attendant upon the services of this church, occupying one of the square pews, at the head of which he always sat, giving devout and reverent attention to the preaching of the word.

Dr. Milledoler was a most useful and excellent man, and at one period of his life his services were sought by some of the most important congregations in New-York and Philadelphia. In the latter city, as the successor of Rev. John Blair Smith, in the Pine Street Church, his ministry was eminently successful, and for several years it was blessed by an almost uninterrupted revival. Previous to the organization of Princeton Seminary, the Presbytery of New-York appointed him the instructor of students in theology, and he had the honor of sending out into the ministry several useful and well-prepared young men. Dr. Sprague has furnished us with the following picture of the man, the correctness of which will be recognized by all who knew him: "Dr. Milledoler was a man of rather more than the medium height, well-proportioned, with a grave countenance, dignified manners, and good powers of conversation. His mind, naturally of a superior mould, was well-disciplined and well-stored. His Christian character was marked by great consistency and a uniformly fervent devotion. His sermons were always highly evangelical, and delivered with a marked vivacity and unction that could scarcely fail to command attention. But nothing pertaining to him was so unmistakable as his prayers; it seemed as if he were literally speaking to his Father in heaven face to face; simplicity, tenderness, fullness, freedom, and variety were their leading characteristics."

We are brought, in the progress of our narrative, to the year 1829. Rapid changes had taken place in the ministry of this church. Dr. Ludlow had hardly become acquainted with his people when the General Synod called him to the Seminary; Dr. Ferris has only commenced his work when Albany calls him to the vacant pulpit of Dr. DeWitt; and Dr. Hardenbergh is induced to accept a new field of labor in the city of New-York after serving this church for about four years. It is not to be disguised that these short pastorates were very unfavorable to the real interests of the church. Frequent occurrence of vacancies interrupted the steady progress of religious work, and agitated the congregation with the natural anxiety respecting a successor. It is almost surprising that the selections were made with such a spirit of unanimity, and that this large church so soon rallied around these young men sent to them by the Lord of the vineyard.

The period of vacancy was short. Dr. Hardenbergh's resignation took effect in December, 1829, and only two months subsequent, namely, on February 23d, 1830, a unanimous call was extended to the tenth pastor,

REV. JACOB J. JANEWAY, D.D.

He had previously been called to the Presbyterian church in this city, as the successor of Dr. Joseph Clark, in 1814, which invitation he declined. Previous to his settlement over this congregation he had occupied some of the most prominent positions in the Presbyterian Church, and at the date of his call had just resigned the Professorship of Theology in the Western Theological Seminary, at Alleghany, Pa. He was not installed until May 26th, though he assumed the charge of the pulpit early in the spring. The church now felt that they had secured a pastor of middle age, who would long remain among them, and give his ripe experience and sound instruction to the upbuilding and establishment of the congregation. He came to this city with a well-furnished mind, a large stock of experience, thoroughly orthodox in his sentiments, and at once, though he had spent his whole ministerial life in the Presbyterian Church, identified himself with all the interests of our denomination. Indeed, he was only returning to his first home. His parents were members of the Collegiate Church, in New-York, into whose communion he also was received on confession of his faith after graduating from Columbia College. His theological studies were pursued under the direction of Dr. Livingston, for whom he cherished an unbounded reverence, first as his pastor, then as his instructor, and through life as his cherished friend. The College testified their confidence in him by electing him a member of their Corporation, and the General Synod by elevating him to the Presidency of that body in 1833.

About the time of his settlement the plan of organizing a church at Middlebush was agitated, and preliminary measures taken to carry it into effect. A memorial was drawn up with great care by that portion of the congregation residing in this district and laid before the Consistory. The commissioners were Henry V. Demott and Frederick J. Van Liew. They argue in this paper the importance of establishing a church not only in that immediate neighborhood, but also on George's Road. The Consistory encouraged the movement, and by immediate resolution proposed to give, as their subscription, the parsonage lot of three acres on Somerset and Hamilton streets. Dr. Janeway was a warm advocate of this measure, and although it was not carried into effect during his ministry, yet he regarded the enterprise as essential to the prosperity of the church; and, marking the indisposition of the people to leave his ministry, in a spirit of great self-sacrifice he immediately determined to resign his charge, hoping that this important plan would soon be accomplished.

The expectation of the church that the ministry of Dr. Janeway would be of long continuance was to be disappointed. The extent of the congregation, the amount of labor incident to a great country as well as city charge, and the need of an immediate organization in some part of this extensive field, induced him to seek from the Classis a dissolution of the pastoral relation, which was effected February 24th, 1831, after serving the church only one year.

After a short residence in the city of New-York, Dr. Janeway returned to New-Brunswick, and in 1833 was called to the Vice-Presidency of the College, and to the Professorship of Belles Lettres and the Evidences of Christianity, which positions he filled with eminent ability until his resignation in 1839.

He died at his residence in Livingston Avenue on Sabbath evening, June 27th, 1858, in the eighty-fourth year of his age; a man greatly beloved for his many virtues, and of distinguished position in the church. It was a sentiment to which this entire community responded, uttered at his funeral by his intimate friend Dr. Hodge, "After a life devoted with singular simplicity of purpose to the service of his Master, he descends to the grave with a reputation without a blot, followed by the benedictions of hundreds and by the respectful affection of thousands. A long, prosperous, happy, and useful life has been crowned with a truly Christian death."

The resignation of Dr. Janeway in the winter of 1831 again left this church vacant. After making an effort to secure the services of Rev. Samuel A. Van Vranken, and having the pulpit supplied by Rev. Henry Hermance for about six months, the choice of the church, as the eleventh pastor, was my immediate predecessor,

REV. SAMUEL B. HOW, D.D.

Dr. How was born in the city of Burlington; graduated from the University of Pennsylvania in 1811; was licensed by the Presbytery of Philadelphia in 1813; first pastor for two years of the church of Salisbury, Pa.; then five years of the church of Trenton, N. J.; then two years as the minister of the First Presbyterian Church of this city; then for seven years pastor of the Independent Church of Savannah; and after laboring for a short time as President of Dickinson College, Pa., and also in a new enterprise in New-York, he was called to this church May 18th, 1832.

You have now followed me to a period in the history of our church within the recollection of nearly every middle-aged man. The pastor who now filled this pulpit is still living, and the time has not yet come to form an estimate of character or to sum up the record of results. The briefest statement of facts occurring within the next thirty-five years will be all that is expected previous to closing our narrative.

The period that now comes under review may be regarded as the era of church extension and revivals. In both of these departments there has been an advance beyond that of any preceding period. In regard to the muliplication of churches, the following facts will arrest attention: Of the ten organizations now constituting the Classis of New-Brunswick, when Dr. How commenced his ministry, only two, in addition to our own, were in existence—the churches of Six Mile Run and Hillsborough. The original Classis, numbering fourteen churches and eleven ministers, extended from Middletown, in Monmouth county, to Lebanon in Hunterdon, and embraced also three churches still farther north, in Orange county, N. Y. Now, within the same territory we have three Classes, thirty-four churches, with a body of forty ministers. That we have multiplied to the extent that we should in all parts of the field is not to be presumed, and the question should press upon us whether we ought not to stretch abroad the curtains of our habitation.

Almost the first act after the settlement of Dr. How

was the organization of the long talked of church in the country portion of his charge. Once more the subject came before the Consistory in a memorial from that part of the congregation residing in the vicinity of Middlebush, and an earnest resolution was adopted that the time had now fully come in which to arise and build. The concurrence of the surrounding churches having been secured, by an act of Classis the Reformed Dutch Church of Middlebush* was organized March 17th, 1834, by a committee consisting of Rev. Messrs. Jacob I. Shultz, H. L. Rice, and A. D. Wilson. That church has always been looked upon with interest as our own enterprise, and nothing affords the old First more joy than to learn of their prosperity. And to-day we offer our congratulations that, under the administration of her young pastor, she is assuming new vigor, and is beautifying the sanctuary of the Lord.

It pleased God, in the year 1837, to pour out his Spirit in a remarkable manner upon New-Brunswick, and bless this church with a revival of religion such as is seldom enjoyed. The work of grace commenced in the Baptist church some time in the month of March, and soon spread through all the other congregations. Of this revival, two interesting narratives were published at the time in the religious newspapers; one by Dr. Jones, pastor of the Presbyterian church, and the other by Dr. How, giving a detailed account of the work in his own charge. In respect to this congregation Dr. How states that "for several years previous it had been peaceful and prosperous, and had steadily improved in its spiritual interests." Two events are spoken of in the nar-

---

* The pastors settled at Middlebush have been Rev. J. I. Shultz, (1834–38,) Rev. John A. Van Doren, (1838–66,) and Rev. George W. Swain, the present pastor.

rative as seeming to prepare the way for this great awakening; namely, the visitation of the cholera in 1832, and the desolating tornado which swept through the city in June, 1835, laying whole streets in ruins and destroying several lives. The minds of the people were arrested and solemnized by these events, and in many instances saving impressions were produced. But in the latter part of May, 1837, the entire congregation seemed to be affected with a religious awe, and it was rare to meet with an individual who was not willing to converse with his pastor on his spiritual interests. Religious meetings were thronged, Sabbath days were seasons of refreshing, conversions were multiplied, and the entire population was moved by the Spirit of God.

The result of this work of grace in this church was the addition of one hundred and thirty-seven to the communion, and about five hundred to all the churches in the city. The work was very powerful in the College. In the graduating class of that year not one was left unvisited. Out of the number who united with our church nine entered the gospel ministry, of whom two are now professors in our Theological Seminary—Rev. Drs. De Witt and Demarest. Many who were received into the membership of the church had been under serious impressions for six, nine, and twelve months, and some for two or three years.

The means employed were the ordinary and established ordinances of grace, and no new measures or novel doctrines were resorted to in order to feed a mere excitement. Religious meetings were indeed multiplied, but they were for prayer and the preaching of the Word. The aid of other ministers was sought, but they were the pastors of neighboring churches and the professors in the institutions. The morning prayer-meeting at six o'clock was uniformly crowded, and those who attended them will never forget the solemn awe that rested upon the assemblies. While there was far from the exhibition of any opposition, every one spoke of the revival with interest, and all seemed to come under the power of an influence which was not of man but of God. Dr. How remarks, in his narrative, that "there was no disorder, no confusion, no wild, misguided zeal. All was serious, solemn, calm, devout, and at times deeply affecting." And months after the work had ceased, the pastor states, as the effect produced upon the congregation, that there has been "an increased spirit of harmony and love among the people of God, and never was the congregation in a state of more entire peace or of greater prosperity than it now enjoys."

This is one of the brightest spots in the history of the church, and it will be long before the members of this congregation and the citizens of New-Brunswick will cease to speak with the deepest emotion of the revival of 1837.

In subsequent years it was the happiness of the pastor to witness other special seasons of ingathering. In 1843, thirty-three were added to the communion; in 1853, twenty-seven; and in 1858, fifty-four; but the powerful work of grace in 1837 stands without a parallel in the whole history of the church.

Year after year there was the evidence of increased prosperity, and during the ministry of Dr. How the congregation had so enlarged in numbers that he reports to Classis three hundred and fifty families, and five hundred and forty-nine communicants upon the rolls. It was God's blessing poured out upon the faithful preaching of the Word, and great diligence in the discharge of pastoral work. So will God bless us as we are faithful to his truth, and conform ourselves to the sure teachings of his Providence.

The large accession of numbers and growth of the church called for the organization of a second congregation of our order in the city. The blessing of God upon the labors of the pastor had filled this building to its utmost capacity, every seat was occupied, and it was felt that to send out a colony was not only desirable but an absolute necessity. Those who were the original movers in this enterprise, while they no doubt felt deeply the sundering of the tie by which they were bound to this ancient church, and could not but express regret at their parting from brethren to whom they were tenderly attached, and to a ministry that had been eminently blessed, were at the same time actuated by a conviction that another church was needed to meet the growing religious wants of this city. The plans of the organization having been perfected, February 14th, 1843, there was organized in this building the Second Reformed Dutch Church of New-Brunswick, by a committee of Classis; and upon Rev. Dr. How devolved the pleasing duty of ordaining the first Consistory. Very soon after, the Second Church called as their first pastor Rev. Dr. Demarest, now of the Theological Seminary.*

The subsequent history of this church proves that the men who originated it did not misinterpret the indications of Providence. And while we with them thank God for all the success with which they have been crowned, and bless Him for the tokens of His favor in

---

* The following pastors have been settled in this church: Rev. David D. Demarest, D.D., (1843-52,) Rev. Samuel M. Woodbridge, D.D., (1852-57,) Rev. Hugh M. Wilson, D.D., (1858-62,) Rev. John W. Schenck, (1862-66,) Rev. Chester D. Hartranft, since 1866.

their rapid and healthy growth, we will pray that both of these churches in harmonious coöperation may seek the extension of the Redeemer's kingdom, and from our communions there may go up to the heavenly mansions, a host of redeemed and sanctified souls swelling the company of the ransomed around the throne.

The failure of Dr. How's health in the winter of 1860 led him to seek rest from mental and physical exercise. Failing to receive the benefit which he hoped to derive from this temporary cessation from the labors of the ministry, he felt that the time had come for a dissolution of the pastoral connection. Accordingly, June 14th, 1861, he resigned his call into the hands of the Consistory, and his relations as the pastor of this church ceased. During his ministry there were received into the membership of the church five hundred and thirty-eight on profession, and two hundred and twenty-five by certificate from other churches, in all the large number of seven hundred and sixty-three. It is a pleasant record that "this relation had been continued nearly thirty years in a spirit of entire harmony, and that he left them in a highly prosperous condition." *

A long vacancy now ensued. But in the mean time the Consistory was not idle. In the summer of 1861, the old square pews were removed, and the building reseated and refurnished in the present modern and attractive appearance. The former dependent method of raising the salary by subscription was abandoned, and the present mode of making the pews assessable for the expenses of the church was adopted. Rev. Joseph A. Collier was called, but failing health induced

---

* By the will of John B. Egerton, in 1857, the church came into possession of $1000, to be invested, and the interest used for the benefit of the Sabbath-school; and also $3063, "the interest of which shall be used as occasion may require for the church edifice and its appurtenances."

him to decline the invitation. An unsuccessful effort was also made to settle Rev. J. L. McNair.

The pulpit remained vacant until December 3d, 1863, when your present pastor was installed. The sermon was preached by Dr. How, from the words, "Who is sufficient for these things?"

During the short period of my ministry the church has come into the possession of the adjoining property, known as the "Old City Hall," by the gift of John Clark, at an expense of $3400. A beautiful and commodious parsonage has been purchased, 106 George street, under the management of a committee consisting of John Clark, Johnson Letson, Joseph Fisher, Ira C. Voorhees, and John Johnson. The amount paid for the purchase and improvements was $5580. The ladies of the congregation have purchased and placed in the gallery a noble organ at an expense of $2625.

There were upon our church rolls, in June, 1863, three hundred and sixteen communicants. We have received during my ministry one hundred and sixteen by profession and seventy by certificate, in all one hundred and eighty-six. Our present communion embraces four hundred and sixteen members.

I have thus traced the history of this church during a period of one hundred and fifty years. Great changes have been witnessed since your fathers laid the foundation of our civil, religious, and literary institutions. The insignificant hamlet that had grown up around Inians's Ferry of a few hundred inhabitants, has spread into this goodly city, with its churches, and College, and Seminary, and schools, and advantages of commerce and trade. The dense forests that surrounded New-Brunswick have given place to well-cultivated farms, and the thrift and enterprise of our rural population. The Raritans, who have given a name to our beautiful river, have long since disappeared. The obscure paths through deep forests along which Dominie Frelinghuysen found his way to his distant preaching places, have been exchanged for these iron roads that course our State, the route of a mighty traffic. The little church in Burnet street, scarce accommodating three hundred worshippers, has given place to two flourishing congregations, with these ample buildings inviting more than two thousand souls to hear the Gospel.

That God was with your fathers is the record of our history. Since January, 1720, twelve ministers have held the pastoral office. Of this number four, Frelinghuysen, Leydt, J. R. Hardenbergh, and Condict, died while in the service of the church. Five of your ministers have held professorships in our literary and theological institutions. Four are still living.

One fact in our history worthy of special interest is the large number of young men who have been connected with our church and have entered the gospel ministry. We have upon our roll of communicants the names of fifty-one who here made a profession of their faith in the Lord Jesus Christ, and have been commissioned to preach the Gospel of salvation.* In addition to this number, upward of fifty were received by certificate from other churches, and were subsequently numbered among the ministry. While we have reason to thank God that He has raised up from the midst of us so many whom he has honored to be standard-bearers in His army, we will remember with even deeper gratitude that among the most devoted of our foreign missionaries, Rev. David Abeel, D.D., Rev. Frederick B.

* See Appendix V.

Thompson, and his wife, Catherine Wyckoff, "were born in this city, were baptized and educated in this congregation, were members of the catechetical class and Sabbath-school, and were here received into the full communion of the church."

We have gathered together some items in our history, but have made no attempt to sum up the actual amount of good accomplished by this Christian church. The souls that have here been educated for heaven, the benefactions that have here been poured into the treasury of the Lord, the influence that has gone forth from this house of prayer, the power that has here been felt, is known only to God. The existence of a single Christian church in a community is an unspeakable blessing, and eternity alone can unfold the results of her mission.

While gratitude is awakened in view of the past, our history calls us to be faithful to the present. We in our generation are making a history, and those who come after us will write up the record of our lives and doings. Shall our history be as worthy as that of the fathers? We meet, to-day, a congregation of the living in the midst of the dead. Around us are the monuments of the departed. The sacred dust of ministers, elders, members of this church, Presidents and Professors of our College and Seminary, surround these walls. This ancient graveyard is the resting place of the illustrious dead. Perhaps no spot of ground has crowded within its inclosure names so dear and honored throughout the whole bounds of our denomination as that which lies beneath the shadow of this venerable building. A walk through this unpretending cemetery will bring before your eye the names of men which are common property to the Church of Christ. Aside from the patriots of the Revolution who are resting here until the morning of the resurrection; and elders who in their infancy were baptized by the hand of Frelinghuysen, and in their maturity were received into the communion under the ministry of Leydt; and women who helped in the Gospel of Christ; there are beloved pastors, and learned professors, and noble benefactors, who will awake when the dead hear the voice of the Son of God, and come forth. It is meet that the precious dust of Hardenbergh, and Condict, and Livingston, and Woodhull, and De Witt, and Schureman, and Van Benschoten, and Ludlow, and Van Vranken, and Cannon, and Theodore Frelinghuysen should here repose in waiting for the glorious resurrection unto eternal life. We do not wonder that, on reading the inscriptions on these monuments, one has been reminded "of that place of sepulchre in the neighborhood of London called Bunhill Fields, where are deposited the remains of such men as Bunyan, and Baxter, and Watts, and a host of others of whom the world was not worthy."

Blessed indeed is the memory of the fathers of this church, and noble their toils and sacrifices for the advancement of the Redeemer's kingdom. "The Lord our God be with us as he was with our fathers." They have left their names and deeds, and have passed away. Do they not appeal to us to do more for Christ than they have done? The circumstances that surround us for promoting the Redeemer's kingdom are far more favorable than those which the fathers enjoyed. We have grown in numbers and in resources; we may derive advantage from the experience and study lessons from the errors of the past; while all these organizations of modern times were unknown to those who have gone before us.

Though the oldest organization of our city, this church

has not outlived her influence. Shall we not recognize our responsibility, awakened by the position we occupy and the history of God's dealings with us? Am I wrong in cherishing for this ancient church the brighest hopes? Progress is the law of Christian life. May we not, then, anticipate growth in the piety of her members, in the liberality of her benefactions, and in the efficiency of her labors for Christ? The most wonderful developments of Divine Providence are now in progress. Movements are going on in our world which are tending to advance the kingdom of our Lord. Let us watch the signs of the times and make our church life throb with the impulse of a Christian activity. And let this church always stand among her sister churches of this city, established upon the true principles of the Gospel, maintaining the faith of our Lord Jesus Christ in its purity, and built on Him as the chief corner-stone.

Part Second.

ANNIVERSARY EXERCISES,

And a Sermon

BY

RICHARD H. STEELE, D.D.

ANNIVERSARY EXERCISES.

At a meeting of the Consistory of the First Reformed Dutch Church of New-Brunswick, N. J., held April 11th, 1867, the pastor stated that the church would complete the one hundred and fiftieth year of her history during the present season. Whereupon, the following action was unanimously adopted:

"*Resolved*, That we hereby express our devout thanksgiving to God for the establishment and preservation of this church during so long a period, and that the event be celebrated with suitable commemorative religious exercises.

"*Resolved*, That we cordially invite all who have been associated with our church, or who are interested in our history, to unite with us on the interesting occasion of the celebration of our one hundred and fiftieth anniversary.

"*Resolved*, That our pastor, Rev. Richard H. Steele, be invited to deliver, on the day which shall be appointed, a historical discourse, commemorative of the founding of this Christian church."

The committee who were appointed to take charge of the arrangements for the occasion selected Tuesday, October 1st, for the proposed celebration. The day of the anniversary was one of the most beautiful of the season. The invitation which had been circulated brought together hundreds of the friends of the church and former members of the congregation, to unite with us on this commemorative occasion.

MORNING EXERCISES.

At ten o'clock, the venerable church edifice, which had been tastefully decorated for the occasion with evergreens ornamented with flowers, was filled with a large congregation.

The portraits of Drs. Ira Condict, John Ludlow, and Jacob J. Janeway, former pastors of the church, were suspended behind the pulpit. In the centre was a painting of Dr. John H. Livingston, beneath which was a drawing of the old stone church erected in 1767, on the site of the present edifice. At the right and left of the pulpit were placed the figures 1717 and 1867. Around the gallery were displayed the names of the twelve pastors of the church. Over the pulpit was inscribed the motto, "The Lord our God be with us as he was with our fathers." In front of the orchestra was the appropriate sentence, "Praise ye the Lord."

The pulpit was occupied by the pastor, Rev. Isaac Ferris, D.D., Rev. Gabriel Ludlow, D.D., and Rev. Thomas De Witt, D.D.

Besides these, the following clergymen were noticed in the audience: Rev. Drs. Berg, Woodbridge, John De Witt, Demarest, Campbell, Sears, Kip, Hageman, Cole, Du Bois, P. D. Van Cleef, C. C. Van Cleef, See, B. C. Taylor, W. J. R. Taylor, Proudfit, and Stryker; and Rev. Messrs. Ten Eyck, Brett, Corwin, W. H. Steele, Alonzo Peck, Lloyd, Bodine, Van Neste, Swain, Willis, Buckelew, Le Fevre, P. Q. Wilson, Manley, Peter Quick, Ward, F. Wilson, C. Wyckoff, A. V. Wyckoff, David Van Doren, A. M. Quick, Enyard, H. P. Thompson, Hartranft, D. A. Jones, McKelvey, Suydam, Riley, Doolittle, and Phraner, of the Reformed Dutch Church; Rev. Dr. Devan, of the Baptist; Rev. Dr. Boggs, of the Episcopalian; Rev. Jacob Cooper and Rev. Robert Proudfit, of the Presbyterian; and Rev. Messrs. Lawrence Dunn and Thorn, of the Methodist.

The religious services commenced with an invocation by the Rev. Dr. Ludlow, who also read the One Hundred and Thirty-second Psalm. A select piece was then sung by the choir, after which prayer was offered by Rev. Dr. Ferris. The following hymn, written for the occasion by Rev. Peter Stryker, D.D., was then sung:

CELEBRATION HYMN.

Tune—Varina.

A HUNDRED years have come and gone,
    And fifty more have flown,
Since Thou, O Lord! this church ordained,
    And called this flock thy own.
The men who then were in their prime,
    And children in their bloom,
With myriads more, who since have lived,
    Are sleeping in the tomb.

Time, on its rapid flowing tide,
    Sweeps all our race away;
Pastors and people seek the dust,
    And buildings show decay.
But 'mid the wrecks of hoary time
    The church securely stands,
Increasing only with its age,
    And sending forth its bands.

And now, O God! we crowd thy gates;
    We join in psalms of praise;
With angels and the host redeemed
    Our fervent songs we raise.
We give Thee thanks for blessings past;
    We plead for grace to come;
Oh! lead us in our future course,
    And bring us safely home!

Come, Holy Spirit, like the dew,
    And fertilizing showers,
That fall on Hermon's lofty peak,
    And Carmel's blooming flowers.
O Father, Son, and Holy Ghost,
    Visit this flock to-day!
Be thou their God for centuries yet,
    Their Everlasting Stay.

The Historical Discourse contained in the preceding pages was then delivered by the pastor, after which the following ode, written for the occasion by Professor David Murray, was sung:

Tune—*Auld Lang Syne.*

All honor to the names of those
  Who first these regions trod,
And in God's fear, here sought to rear
  This Zion of our God.
    Chorus.—Let hearts be glad and lips rejoice
      At what we see to-day;
      With organ peal and living voice
      Unite our thanks to pay.

With brave old Holland hearts they crossed
  Through ocean's wave and wind;
And naught of trust in God they lost,
  Nor left their faith behind.
    Chorus.—Let hearts, etc.

Here in the wilds, they sought to raise
  An altar to their God;
And train their children in the ways
  In which their fathers trod.
    Chorus.—Let hearts, etc.

And while they plowed with zeal and thrift,
  And filled their barns with corn;
They sought from God the better gift
  Each evening and each morn.
    Chorus.—Let hearts, etc.

From Heidelberg and Dort they brought
  The dear old creed and psalm;
And with their quaint old music broke
  The wilderness's calm.
    Chorus.—Let hearts, etc.

Through all these years, what burdening fears
  Have here besought relief!
Here sorrowing saints have dried their tears,
  And soothed away their grief.
    Chorus.—Then let our hearts and lips rejoice,
      And cheerful music raise;
      With organ peal and living voice,
      Give God his due of praise.

The morning services were concluded with the benediction by Rev. Thomas De Witt, D.D.

In the old court-house, adjoining the church, the ladies of the congregation had prepared a bountiful collation, to which the hundreds of friends who were in attendance on the anniversary were invited.

AFTERNOON EXERCISES.

At three o'clock, the audience again assembled in the church, when the services were opened by an appropriate voluntary by the choir.

The venerable Rev. Thomas De Witt, D.D., having been invited to preside, made the opening address.

He expressed the pleasure he had enjoyed in listening to the thoroughly-prepared discourse commemorative of the history of this ancient church by its pastor. It is the mother church of many in the adjacent field, which has ever been so interesting and valuable a portion in our Reformed Dutch Church.

The name of the first Dominie, Frelinghuysen, is well known, not only in the annals of our own church, but also in those of the religious history of our country. Dr. De Witt remarked that, not many years ago, he found in the hands of a Hollander a volume entitled, "Life and Letters of Sicco Tjadde." Tjadde was a devoted and successful minister in Friesland. He had been written to in reference to procuring a minister for the early settlements in New-Jersey. The circumstances connected with the acquaintance he gained with Mr. Frelinghuysen shed light upon the character he sustained of great spirituality of mind, close evangelical preaching, and entire fidelity and faithfulness. It is to be regretted that this volume was not secured at the time. It contains several letters between Mr. Frelinghuysen and Tjadde, after his removal to America. A powerful revival attended Mr. Frelinghuysen's labors, the fruits of which are noticed by Tennent and President Edwards as existing previous to the great revival under Whitefield. Salt was then spread around, which still is found, not having lost its savor. Dominie Frelinghuysen had a particular friend of his early days—Dorsius, of the German Reformed Church, in Bucks county, Pennsylvania—and a helper to him in revival scenes. They each of them received classical students, and several of the American ministers, as Goetchius, Verbryck, Thomas Romeyn, etc., were educated under Mr. Frelinghuysen. The subject of creating an academy was early advocated before the Classis of Amsterdam, without any action resulting. After the disruption of the churches, in 1755, into Coetus and Conferentie, on the question of independent ecclesiastical judicatories and the education and training of our ministry here, in 1758 Rev. Theodorus Frelinghuysen, of Albany, son of the elder Frelinghuysen, was commissioned to Holland, to labor for the erection of a college, by obtaining the consent of the judicatories in that country. He was lost at sea on his return. Ecclesiastical recognition was refused, until Dr. Livingston, pursuing his studies in Holland, returned with the olive branch, and the breach was healed. This was the same year, 1770, when the charter of Queen's College was obtained.

Dr. De Witt then referred to Dominie Leydt, who is first heard of in Dutchess county, near one of the congregations over which he was placed in his early ministry. The testimony of aged persons with whom he conversed represented him as of great respectability of character, and honored by the church and community. He took a leading part in the Coetus controversy, and published two or three pamphlets. Dr. Hardenbergh was from one of the most distinguished families in Ulster county, not far from the place of Dr. De Witt's nativity. During the years of his ministry at Marbletown and Rochester, in that county, he was the pastor of his mother's family. The uniform testimony given by those acquainted with him there exhibits him in the same character of mental, spiritual, and official excellence which rendered him so distinguished in New-Jersey.

In 1810, when Dr. Livingston removed from New-York and opened the Theological Seminary, Dr. De Witt entered it, and had the privilege of being received into the family of the Rev. Dr. Condict, and had thus an opportunity of forming an estimate of his character. With little of animal spirits, and, perhaps, in the depth of his humility, inclined to despondency, there was a uniform breathing of deep piety. His counsels were always wise, and marked with practical sound sense.

His preaching, without brilliancy, was always sound, instructive, and experimental. At this time, Queen's College had been revived, and he was the acting President. He stood among the most distinguished in the church for faithful and useful labors in the revival of the College. In the summer of 1811, he was seized with violent disease. During the progress of the sickness, his soul was in conflict as to his spiritual state. On the night of his death, when it was supposed he was sinking fast, he aroused, and spoke calmly, deliberately: "Jesus is mine, and I am his. I know whom I have believed. He giveth me the victory." On the Sabbath following the death of Dr. Condict, as the work of pulling down the old church had commenced, Dr. Livingston preached a sermon in the Presbyterian church on the text, "I AM THE GOD OF BETHEL," which was one of the most powerful he ever preached. His allusion to the cotemporaneous breaking down of the earthly tabernacle of Dr. Condict and of the church edifice wherein he had labored so long was most happy.

ADDRESS OF REV. SAMUEL M. WOODBRIDGE, D.D.

Dr. Woodbridge represented the Theological Seminary, and spoke substantially as follows:

I bring to this venerable church the salutations of the most ancient theological seminary in America. It is proper we should mingle in your festivities; for not only have the interests of the church and the school of the prophets been almost identical, but we have received from you benefits we ought and do now gratefully acknowledge in the name of generations of the sons of the prophets. It is not merely that you have assisted the Seminary pecuniarily, nor that you have given two of your pastors to be its professors, but that to your solemn assembly we have been permitted to come from week to week to gain strength for the duties of life, and to express publicly to God the adoration of our spirits. For there is nothing can take the place in the Christian life of the worship of the great congregation; no private study or meditation, no instructions in the lecture-room, no private or social prayer. It is to the house of God the Christian turns when he would find rest, and here he finds the special supply for the great want of his spiritual nature. Here hundreds of our ministry, perhaps the majority of those now living, have joined in praise and supplication, here have listened with gladness to the sounds of the blessed Gospel, and here have gathered around the holy supper to commemorate the dying love of the Lord, and gone away refreshed, and to carry the influences here received through all future life. I have felt for years, and the feeling increases, that we can hardly overrate the influence of the pastors of these churches upon the students who look to them as living exemplars of what, in the Seminary, can only be taught as theory; and I can not here forbear giving testimony (and I am sure I speak the sentiment of all who have been witnesses) to the faithfulness of that servant of Christ who yet lingers amongst us, and who for thirty years ministered to this people; and I am sure all my brethren will agree in saying that never have we seen in him an act unbecoming a pastor over the flock of God, nor have heard from him a sentiment unsound or unevangelical. But the church has also received great benefits from the Seminary, too great to be told. Here its professors, one after another, have preached the Word of Life. I shall never forget the impression made upon me when I first entered this house and thought of the eloquent, and venerable, and godly men who had here proclaimed the truth. It seems as if upon these walls yet lingered the echoes of their voices—the voices of Livingston, Schureman, Woodhull, De Witt, Ludlow, Cannon, Van Vranken, and McClelland. These stones may be silent, but the words of these men yet resound in living hearts.

What thoughts arise at the mention of a hundred and fifty years in connection with the history of this church! As Dr. De Witt was speaking of the death of Dr. Condict, I was led to think of the *unwritten* history of the Church of Christ. How little we know of the true glory of the church, buried out of our sight, seen only by the eye of God and of angels! Those deep experiences of the saints, those inward joys and griefs with which no stranger intermeddleth, those prayers with strong crying and tears, those triumphs of the soul over fear, and death, and hell—what know we of these? We see but just the surface of this great ocean, whose depths are penetrated by the eye of Him who searcheth all things. How glorious must have been this secret history for a hundred and fifty years!

What a work, too, has been accomplished here, a work so wonderful that the angels have gazed upon it with joy and praise! The arrest of the sinner on the path of death, the conviction, the illumination, the conversion, the repentance, the faith on the Son of God, the struggle against sin, the wrestling of the soul against principalities and powers, the victory—who can doubt angels have been within these walls anxious spectators? A greater than angels has been here in the midst of his brethren; and he also, who on the day of Pentecost came down like a rushing mighty wind, has made this place awful and this city tremble by His presence. How many of those now in their graves have been cheered and comforted here; and this leads us to think of the close connection of the earthly and the heavenly church. The living and the dead are one in Christ, nay, the dead are the living. We have sometimes regretted that our cemeteries are being so removed from the churches. There is a beauty in the spectacle of the graves by the house of God, as if signifying that the church has not lost its interest in those reposing in the dust. They are still citizens in the kingdom of Christ, that glorious kingdom which disregards death, extending into the heaven of heavens, and in its vast circumference taking in the general assembly and church of the first born, and the spirits of the just made perfect, reaching also to our poor world and embracing the miserable and fallen, the trembling sinners who seek refuge in Jesus.

And we are reminded, too, of the perpetuity of the church. Our fathers, where are they? and the prophets, do they live forever? The fathers are gone, but instead of the fathers are the children. The church can not perish, because God is her life. Human associations rise and pass away, but the society of Jesus, by a few simple appointments of her divine head, sends down her name and principles from generation to generation. In her history a century and a half is but a brief period. She counts her years by thousands. Arts, codes of laws, kingdoms perish, the earth may be removed, and the mountains carried into the midst of the sea, but the city of God remaineth.

ADDRESS OF REV. CHARLES S. HAGEMAN, D.D.

Dr. Hageman represented the ministry that had been reared by this church. In a feeling and impressive manner he described the scene when thirty years ago he stood here and gave himself to God and to the ministry of reconciliation, and gave some interesting incidents connected with the great revival which shook the city and brought so many into the church, when so many of his class were converted and dedicated themselves to the ministry. He alluded to the ability, the fidelity, and zeal of the former pastor of this church, (Dr. How,) and to others who had preceded him, to illustrate the influence of the ministry, and to show the influence of this church; that the fires that had been kindled upon this altar had burned upon many other altars lighted by those who had gone from this church; that by her ministry she had exerted an influence both in church and state which could not be fully known. The influence of a ministry of one hundred and fifty years was inconceivable; that such men as Frelinghuysen and Leydt had prepared the way for the establishment of our institutions, and of civil and religious liberty; that they had been faithful to the cause of their country, had labored arduously and successfully for God, and their country, and humanity during the Revolution, and others with their spirit had battled nobly for truth, and justice, and liberty in the conflicts of later days, and helped to free it from oppression.

He hesitated not to affirm that the state, with her illustrious names of senators, governors, statesmen, owed more to the ministry for the welfare of the country than she would acknowledge.

Some of these men had lived previous to the establishment of our literary and theological institutions; before the great benevolent enterprises of the church were undertaken; they prepared the way for them, and indeed made their organization necessary.

He referred to the fact that no record had been found to indicate the burial-place of the first pastor of the church, as an illustration of the neglect with which great men are sometimes treated.

One of the striking results of the labors of some of these pastors was that many young men were induced to enter the ministry. In this respect they were worthy of our example.

He said that the influence of the ministry that had gone forth from the church was inconceivable. To have some idea of it, it would be necessary to collect together those who had been saved by them, all the kind words spoken, the hearts comforted, the minds impressed and directed; to look into the golden censer and see the prayers offered by them, to see the harvest from the good seed sown, and even to look within the vail to those redeemed and saved through this ministry. The influence of a faithful ministry was cumulative, like the rising sun culminating in noontide glory, like the flowing tide increasing in volume and strength until it overflows the strand.

He urged his brethren to thank God and take courage, for though ministers died and passed away, yet the Lord lived and his church would triumph.

ADDRESS OF REV. WILLIAM H. CAMPBELL, D.D.

Dr. Campbell, President of the College, said:

I find the meaning of this day's exercises, as well as the warrant for them, in Psalm 48: 12-14, "Walk about Zion, and go round about her: tell the towers thereof. Mark ye well her bulwarks, consider her palaces; that ye may tell it to the generation following. For this God is our God forever and ever: he will be our guide even unto death."

In obedience to the command, we have walked about this Zion; we have gone round about her for the hundred and fifty years of her history, we have told her towers, marked well her bulwarks, and considered her palaces. And now in view of it all we cry, "We have thought of thy loving kindness, O God, in the midst of thy temple." "Out of Zion, the perfection of beauty, God hath shined." It is emphatically a history of divine loving-kindness. And with grateful hearts and strong confidence in a covenant-keeping God this church will tell to generations following what God has done for them, and will assure the children and the children's children that this God, who has done all these great things for the fathers, is our God forever and ever; he will be our guide even unto death.

And now, in a word, what has God done so signally for this church? What are these towers, bulwarks, and palaces which he has here erected? Let us have definite notions on this point, for indefiniteness here will be imparted to our thankfulness, and to all the experiences and duties which are founded upon it.

And the great noteworthy fact in this history of a hundred and fifty years is this: *God has made this church a uniform attestant, in doctrine and life, of the truths for the teaching of which he founded the church.*

The great purpose of the founding of the church is given by Zechariah, in the fourth chapter of his prophecy. The symbol of the golden candlestick, with its seven branches and its seven times seven pipes for the full supply of the oil of illumination, teach, that the church is to shed abroad the light of divine truth in the world; and the "two anointed ones," (verse fourteen,) denoting Joshua the high-priest and Zerubbabel the king, the two official ones of the theocracy at the time of the vision, symbolize the two great doctrines of religion—the high priest Joshua symbolizing the *atonement*, the divinely appointed sacrifice for sin; and Zerubbabel the king symbolizing the doctrine of obedience, in other words, the *sanctification* of those for whom atonement had been made. These two truths are the great doctrines for the dissemination of which the church was founded. And here for a hundred and fifty years, in the pulpit and in the life of this church, these two doctrines have been uniformly, persistently, unceasingly held up to the world. Here hundreds and thousands have heard these truths, and witnessed the influence of them, and been blessed by the preaching and example. All the life of this church has been spent in exhibiting these truths and in furthering the influence of them. What church can show such a galaxy of pastors as this? They, twelve in number, from Frelinghuysen down, may be fitly called the twelve apostles of this church.

It was for the furtherance of these two great truths that Queen's, now Rutgers, College was founded. The thought of the College originated with Frelinghuysen, the pastor of this church, and the thought was carried out and made a fact by Dominie Leydt, Dr. Condict, Dr. Hardenbergh, *and all the others*. And the College was placed here rather than elsewhere just because this church was here, and because the College was the natural outgrowth of the life of this individual church. And whatever Rutgers College now is or may hereafter become it owes, in large measure, to this church, just as the child owes its future well being to the parent. Rev. T. J. Frelinghuysen, as I have already said, conceived the idea of the College. And you have heard from the Historical Discourse of your pastor, delivered this day, what the pastors Leydt, Hardenbergh, Condict, and Schureman, and the others, did for it. This church gave the time of Drs. Hardenbergh and Condict as instructors in the College; it has always given money liberally for its endowment and prosperity. On the last effort for its endowment the work began in this church. Dr. How, the pastor, presented the subject to the people on the Sabbath morning and declared that the success of the measure depended upon what the members of the Dutch churches in New-Brunswick thought of the College and did for it. He said the College must have a recommendation from our churches in New-Brunswick in form of a large subscription to endowment, or it could not succeed. Then on the next day he called on you at your houses, and you, as well as himself, did give nobly. And as Dr. How, your pastor, and you, the people, then did, so your pastors and this people have ever done for the College from the beginning down to the present day. And all this has been done that Christ, the atoning sacrifice for sin, and the Holy Ghost, the sanctifier for pardoned sinners, might be known, believed on, and everywhere influential. And thus the great purpose for which the College was founded was to hold up these two great truths.

How great, then, the influence of this church! Dr. Thomas De Witt, a few moments since, compared that influence to a river. The figure is eminently scriptural. How beautifully and clearly is all this brought to view in Ezekiel's vision of the Holy Waters, (chapter 47.) The prophet sees waters issuing forth from the house of God, and they pass along at the south side of the altar of atonement. Now, these waters are the streams of influence for good which go forth from God's house and God's people. Their flowing forth from the sanctuary, and in such close proximity to the altar of burnt offering, shows not only the source whence the influence comes, but also the only ground upon which any influence can be availing for good; it must stand in the closest connection with the atoning sacrifice of Jesus Christ. Mark, too, the growth of the stream. At a thousand cubits from their source the waters reach to the prophet's ankles, a thousand cubits further they reach to his knees, a thousand cubits further they reach to his loins, a thousand cubits further and the waters had become a river which the prophet could not pass over; the waters had risen and had become waters to swim in. How vast, then, the growing influence of good men! Mark, too, the effects of these constantly augmenting waters. They flow on in full stream to the Dead Sea, the Sea of Sodom—that spot which, above every other on earth, stands as the symbol of spiritual death and of the wrath of God. And as soon as the full stream reaches the desolate spot, all revives. The waters of the Dead Sea are healed, they abound with fish, and men spread their nets from town to town upon its once more thickly populous shores.

How striking and beautiful is this lesson of the prophet! The influence of the church, exemplifying in teaching and life the renewing and sanctifying doctrines of Christ, shall convert the spots of earth where spiritual death reigns into a paradise of God. Such is the history of this church which you are to tell to the generation following, assuring them that "this God is our God forever and ever; He will be our guide even unto death."

ADDRESS OF REV. P. D. VAN CLEEF, D.D.

As we follow the history of the church of God, we seem to be tracing the course of some noble river as it rises in a clear mountain spring, and rolls on through rocky gorges and verdant meadows, fertilizing every land, and bearing upon its bosom rich argosies freighted with the happiness and the hopes of humanity. The history of each congregation resembles that of the church at large, and is marked, both in its origin and progress, by the same wonderful providences. With deep interest and devout thankfulness we have followed your beloved pastor this morning, as he piloted us along the course of this tributary of the great river of life. We have rejoiced in the shade, and have been refreshed by the fruit of the trees that lined its banks. This stream, like the famous river of Egypt, has diverged into numerous branches, which have irrigated many a harvest-field. One of these water-courses it has been made my pleasing duty to explore, and I bring you some of the fruits found growing in the fields it has fertilized.

We have heard of the long line of pastors who, for the space of one hundred and fifty years, have served this church. Let me speak of those who have been converted under their ministry, and have gone forth to perpetuate their influence. In this way we may gain some conception of the moral forces that have been developed here during five generations. The influence of this church has no geographical limit. The world has been its field. The good it has done is not to be estimated by the number who have gone from this sanctuary to swell the redeemed throng before the throne of God and the Lamb. How often have angelic messengers ascended to heaven with glad tidings, as one after another, parent and child, through successive generations, has been born into this household of faith, and taken his place at the sacramental table, and become a light in the world, and a grain of salt to spread the savor of a godly life. But how grandly that idea of influence looms up when we remember that nearly fifty young men, admitted to their first communion here, have gone into the world to preach the everlasting Gospel. Some of them, doubtless, had been trained in youth under other faithful pastors; but here they first publicly gave themselves to Christ.

It can not be out of place on this memorable day to recall the names of our brethren who, though absent in body, many of them, are with us in spirit. The following list includes only those who were received on confession of faith. (For a list of members who have gone from this church to preach the Gospel, see Appendix V.) There are nearly as many more who were members by certificate at the time of their licensure; for at one period the most of our graduates were, for the sake of convenience, licensed by the Classis of New-Brunswick.

Many of these have ceased from their labors on earth; the remainder, with a few exceptions, occasioned by age or physical disability, are actively employed. Time will not permit me to speak of all these brethren and fathers. I must recall the name of one, however, who was cut off in early life. Abraham V. Wyckoff was a child of this church. Amiable, studious, and consistent, he was beloved by all. His examination for ordination took place at the same time with my own, before the Classis of Greene, within the bounds of which he spent the greater portion of his ministry, which it pleased the Master to limit to six short years, when he was called to receive his crown.

And now pause and reflect upon the influence that has gone forth from this church through the sons she has given to the ministry. The average ministerial career of thirty-six of these pastors is, up to this time, twenty-three years, and the aggregate, eight hundred and twenty-four years. They have probably preached a hundred thousand sermons, and have been instrumental in bringing many others into the ministry. And yet how feeble the conception we can gain from all this of the power of a single church among the moral forces which, under Providence, control the destinies of the world.

But the sons of this church have been called to other positions. Four of them have filled, and three are now occupying professorial chairs. Others have carried the Gospel to the heathen. The records of the church are adorned with the names of David Abeel, Frederick B. Thompson, and William H. Steele. These were the men who hazarded their lives for the Gospel. The first was the pioneer missionary of our church to the Chinese Empire, and the others remained and labored on the island of Borneo until the last hope of establishing our mission there had expired. Yet they labored not in vain. The Dyak people were not converted and made a Christian nation, as we fondly hoped; but may we not indulge the pleasing thought that at least one Dyak voice shall at last mingle with the hundreds and thousands from China in the everlasting song of the redeemed; that some will rise up from the Archipelago, as well as from the Celestial Empire, to bless this church, and to bless the men who carried the Gospel to benighted Asia? Thus this church has spread like the great banyan tree of the East. A branch has stretched across the continent and taken root in the fertile soil of the West. Another has reached over the ocean and rooted itself in the eastern hemisphere. These spring up, and in their turn take root again; and thus the process will go on until all the living churches of God shall have intertwined their spreading branches, and formed one vast tree of life under which the nations shall find a shelter.

It would be interesting to know by what steps God, in his providence, has conducted each of his servants into the ministry. I can not speak for others, but may be pardoned for saying that, in reviewing the chain of providences that led me to become a minister, the link that I recall most distinctly was a simple question from my pastor, the Rev. Dr. How, when, a Sabbath-school scholar, during the precious revival of 1837, I was examined for admission to the communion of this church. He said, "Have you thought that you would like to study for the ministry?" I could give no direct answer, but the words dropped like seed-corn in the soil of memory and reflection, and they germinated and grew into a desire, and then ripened into a purpose to preach the Gospel. Oh! how much a faithful pastor can do, by the most simple and easy methods, to kindle a desire for usefulness in the young heart, and how great the debt of gratitude he has a right to claim from those whom he has instrumentally led into the gospel ministry. I take pleasure to-day in recognizing this obligation to my former venerated pastor, to whose repeated conversations in his study I was so much indebted, when, with unwearied kindness, he instructed me, removed my doubts and difficulties, and threw the light of wisdom and experience on my path.

Pardon this personal digression. Do not weigh in the balances of cold propriety words forced from the lips by the gushing memories of the past, those "happy, golden days," when even the sky seemed brighter and the earth greener after the reviving showers of the Holy Spirit. Who can forget a revival, when associated with the memories of his early Christian life and love? Who can forget the communion Sabbaths that dawned so beautiful and bright? I recall one of them. It was a lovely September morning, in 1837. Memory brings back the crowded congregation; the tremulous voice of Elder Stothoff, as it rose from this platform and mingled with the swelling volume of song that filled the sanctuary with the fragrant incense of praise; the earnest prayer; the rich gospel sermon; the old sacramental form, so redolent of Calvary and Gethsemane; the long list of names of those welcomed for the first time to the table, and mine among them; and then the bread and wine touched with trembling hands and quivering lips; the words of exhortation; and the hymn of thanksgiving. My vision of that sacramental Sabbath would not be complete without the tall form of gray-haired Cæsar leading the large number of colored communicants from the gallery up the aisle to the table, where our pastor welcomed them with the same invitation to the gospel feast. And I used to think he sometimes kept his best thoughts for them, and his words were so simple and touching as he spoke of the dear Saviour who promised that all his people should drink with him

"The grape's first juice,
Fresh from the deathless vine that blooms in heaven."

But I must close. Let me leave as a theme for reflection, *The self-perpetuating power of the church through the ministry which she is raising up.* You remember the incident of the conversion of a Hessian drummer-boy, under a sermon of Dr. Livingston, in a barn at Poughkeepsie during the Revolution. That boy was Christian Bork, under whose ministry John Scudder was converted, the father of our beloved missionaries in India. Let the church remember the promises of enlargement and triumph which Christ has left her, and never forget his command to "pray the Lord of the harvest that he would send forth laborers into his harvest."

"He who slumbereth not nor sleepeth,
His ancient watch around us keepeth;

> Still sent from his creating hand,
> New witnesses for truth shall stand—
> New instruments to sound abroad
> The Gospel of a risen Lord."

ADDRESS OF REV. D. D. DEMAREST, D.D.

I feel honored in having been selected to present on this occasion the salutations of the churches that have been organized chiefly with members from this venerable congregation. The daughters come with hearty and joyous greetings to their mother, and on this her one hundred and fiftieth birthday anniversary compliment her on her continued freshness and beauty, and the proofs she is giving of undiminished vitality and energy. They come with prayers that God will bless her as she has never been blessed before, and that in the time to come many daughters may be born to her who shall rise up and call her blessed.

A little band of three sisters appears to-day. 1. Spotswood, organized about the year 1820, and so approaching the close of her first half-century. A church that, owing to the force of circumstances beyond human control, has never reached a point that entitled her to be called a strong and influential church. Yet she has been a steadily shining light. Through all these years she has perseveringly maintained the public worship of God, and furnished healing, rest, and a home for many a sick and burdened and wandering soul. The little band of disciples there are to-day proving the reality of their spiritual life by zealous and self-denying efforts in the erection of a new house of worship.

2. Middlebush, organized about thirty-three years ago, and which has given the ordinances to a generation. Faithfully have all who have there worshiped been instructed and warned, and well have the young there been trained in the doctrines of godliness and in the spirit and forms of devotion. Nobly has the church of Middlebush done according to her ability for the work of church extension by her regular and liberal contributions to the cause of missions. She is now repairing and beautifying her house of prayer.

3. Second New-Brunswick, organized early in 1843, and

consequently within a few months of the end of the first quarter-century of her life. Of the feeble beginnings of this church, of her early struggles, of the devotion and perseverance of her founders, I would love to speak if it were proper. Yet I can not allow the occasion to pass without bearing testimony to the purity of the motives of those who went forth from this church to form that new organization. They loved their old home none the less because of their attachment to the new. I would also love to indulge the feelings stirred up by memories and associations connected with the most interesting portion of my own early ministry. Surely I may to-day mention with gratitude that for eight and a half years I was permitted to labor in cordial coöperation with the faithful servant of God who so long ministered at these altars, and who, having finished his public work, is now waiting for his crown. We regret his bodily absence to-day. We thank God that he is present in spirit. We call to remembrance the former times, and we all rejoice together in the prosperity of that young and vigorous church. From her contracted tabernacle, dear to some of us as the place where the few were wont to meet, she has gone forth into her spacious and beautiful edifice, in which we hope that many will, through many generations, be born into the kingdom.

I wish that I could speak in behalf of a larger band of sisters. But it is not for me, and on a day like this, even to hint that there should have been a larger family. It is not for me to intimate that within the limits of the territory originally solely occupied by this church there is room for more of her order, or that Providence has clearly indicated a path of duty that has been shunned. On the contrary, I believe that there are laws that govern the multiplication of churches in this land that carry themselves into effect. We have no State authority to regulate this matter, no geographical division into parishes fixed by law. We usually do not even look to ecclesiastical bodies to take the initiative. Wherever and whenever Christian people feel that there is a time and place for a new church, they will move in the matter, asking only the countenance and authority of those who are over them in the Lord, and the sympathy and prayers and Christian help of those from among whom they go.

I will go further, and utter an earnest protest against the heedless and unreasonable censures that are often brought against our fathers for having been so slow to extend the denomination and organize new churches, and for suffering the ground to be occupied by others. Ignorance is the most charitable excuse for such censures. Let any one study the history of the struggles of our church for more than one hundred and fifty years to maintain an existence in this country in the face of tremendous and overwhelming difficulties, and he will admire the perseverance and rejoice in the success of the fathers. Extension! Progress! Formation of new churches! Why, the question was one of life, not of growth; of holding fast, not branching out. Let any one but consider the speedy passing away of the Dutch authority from New-Netherland and the check to immigration, the obstinate adherence to the Dutch language, ecclesiastical dependence on the mother country, difficulty of obtaining ministers, troubles of Coetus and Conferentie, and he will prate no more about the slow and deliberate movements of the fathers. And how can any one, in view of these hindrances, say that it is disgraceful that the Reformed Dutch Church is not now the leading church among nearly a million of people in the city of New-York, because two hundred years ago she stood alone in New-Amsterdam a Dutch village of 1500 inhabitants, one tenth the present size of our little city of New-Brunswick?

Besides, it is the glory of our land that no denomination has the right of preëmption or preoccupancy to any part of the soil. We have religious liberty. A church long established may not forbid one of another order to spring up by its side. There is room, it is true, for Christian courtesy and charity, especially among those essentially alike, which should prevent an unnecessary multiplication of feeble churches. But how can it be otherwise than that in places of importance all the leading denominations should be represented, no matter which was first on the ground? A church should look after the members of its own household; but how can it expect to bring under its care those whose preferences are in other directions? I for one say, let us rejoice in the dwelling together of Presbyterians, Baptists, Episcopalians, Methodists, Reformed Dutch, and give thanks for the practical proof that there can be unity of spirit and aim where there is diversity of form. If our own church be small among these divisions of the sacramental host, let us remember that an eloquent Methodist brother, now in glory, has called us the heavy artillery, which part of an army is always small in numbers in proportion to the weight of metal thrown by it into the ranks of the enemy.

But the time for progress and extension has come, and there is a wide field before us. Instead of blaming the fathers, let us ask ourselves what are we doing. As the spokesman for new churches, I am here the representative of progress. Our doctrines and order should spread among the American people. We have a work to do for Christ. We must not sell our birthright. We must improve it. Growth is essential now to life. This church is sound in the faith on that point. Her sons are at work in heathen lands and in our western domain. Shall she not also look nearer home? Shall she not ask, What could be a more fitting memorial of these one hundred and fifty years than a church rising in some portion of our city where needed, where the members of our own household, sent forth with our blessing and help, may worship God according to the customs of the fathers?

During the exercises Prof. David Murray read the following poem, which he contributed to the occasion:

"THE OLDEN TIME."

'Tis good for our pride
To throw things aside—
The business and pleasures to which we are tied,
The burdens we carry, the hobbies we ride,
The projects we form, and the plans we have tried—
And linger an hour, or even a day,
O'er the records of things which have passed away;
Bring out the old papers and family scraps,
Overhaul the old boxes, and bureaus, and traps,
And if you can bear it,
Poke round in the garret,
Bring down the old love-letters, in which long ago
Our sainted old grandmothers conclusively show

ANNIVERSARY EXERCISES.

That they used to make love in that earlier day
Very much, after all, in the modern way.
Then while you are at it, go empty the barrel
Which holds some Dutch ancestor's best Sunday apparel;
And trig yourself out in his coat and his hat,
And his best Sunday waistcoat, be careful of that;
'Tis not to be sneezed at, although, like enough,
It may still hold a scent of the old fellow's snuff.
   Be sure try his breeches
   Of a length that just reaches
Adown to the knee, whence a stocking so neat
Completes the remainder down to the feet.
   And then, if you choose,
   You may try on his shoes,
And have them well polished before put in use,
And rub up the buckles with the least bit of leather,
For copper will tarnish in this sort of weather.
Then he wore down behind a long, slender cue,
Tied up in an eelskin with ribbon of blue,
Which looked all the world, folks have profanely said,
Like a frying-pan handle stuck on his head.
Go look in the glass in this fancy old rig,
And if you are not a conceited young prig,
I am sure you will own that old Diedrich then
Was not such a bad-looking specimen.
   Now when we've begun,
   Why, under the sun,
Can't we go a bit further, and just make a run
On our grandmother's bandbox and presses,
And bring out from thence a few of her dresses?
By the by, she was noted a belle in her day,
And quite turned the heads of the men, they say;
And even Lord Howe, the British commander,
Is said to have sat by her side and fanned her.
But good Dame Katrina quite stirred up his dander
By marrying Diedrich, whom he thought a gander.
 Let one of these damsels I hold in my eye
Be pleased just for once these dresses to try,
And show us Katrina in Sunday attire
All ready to walk to the church with our sire.
   This lilac brocade,
   With bright silver braid,
Ah! this will become you now to a shade,
A little bit faded, but what of that?
A little too full, for Dutch dames were fat;

But a very good dress, notwithstanding that,
And fit to adorn the queen who sat
At Solomon's feet to hear him chat.
You will see it is short, and meant for the street,
And did not quite cover Dame Katrina's feet;
For who so cruel would try to hide
Those bright silver buckles, Katrina's pride?
    Now try on this bonnet,
    And depend upon it,
You will cut a figure when you once don it.
But first you must add a few inches more
To the height your waterfall had before;
And one "heart-breaker" must hang down behind,
To be played with and tossed by the wanton wind.
Then put on the powder, and do not spare,
For Katrina was proud of her golden hair.
Now on with this "coal-scuttle," large and wide,
With good broad ribbons securely tied.
Why, bless your heart, there's enough of that,
If only the stuff were spread out flat,
To make a good dozen, as large as the mat
Which ladies now wear, and call a hat.
    Good Diedrich, he was grave and stout,
    And his wife was nowise thin;
    And a dimpled smile kept playing about
    The good little woman's chin.
And on Sunday morn, when the church-bell rang,
They always started when they heard its clang;
And walked to church like a godly pair,
While bright little Volkert, their son and heir,
Went trotting before, and always were there
A good many minutes before the first prayer.
    Good Diedrich took, in the winter weather,
A foot-stove of tin, well-soldered together,
And filled with water at a boiling heat,
To protect from the cold their freezing feet.
On very cold days, as a very great treat,
It served little Volkert as a nice warm seat,
Where the boy might be broiled like a piece of meat.
For, remember, that no one ever hears
Of a stove in a church back a hundred years,
Still less of a furnace, or as it would seem,
Of even a patent for heating by steam.
    The church was old, the church was queer;
    Would you like to look in on the Sabbath-day,

And witness their strange, old-fashioned gear,
And gather a hint of the ancient way?
The walls were plain, the roof was square,
The carpets—ah! well, they were not there;
And the pews—of course, they were better bare,
For cushions were deemed a carnal affair.
In the centre aisle the bell-rope hung,
Where the sexton stood, when he puffed and rung;
And the people said he was cross as a bear
If any one jostled against him there.
And the boys in the pews had a wholesome fear
Of Johannes's anger, when he was near.
At the pulpit-front the vorsinger stood—
His nose was large and his voice was good—
And he pitched his tune as he pitched his hay,
To the right and left in a frantic way.
And the old Dutch psalms made the welkin ring,
For Dutchmen are strong when they come to sing.

But the pride of the church, the glory of all,
Was the pulpit which towered against the wall.
'Twas set so high, said the wits of the town,
For the preaching was heavy, and would settle down.
Like an egg-cup it stood on a narrow base,
While the good old dominie held the place
Of the spoon in the empty shell,
To stir in the pepper and salt, and he stirred them well.
Over his head a sounding-board hung,
Like a vast extinguisher, above him swung,
Ready to fall and put out his light,
As candles are quenched at dead of night.
Will somebody put a contrivance so neat
Directly over each congressional seat,
So that Colfax then by pulling a string
Might the noisy men to silence bring?

  Well to the front the deacons sat,
   All in a goodly row,
  Grave and sober, and generally fat,
   With linen as white as snow.
Gravely they sat till the sermon was done,
Then gravely they rose for their task, one by one;
And taking the bags from where they had been,
Passed them to gather the pennies in.
Each bag was hung to the end of a pole,
And a little bell swung beneath the whole,
Whose tinkling might serve the sleepers to wake
From the nice little naps they sometimes take.

There, look for a moment and admire the style
Of him who is gathering the middle aisle.
Hear the tinkling bell and his creaking shoes,
As he passes along among the pews.
Back in his garden, yesterday night,
You might have seen him, while it was light,
Practicing over his work for to-day,
Rehearsing the part he would have to play.
Armed with an oven-swab, there he goes,
Passing it up and down the rows,
Giving to each big cabbage-head there
An equal chance to deposit his share.
Do you wonder now at the exquisite style
Of the deacon doing the middle aisle?
We commend the example to others, too;
Have you a task that is hard to do?
Into the garden-plat haste to repair,
And try it first on the cabbage-heads there.

Time can strengthen, time can kill;
  Things will last, though men will die;
While the house is lasting still,
  Graves about it scattered lie.

Generations here grow gray;
  Others flourish in their stead;
Pastors perish, people lay
  Here their kindred dead.

But the church in faith holds on,
  Stronger with its growing age;
Proud to point to records gone,
  Eager yet to add a page.

Let another fifty years go by;
  What shall then its record be?
Call a meeting then and try,
  And may we be there to see.

Brief addresses were also delivered by Rev. B. C. Taylor, D.D., Rev. David Cole, D.D., Rev. W. H. Ten Eyck, and Rev. P. D. Oakey.

On motion of Rev. Dr. Cole, it was resolved that the meeting deeply appreciate the excellent Historical Discourse delivered by Rev. Dr. Steele this morning, and that the Consistory of this church be requested to secure the same for publication.

Prayer was offered by Rev. Peter D. Oakey, and after singing the Doxology the benediction was pronounced by Rev. Dr. Taylor, of Bergen.

EVENING EXERCISES.

The evening exercises were opened with a voluntary by the choir, after which the forty-eighth Psalm was read, and prayer offered by Rev. Prof. Joseph F. Berg, D.D.

The congregation then united in singing the following hymn, written for the occasion by Rev. John B. Steele :

"THE THIRD JUBILEE."

Tune—*"Harvey's Chant."*

1. The silver trump of jubilee
   The pastors thrice have blown,
   Since first a royal priesthood laid
   Our Zion's corner-stone.

2. The pillar, on the rocky base
   Our fathers reared of old,
   Has wide displayed the truths of God—
   The purest, finest gold.

3. From year to year the altar's fires
   Have never ceased to shine ;
   And men of God have ever stood
   Within our holy shrine.

4. The Saviour here has gathered gems—
   His jewels rich and pure,
   To shine in His celestial crown,
   Forever to endure.

5. A cloud by day, a fire by night,
   Our covenant God has given:
   Beneath the folds of light and shade
   We journey on to heaven.

6. On this good day, with grateful hearts,
   We set our symbol stone ;
   And look to God, in faith and hope,
   For help in years to come.

Rev. Isaac Ferris, D.D., the senior ex-pastor of the church, then delivered the following address:

ADDRESS OF REV. ISAAC FERRIS, D.D.

My Respected Friends: It is now about forty-six and one half years since a young man, twenty-two and one half years old and about ten months from the Seminary, assumed the pastoral charge of this church and congregation, then embracing three hundred families, and these dispersed over an area five miles square; and having in his audience three professors, and some twenty-seven theological students, earnest young men with cultivated minds. It was a most responsible position for such an one to occupy, and it was in some degree realized, and would not have been assumed but from the conviction that the finger of God was clearly in the call, which came as unanimous from a people who had been distracted for years by a dividing question, in whose discussion very unhappy feelings had mingled.

The relation continued for three years and eight months, and was broken up by the renewal of the old dividing question. It may not be amiss to state it briefly, as it is a thing of the past. This congregation embraced a city and a country population. In the settlement of a minister it had been the usage, from the founding of the church, to have the second service on the Sabbath, during the summer, occur after an intermission of one hour. In the process of time the city population grew so large as to make it desirable and even important to have the service fixed at an hour convenient to the city congregation, and as were the services of other churches. Strong feeling and parties arose, each claiming what they sought as a right. The discussion had caused the resignation of Rev. Jesse Fonda. Dr. John Ludlow did not encounter it, as his pastoral relation continued only a little over a year. As I now look back on the merits of the case—indeed, as I then thought—the *right* was with the country people, but the *policy* was with the city, until the question was settled in the call of the pastor. In the call of my successor the matter was put forever at rest. The subsequent course of things has proved the wisdom of this final action. The increase of population to any important extent, as was expected would be, has been in town. The growing families here have been preserved to the original fold. And now, on this ground, you have two large, vigorous churches, while an outgrowth at Middlebush has constituted a blessed church-home to the more distant families. I rejoice in the prosperity and the expanding usefulness and power of my first charge. To come back to this spot has always been to me a pleasure, and to meet, as I have always done, the warm greeting and cordial good wishes of those to whom I had ministered, both the fathers and the children, in the greenness of my ministry, is among my most pleasant memories. The fathers have gone, and the children have mostly gone, and now I have before me the children's children, and to them I submit my remarks on what occurred in their fathers' fathers' day.

A ministry of three years and eight months will ordinarily furnish few events of special moment, and their tale is soon told. But I feel I may take a wider range, that I may submit some statements concerning the honored dead, and thus pay my tribute to those whom I shall never again see in the flesh. My thoughts have taken this direction as I have anticipated this interesting occasion: that I would first notice some special points during my ministry, and then speak of my hearers and my co-laborers.

As to the particular events referred to, let me speak first of the additions to the church. It pleased God to give me early seals to my ministry. His word was made effectual, and I was permitted to hear from one and another the earnest inquiry, "What shall I do to be saved?" Some of the most precious cases occurred in connection with pastoral visitations and special interviews with those who offered their children for baptism before they had given their own hearts to Christ.

Among the early accessions was that of David Abeel, the devoted missionary. With his religious inquiries I had nothing to do; he had obtained Christian hope in the winter of my settlement, and found Dr. Livingston his faithful and tender counselor. But we were brought closely together in his early Christian life, and it was my privilege to advise him concerning his public consecration and to receive him to the fellowship of the family of Christ. Our walk together was very pleasant, and through his whole life we were dear friends and coöperators in Christ's work. Very pleasant was it, in the second and third summers of my settlement, as I had invited those who felt an interest in the matter to come together every Sabbath morning, at six o'clock, for prayer for one hour, in the old Lancaster school-house—very pleasant was it to see David, with his excellent mother and sisters, coming over the hills from their rural home to the place of meeting; and very animating and invigorating were those meetings, for the Master crowned them with his presence and blessing. They are bright spots in memory.

We were not favored with what would be called revivals; but we had times when the dews of divine grace distilled sweetly among the people. On several occasions we received sixteen to the communion on profession, and in the course of three years and a half seventy-eight, with thirty-two by certificate, making one hundred and ten. After my ministry terminated, it overwhelmed me to hear from the precious man and devoted missionary, Frederick B. Thompson, that the word at my lips had been made the word of life to his soul.

I regard it with interest that I was the first pastor who instituted a stated and regular weekly evening lecture in our city congregation. As there was no church lecture-room at the time, through the kindness of the proper authorities we enjoyed the use of the Lancaster School-house, which I think was one of the early buildings of Queen's College. The excellent system (which I have never ceased to admire) of having a weekly catechising and lectures in connection, in several distinct neighborhoods in succession, throughout the congregation, was in use. One point was Poole's Landing; another, Middlebush; a third, Three Mile Run; a fourth was George's Road Poorhouse; while the catechising in the city was weekly. These services in the country districts were attended by almost every person, young and mature, and were regarded as hallowed seasons. Their observance had the effect for generations of securing an amount of sound Bible knowledge which gave the highest character for Christian intelligence to the people of Middlesex and Somerset counties; for they constituted the prevailing system of all our churches in this region, and they trained the most faithful church-going population I have ever seen. The work of the pastor became increased, but it was delightful.

By arrangement with the Consistory, one sermon on the Sabbath was given in the church the first year of settlement; but the country and city lectures made three preaching services per week. The second year, there were four weekly; while funeral sermons, and sermons at the houses of sick or infirm or aged persons in the country, made them not unfrequently five. One not actually in the work in a large charge can scarcely realize how the demands for service press a willing man. But it is well, for it is the Master's work; and while a man is in health, what can he better do? As for myself, I was a stranger to sickness or ailment of any kind at that period.

Another circumstance of great interest at the time was the fact that, in compliance with my desire and the appeals made, the observance of the Lord's Supper four times in the year was introduced. The usage had been to celebrate that ordinance at intervals of six months. On this subject there has been in a lifetime a very general conformity in our churches in a quarterly communion, while in a few cases a change has been made to six times in the year.

When we consider primitive usage, we can not but wonder that there should have been so great a deviation from that example as a commemoration once or even twice in the year. The idea of frequency is distinct in the words of the institution, and it should be such as to maintain at the same time the idea of the hallowed character of the service.

But that to which I confess I look back with great satisfaction, as most important to myself in its various bearings, was the ground publicly taken on one of the most destructive of social usages.

In the fall of 1820 occurred the suspension from his ministry, under the charge of intoxication, of one of our most distinguished ministers by a northern Classis. He was reported the most accomplished pulpit orator in the northern part of the State of New-York—a fine scholar, a gentleman of very wide influence. His fall grieved many hearts, while it broke up his pastoral relations, and covered his later life with a dark shadow from which he never emerged, though that which caused it had been corrected. It was apparent to me, as a looker on, that he had no more natural appetite for strong drink than any other man, but was the victim to the usages of social life—ruined by his friends, who became afterward his accusers. Every man of any position had his sideboard in his parlor, and that well stocked with the choicest of stimulants. Every visitor was expected to take his sip whenever he called. It was ungenteel—it was a slight, a reflection—not to drink a glass. And in making a half-dozen calls in the course of two or three hours and taking as many drinks, how, as a matter of course, was an appetite formed. The wonder was, not that there were so many drunkards, but that every body was not such. To my mind, the usage was horrible; and my determination was, wherever I settled, on the first public exercise, to relieve myself forever from compliance with the tyrant custom. Never can I forget the scene. This sanctuary was crowded in every part, as there was great curiosity to hear the first sermon of the young pastor elect. At the close, with the case which had occurred full in my mind, and which I stated, I solicited the people never, under any circumstances, to offer me strong drink, and not to consider me impolite or churlish if I peremptorily declined, should they forget themselves.

I remember well how the smile passed at my expense over the face of the whole congregation. It was a bold step for so young a man; but it was most important. It was shutting down the gate of access to a course which has been ruinous everywhere. It made its impression for good, as it fastened itself upon the minds of my people from its peculiarity and novelty. Need I say that step was never regretted?

As was proposed, let me give some sketches of my hearers. It may be said, probably, that, as are a man's hearers, such is his ministry. He will be influenced by the description of persons who are to sit in judgment on his performances. The intelligent, the cultivated, the discriminating will stimulate the young man to corresponding efforts. Every locality which has public institutions, in which and around which strong and educated men cluster, will have its terrors to the beginner in public services, while it will furnish strong encouragement to fidelity and earnestness, for it is in the best degree appreciative.

It was my privilege to have as my constant hearers a noble band of twenty-five or thirty young men of the Theological Seminary, quite a proportion of whom was near my own age, whose feelings and warm interest were with me. Ours were most pleasant relations, as I was so recently one of them. How many have gone to the grave, having done a good work for the Master! A small proportion remain, and they have become the fathers in our Israel. Thus we pass along, class after class, to various fields, encountering the wear and tear of life, but never losing the tenderness of that tie which bound us together in the Theological Hall and in our Christian associations. I said noble young men. Let me not leave an impression that I look upon them as an exception *par excellence*—by no means. My relations to the Seminary have been such as to bring me often, in the intervening years, in contact with the young brethren gathering here for training for the ministry, and my opportunity of seeing other young men has not been limited; and I say unhesitatingly, notwithstanding insinuations in some quarters, that I have never seen a higher class of mind and character than gathers here in preparation for ministerial work.

At the head of the school of the prophets was the venerable and venerated Dr. Livingston. His seat was always here, at the head of the elders' pew, and he was ever the object of interest on which the stranger would fix his admiring gaze. He presented the most perfect specimen of an old gentleman of the continental school of a hundred years ago; rather tall, fully developed in physical system, calm, dignified in air, yet affable, bland, with his flowing white wig dropping down to his coat-collar, he was a man by himself. His were inexhaustible stores of knowledge, showing that he had been an intense student, comprehending in his course the vast fields of science and literature as well as theology, and having all at command. To him was always yielded the sermon of the sacramental Sabbath morning; and then it was he poured forth the riches of his evangelical resources and his sweet Christian experience—touching, warming, thrilling every heart—making the occasion a festival indeed. His mode of sermonizing was eminently didactic and analytical, turning every thing in his text to account. His grand peculiarity in the pulpit was the large illustration of his subjects by voice and action. In this he has had no successor; some have attempted its imitation, but, as usual in such cases, they have been miserable failures. To him belongs the credit of giving a permanent form to the theological training of the Seminary, and it must be pronounced sound, Biblical, evangelical. Its results, as seen in our ministry, are all we could ask. It was my frequent privilege to accompany the doctor in his walks, and it was always delightful to notice the respect paid him by all classes and ages, and especially to see the satisfaction of the little ones where we called, as he laid his hand on their heads and pronounced his blessing on them. Never shall I forget my first sight of him, in Albany street. It was in the spring of 1819. I was then contemplating joining the Seminary for my closing year, and was here to witness the final examination. He was passing down Albany street, and reached Mr. Blauvelt's house, (now No. 52,) on the stoop of which some half-dozen students sat, who lifted their hats to him. With peculiar dignity, he turned his person squarely toward them, and with both hands took off his broad-brimmed hat and bowed his whole person. To my mind, he stood as the personification of one of the patriarchs.

One of my most cherished memories is that I enjoyed, when I left this charge, his warm love and confidence, and received from him, in his own beautiful penmanship, the expression of them. It was the last time I saw him, as soon after he slept in Jesus.

My closing year in the Seminary was the first year of the professorship of Dr. John Ludlow, who was, in his twenty-fifth year—in June, 1819—elected to his office, and for two years was a hearer. The choice of so young a professor was deemed a remarkable, while it was proved, by the result, a most wise proceeding. The new professor was not to be judged by the years he had seen, but by his mental development and strength of character, and these gave him a very marked preëminence. His was a rare case of maturity of mind at that age; and, while he possessed an iron constitution, with his experience in teaching as a tutor in Union College he was especially fitted for his work. And a hard work it was. It seemed a giant's burden, and manfully he bore it.

He had every thing to prepare, as text-books in several of his departments were few. He instituted the system of hermeneutical and exegetical studies in the Seminary, and gave a character to that branch of preparation altogether new to our students. He was charged with teaching Hebrew, Greek, Church History, Church Government, Pastoral Theology, and Biblical Analysis. Day and night he was engaged, the light in his study being the last extinguished in his neighborhood. He preached occasionally, and then it was with the power of a master. His manner was modeled somewhat after that of his preceptor, Dr. Nott, President of Union College; but the clarion voice, and the piercing eye, and the energetic gesture were his own. He was not emotional, and accordingly his preferred field of topics was that involving power and perhaps terror. He was not rhetorical, in the sense of the florid and metaphorical, but very plain in style; his words just what expressed his thoughts—no more, no less—the right word used, and always in the right place. His aim evidently was, first, to get in his own mind a definite, clear conception of a subject, and then to present it in the most direct and effective manner. He emerged from the Seminary an orator of the first degree, and as long as he preached *ex tempore*, that is, without notes, was everywhere acknowledged such. The distinguished Chancellor Kent, then in his own prime, when he heard Dr. Ludlow in the pulpit, at Albany, in 1822, preach on 1 Cor. 1: 22-24, pronounced it the most commanding pulpit effort he had ever heard. The sermon, as an intellectual production and an exhibition and defense of the Gospel, was a masterpiece.

Dr. Ludlow was a wise and sound-minded man, possessing a most marked balance of mind. No man saw better what belonged to a given occasion or could better unravel what was conflicting. In social life he manifested the warmest affections and the most unyielding fidelity in his friendships. His were capabilities for the most responsible trusts. Had he been a military man, he would have been one of the great captains of the age; had he devoted himself to law, he would have taken rank with the most distinguished jurists; and had he given himself to political science, he would have won renown as the first of statesmen. What a thought it is that this man, so fitted by nature and attainments, was forced to retire from the position he so admirably filled here by the want of funds requisite for the support of a second professor; but his going waked up the church to her duty. In the work of the ministry, in the church of Albany, he won a great reputation; in the University position he occupied, at Philadelphia, he made his mark on every class with which he had to do, and his memory is cherished most tenderly. He was truly one of the leading minds of our church.

A few months only elapsed when, having been chosen to supply Dr. Ludlow's place, the Rev. John De Witt, D.D., of Albany, came among us, truly a man of genius and finely cultivated taste as well as capital scholarly attainments. His had not been the advantages of early theological culture, as those now enjoyed, but he had made up for all by most assiduous study of the best authors and critics of the day. He had, in Albany, in the Second Church, occupied a most influential position, and called around him a large and very devoted people. There I was his hearer for a large portion of a year, and there, as a temporary dweller, I learned to love the doctrines and usages of the Dutch Church; for, though brought up with Dutch boys as my daily playmates and schoolmates, in New-York, and hearing the tongue almost every hour spoken, and learning to speak it in a degree, I had never crossed the threshold of a Dutch Church, as "I was not Dutch." Dr. De Witt soon made himself felt in the Seminary and in the town. He was a most animated man, and infused animation and energy into whatever he undertook. He did nothing (as we say) by halves, and would have every man like himself. He seemed to catch intuitively what others would mine out by hard labor. As a preacher he was polished in his whole style and manner, and eloquent and pathetic. While he developed a subject in a way to satisfy the intellect, he knew how to bring it home to the heart. One of the best defenses I have ever heard of the Saviour's divinity he gave in this pulpit, from the first five verses of John's Gospel. So, too, one of his most moving, practical sermons was from Hosea, "Then shall we know, if we follow on to know the Lord." It has always been to me a matter of wonder that a volume of his sermons was never printed.

There was one form of service he performed, in addition to all his other duties, which was highly valued; he gave special attention to the elocutionary culture of students, after the rules of Walker, on which his own delivery was formed. On the decease of Dr. Livingston, that the Seniors might lose as little as possible from that event, he carried on their course in Didactic Theology, and thus in effect, for several months, he had the whole weight of Seminary instruction resting on him. He was very fond of nature. To him, principally, are we indebted for the fine shade-trees of the Campus, as well as for the fine floral display which was yearly seen and admired at his door. He, too, was the means of the donation of what was known as the Mrs. Chinn's Library, and which he selected.

One personal incident, to me of great moment, I may mention, if for no other reason than to show how judicious Christian friends may benefit a young preacher. We were on intimate terms. One day he said to me, "Have you any idea how you preach?" I told him I had not, and often wished to hear some one preach as I did, that I might see and hear my own manner, and correct it. He asked if he should show me. I solicited him by all means, for I knew that he had a remarkable power of imitation. He gave it to me, and it was the most valuable lesson of my early ministry; it altered my whole manner of preaching from that day.

But I must fill up my picture with notice of another most worthy and most unassuming clerical hearer, and that is Rev. John S. Mabon, who received his Professoral certificate at the same time with Dr. Thomas De Witt. If true greatness is modest and retiring, then Mr. Mabon is entitled to the honor, for he was such. No one could have intercourse with him without being struck with the evidences of his profound and varied cultivation. He was indefatigable in study, and was most happy among the literary treasures (gathered by himself in Europe) which filled his shelves. He never assumed the pastoral office, though, when in health, he not unfrequently supplied pulpits, and had performed missionary work in Northern New-York and in Canada. He was an honored educator, and had the satisfaction of preparing not a few young men for college classes. In the Grammar School of Rutgers College he labored continuously for nine years. On the decease of the excellent and amiable Dr. John Schureman, the General Synod gave him charge of instruction in Hebrew, in the Seminary, until a professor should be chosen. His students remembered his faithful efforts gratefully. He was the warm friend as well as the devoted instructor of young men, sympathizing in their trials and ever ready to help with counsel and other aid.

It was unfortunate that Mr. Mabon confined himself to his laborious avocations so closely that his health was thereby seriously impaired. He was brought into close relations with Dr. Van Vranken, as he married the doctor's sister, a Christian lady, whom I may well remember, as she was the warm and sympathizing friend of my family. Mr. Mabon was a model hearer, being always closely attentive, and entering into all the trying circumstances of a beginner in pulpit duties. As a theologian, no man exceeded him in soundness of views and intelligent apprehension of truth. Bred first under most thorough Scotch training, he completed his course with Dr. Livingston. In his latter days his trials were various and severe, but borne with a Christian spirit. Though personally gone to his rest, he lives in a son, whose privilege it is to occupy a high position among our ministry.

It belongs to my narrative to say that the distinguished George Wood, who reached the pinnacle of fame as a lawyer, was a constant attendant in the morning of the Sabbath. His close attention was calculated to induce care in every effort on the part of a young preacher. James Schureman Nevius, the most cheerful and vivacious of young men, always ready for a joke and never behind in a repartee, and, at the time, a keen, discriminating young lawyer, was my fellow-boarder at his uncle's, and my hearer. With sharp eye and keen ear he always heard the young fledgeling in the pulpit. And then regularly came Dr. Ackerman, whose interested countenance has often come up before me, and whose son has become the benefactor of our missionary brethren.

Shall I not speak of my helpers? They deserve a special place. We have the advantage, through our ecclesiastical system, of surrounding a minister with the best material of which a church is composed. If a man is unfitted, or fails in accomplishing a fair work, he may be easily passed by and another introduced to his place. It was my privilege to have some most capital men in the eldership as well as active men in the deaconship; not all of the same characteristics, but rarely a deficient man—plain for the most part, sincere, possessed of good sense and piety. Mr. James Schureman was a noble specimen of a man, highly intelligent, judicious, and possessed of general influence, and of large and liberal views. He had seen much of public life in honorable positions, and was qualified for the leading place which others assigned him. Frederick Van Liew, of Middlebush, was a farmer, and had enjoyed few advantages; but he was far beyond the ordinary run of men; more than almost any other man he had the confidence of the country part of the congregation, and was their most able advocate. It was my privilege to enjoy always his regard and confidence. Peter Voorhies, of Middlebush, was an aged man in my day; he had long been a pillar in the church. But I can not dwell on the Wyckoffs, Henry Van Arsdale, David Fine, Philip Oakie, Henry Schenck, Lewis Carman, the Outcalts, Judge Nicholas Booraem, George Nevius, and others; the last two still surviving. Another I can never forget. Though not a member of the church, Peter Spader was a most valuable man; his favors were constant. Though separated, by removal, to another charge, I always received a cordial welcome when we met.

Paul charged his true yoke-fellow, Enodias, to help "those women which labored with him in the Gospel;" and what pastor has not reason to cherish a high regard for this class of his helpers? Their place is a most important one. When are they not first in good deeds? When are they not the ever ready coöperators in the plans of usefulness a pastor may commend?

When are they not the most persevering? Here they were to me most valuable. They constituted a valuable band. But there are four whom I have had special reason to remember most kindly: Sarah Van Doren was never weary in well-doing, never could do too much, the Sabbath-school was on her heart; Miss H. Vethake, cultivated, highly educated, retiring, and never self-reliant, regarded no study or labor too much for the cause of piety; the two sisters, Phœbe and Elizabeth Bennett, became members during my ministry, and were most efficient workers and supports. Only within a few years has the last of the four been called home, leaving her blessing behind her in the form of benevolent gifts.

May I say a word about co-laborers, whose work lay around me in this church-field? The ministerial brethren of the Classis were most valuable men. John S. Vredenbergh, of Somerville, was a man of strong, marked merit. His whole heart was in his work, and it was a large work; and in this he had a helper in a wife, who was a second Isabella Graham in the variety and importance of her benevolent works. Few families were more esteemed than theirs, and few are there where unusual culture and intelligent, earnest piety were so strikingly the characteristics, and few have made such personal consecrations to the cause of Christ.

Mr. Vredenbergh went into the ministry from this church. I found his aged father in its fellowship when I settled. The pastor of Somerville was always heard with attention in the councils of the church, for he was a most judicious and wise man. God blessed his work abundantly, and it is remarkable how great its results were after his decease. Not long after that event, a most extensive and powerful revival occurred, and some three hundred and fifty were gathered into the fold. It was the first revival in which I had labored, and it was delightful to hear constantly of some good word or earnest sermon of the deceased pastor as the instrument of awakening.

One of the most Nathanael-like men was John L. Zabriskie, pastor of Millstone, and he was my nearest clerical neighbor. He was an honored instrument in building up what I used to regard as one of the most desirable rural charges in the denomination. He was eminently a man of peace, and of great simplicity of character. Without any pretensions to greatness, his ministry was truly evangelical, and he saw the children and the children's children come into the church. His house was the much-loved place of ministerial meeting.

My valued friend and classmate, both in college and in the Seminary, Isaac M. Fisher, in a few months after my settlement here became pastor of the Bedminster church. A capital theologian he was, and a most able defender of the doctrines of our church. No man among us in the Seminary was so familiar with the system of Dr. Livingston, and could more intelligently explain and illustrate it. His critical acumen had been sharpened by the great Hopkinsian controversy which had pervaded the New-York churches a few years before; and with all its points, both theological and metaphysical, he had made himself at home. A most honest and upright man in his principles, he enjoyed the confidence of all who knew him, and the remarkably upright physical man seemed the index of the spirit within.

Rev. Jacob J. Schultz was located at the White House, and was one of the most earnest of preachers. He labored as one who had the best interests of his people at heart, and was blessed with large ingatherings to the fellowship of the churches to which he ministered. Every good enterprise found in him a hearty coöperator.

And there was Samuel A. Van Vranken, generous, warm-hearted, and ever enlivening by his sparkling remarks. It was said he had settled in Monmouth with solicitude for his health, as he had expectorated blood near the close of his student life. But certainly, on that score, the settlement proved most wise, for he became one of the most vigorous of men. The bosom friend of Dr. Ludlow, he exceeded him in the animation of his style and in the emotional character of his preaching. In the midst of his people, he was in his glory. In view of his health, he did not in his early ministry give himself to books and to sermon-writing. His study, it was said, was the lawn in front of his house; and there, pacing to and fro, he wrought out, without pen or paper, his Sabbath preparations, and among his most intelligent hearers obtained the reputation of a most powerful preacher. It was with difficulty he was induced to leave a place where he was so happy. Providence brought him to the professorial office here after two pastoral changes, and now his remains lie in the westernmost portion of your graveyard.

But the man who out-topped all others was James S. Cannon—noble in form, dignified in manner, careful in speech, wise in counsel, the friend of all, especially of the young minister, and distinguished for his literary and theological attainments.

The doctor was brought into close relations with the Theological Seminary by performing the service of Professor of Ecclesiastical History during the session of 1818 and 1819, (as was the case with Mr. Mabon;) and his interest in the students, which was always warm, became very earnest, and made him their counselor and friend. He seemed like a venerated parent at Six Mile Run, to whom the students loved to repair for converse and advice. He was truly a Christian philosopher, looking out thoughtfully and calmly on the outside world, with its wave-like changes. His preaching was far from the sensational, which rings changes on a few exciting topics. Its range was over the vast field of Bible truth, resting with delight on the Gospel and the sweet experience of its working in the Christian life. He subsequently came into distinct professorial relations with the Seminary, retiring from the pastoral office. And you know well how truly gentlemanly his whole bearing, how uniformly kind, how sympathizing, how exemplary his Christian walk, how elevated and how thorough his instruction, and how completely he secured the confidence and regard of all his pupils, either of the College or the Seminary. He was truly a great man, in the best and most desirable sense of the term.

My friends, I thank you for so kindly allowing me to carry you in a familiar strain through reminiscences to me so pleasant, and, I trust, not uninteresting to you, many of whom are the descendants or the connections of those of whom I have spoken, or to whom I have referred. They are gone; but not without leaving a most solemn work for their successors. The old flock is divided into three folds, each having much to call out our gratitude. I rejoice with you in your enlargement, and in the promise for the future involved in it. To realize all, and still to advance to a higher development of Christian character, requires the earnest effort of all, and what encouragement have you to make it! The God of the fathers is your God. What a glorious starting-point does this day, with its charming services, furnish, and how worthily may this be made the mark of those who are in the vigor of life and of those rising to maturity!

To myself, this has been a most grateful day, and especially as it has followed another of most pleasant character. A week since, I preached to the people among whose fathers my profession of the Saviour's name was made, and my first communion was celebrated just fifty years ago this month, and before whom my first sermon was preached; and now I have been in solemn service with the children, and the children's children, in the sanctuary where my ministerial life began. I ought to be thankful. I trust I am thankful, and I can well leave the future to my divine Master, to whom I would give all the glory.

On the conclusion of the address, the congregation united in singing

PSALM XC. PART II.

Tune—Windsor.

> Our God, our help in ages past,
>   Our hope for years to come,
> Our shelter from the stormy blast,
>   And our eternal home!
>
> Before the hills in order stood,
>   Or earth received her frame,
> From everlasting Thou art God,
>   To endless years the same.
>
> Time, like an ever-rolling stream,
>   Bears all its sons away;
> They fly, forgotten, as a dream
>   Dies at the opening day.
>
> Our God, our help in ages past,
>   Our hope for years to come,
> Be Thou our guard while troubles last,
>   And our eternal home.

The evening service was concluded with prayer and the benediction by Rev. Dr. Ferris, and the great congregation separated.

Thus, through three services, occupying nearly the entire day, the interest of these anniversary exercises was maintained. The expression was general that the occasion was of a most delightful and refreshing character, and had left impressions which would make it forever memorable to all who had been permitted to participate in these solemnities. We had "remembered the days of old," according to the divine direction. The history of God's dealings with the Church during a period of one hundred and fifty years, and of His grace to "the fathers," had been contemplated for our encouragement and strength. Hallowed and tender recollections had been awakened while worshiping in the venerable sanctuary which, for more than fifty years, had invited successive generations within its courts. Blessed seasons had been witnessed here by God's waiting people, on returning Sabbaths, as His Spirit was poured out in answer to prayer. From this communion of saints on earth multitudes have gone, rejoicing in hope, to join the Church of the first-born whose names are written in heaven.

Under such auspicious circumstances has the First Reformed Dutch Church of New-Brunswick celebrated her One Hundred and Fiftieth Anniversary

ANNIVERSARY LESSONS.

A SERMON PREACHED OCTOBER 6, 1867,

BY REV. RICHARD H. STEELE, D.D.

"THE Lord our God be with us, as he was with our fathers."—1 KINGS 8 : 57.

WE have been permitted, in the providence of God, to celebrate the one hundred and fiftieth anniversary of the founding of our church—an anniversary that has awakened attention wherever the children of this congregation are scattered, and which will form an interesting topic of conversation as long as the present generation are upon the stage of life. It seems that, as a fitting conclusion to the exercises of this occasion, your pastor should endeavor to gather together its lessons, and repeat, on behalf of you all, the prayer of Solomon at the dedication of the temple, which was so appropriately selected as the motto of the whole services, "The Lord our God be with us, as he was with our fathers."

Rest assured, my friends, that the interest of this occasion is not transient or circumscribed. It has left impressions upon our hearts which will abide with us always; and, as the facile pen of the reporter shall spread round a circle of unusual width the story of our religious festival, it will form the topic of thought and prayer in many distant families. God has been with us in this series of meetings. If ever Heaven has smiled propitiously upon Christian gatherings, ours is the occasion. The day has been a joyful one in New-Brunswick; and we, who worship at the old altar and dwell at the old homestead, have not misinterpreted the indications of Providence in gathering together the children of the fathers and their descendants to this feast of memory. The broad invitation that we circulated; the recollections that have been awakened; the wonderful history that has been recited of these pioneers of the covenant, who so many generations ago laid the foundation of our institutions of religion, and learning, and government; the rich tone of spiritual feeling that pervaded our assemblies; and the new purposes formed in respect to the interest we shall hereafter take in the cause of Christ, all testify to the hold this anniversary has taken upon our minds and hearts. I repeat it: The story of our coming together on this high festival occasion will be rehearsed around many a fireside and to future generations. An interest which is not transient or local now surrounds the spot where it pleased God to plant, one hundred and fifty years ago, this goodly vine. Those who know us and have worshiped with us, as well as strangers who have never stood within these gates, will fix on us their minds as they speak of our remarkable history.

In making the improvement of the occasion which the whole subject suggests, I will not follow any formal analysis of the theme, but will lead you with me along a path of familiar reminiscence and encouragement, entreating the blessing, "The Lord our God be with us, as he was with our fathers."

Our fathers, and God with them. After the record which has been reëngraved upon their monuments, can we doubt the reality? I think of these men once more, as we have read their names and refreshed our memories with their virtues. When we reflect upon the hardships experienced by the first settlers in this new land, the privations, the labor, the dangers incident to this then unbroken wilderness, can there be room to doubt the special providence of God in selecting the agents who should found, and in leading them to the place where they should erect, this temple of worship and praise, the first religious organization in our goodly city? Was it the merest accident that they were led to pitch their habitations in this fertile land, coursed by this noble river, surrounded by these broad fields of inviting husbandry, in this genial climate, midway between the stern winters which crown with frost and ice the northern latitude and the enervating heat and sickness incident to a southern clime? Let those believe who may that such a movement as this is only human in its conception and results; that the order of events that peopled this section of our State with that sturdy Batavian race, whose excellences we have commemorated, was a mere random adventure of men who knew not where they were going, or what was the end of their mission; we, who have faith in Providence, not blind but wise, not a coercive necessity but an intelligent purpose, will believe that the Lord Jehovah was with our fathers.

When I think of those praying men who crowded around that noble minister, Rev. Theodorus J. Frelinghuysen, who broke ground for the Gospel in this new territory, the companion and colaborer with Gilbert Tennent, George Whitefield, and President Edwards—whose grave, like that of Moses, no man knows unto this day; when I think how the good minister, Mr. Leydt, passed almost from his pulpit to the grave amid the lamentations of the people; when I think how all the expectations of this church were disappointed as they bowed in submission to the will of Providence in the early removal of Dr. Hardenbergh, while they received the consolation administered to them in the funeral sermon preached at his burial by Dominie Van Harlingen, from the text, "My father, my father, the chariots of Israel, and the horsemen thereof;" when I think how hearts were almost broken at the great bereavement experienced in the death of Dr. Condict; when I recall the names of all these ministers and their successors, and behold the foundations they have laid, the seed they have sown, and the harvests they have gathered, I am ready to repeat, what has come out all along in our narrative, "This is the Lord's doing; it is marvelous in our eyes."

How different is our position to-day from that of those who first came to this field with the Gospel of salvation! It has been impossible for me, during the preparation of my Historical Discourse—and I confess that it has given me two years of labor and thought, in the midst of other duties, feeling my way through a wilderness which had never been traveled, and gathering materials for the first one hundred years from letters, scraps of newspapers, old wills and deeds, Bible records, and inscriptions on the old brown tombstones—it has been impossible, in the midst of it all, to keep from my mind that old building, with its shingled sides, and steep roof, and unpainted interior, and uncarpeted aisles, in Burnet street, where your forefathers worshiped God in the olden time, and contrast it with the quiet Sabbaths which have shed around us their hallowed influence in this ample tabernacle and these crowded congregations. We can not but view with emotion the obscure origin of some vast river, and trace it in its expanding flow onward in its course until it mingles its waters with the great reservoir of ocean. Then it is the little rivulet tinkling through the valley; now it is the broad river on whose bosom the commerce of a nation floats. So, with emotions of wonder and thanksgiving to God, we trace the origin of those streams of moral and spiritual influence which have blessed our world, and are still accumulating strength and vigor with the lapse of years, and whose ultimate power for good it is almost impossible for us to conceive. Truly, that little band, who first planted here the Gospel of our precious Saviour, the Lord Jesus Christ, might well be spoken of, in the beautiful figure of the Psalmist, as "an handful of corn on the top of the mountain." And even now the prediction has been fulfilled, for the fruit thereof has shaken like Lebanon.

> "They little thought how pure a light,
> With years, would gather round that day;
> How love would keep their memories bright;
> How wide a realm their sons would sway!"

A review of the history of our church, when it shall be spread out before you, will exhibit the fact that the early founders of our religious institutions were men who *loved the word of God*, and who made their appeal to it as the *only infallible rule of faith and practice.*

There are still in existence a few venerable copies of the Bible, in the native language of the Hollanders, preserved as heir-looms in the families of their descendants. These well-read pages attest how intelligently and tenaciously they adhered unto God's testimonies. If they sought for comfort, they found it in the Holy Scriptures; if they needed inspiration, they caught it from the Old and the New Testament; if they desired strength, they sought it in these lively oracles; if they panted after holiness, they communed with the Holy Ghost in the volume which was written by Him. They had few books to adorn their dwellings; and in most instances a large family Bible, with its antique binding and strange plates and clasps of ponderous brass; a psalm-book; and a volume of sermons prepared by some famous divine of the Netherlands—a Brakel, a Van Derkemp, a Hellenbrook, a Marck—constituted the entire religious educational apparatus of the household. But this word of God they loved. Some of you remember how these pious men and women of the past generation pored over these sacred pages. Amid all privations, they were sustained by the principles and promises treasured, as they believed, for God's people in the Book of the Lord. Its biographies of the patriarchs, its historical narratives, its predictions of the Messiah, its precious psalms, its proverbs and parables, its Gospels of the Saviour, its apocalyptic vision of heaven, were familiar lessons from infancy to old age. They read the Bible daily, and large portions of it were committed to memory. They taught their children to read it and reverence its inspired teachings. And some of those godly men became expounders of the word of God, and their names have been handed down to us as "helpers" in the Gospel of our Lord.

My friends, in the reverence in which they held, and the attachment which they cherished for, the Bible, the Dutch fathers are examples to us. It is emphatically *the book for the family and the race.* To it we must come at last for all that higher knowledge which relates to our origin and our destiny, the true aim of life and the real dignity of rational and intelligent beings. Let the pleasing custom be perpetuated of preserving the genealogical record of the household in the family Bible, written between the Old and New Testaments, to be consulted by those who come after us, telling the story of births, and baptisms, and marriages, and burials, from generation to generation. Familiarize your own minds with its blessed language, teach your children its lessons of heavenly truth; and as did the fathers, so do you take this best of all books as the guide, the instructor, the light, and life, and law of the house. "There," said one of the pastors of this church, when he was dying, "there is the word of God, which has an abundance of knowledge and grace. The Lord has given you reason, and a capacity for knowing and loving him; let that word be your teacher, and you will experience riches of grace."

Again, *the fathers of this church were men of intelligent and earnest piety.* I speak now of their religious character, as moulded and developed under the instructions of the early ministers of this church. After the great conflict through which Dominie Frelinghuysen passed with the formal element which prevailed throughout this whole region, he gathered into the communion a body of men who were spiritual, praying, and devoted to the cause of Christ. They were sound in their views of the truth; in their system of religious belief, they adopted the catechisms and confessions of faith of the Reformed Church; in their method of instruction in the household, they followed the direction of the Scriptures, and taught their children out of the word of God, and trained them systematically in the doctrines and standards in which they themselves had been educated in the fatherland. They were the children of the covenant. They had faith in God, and made sacrifices to promote his honor. They looked beyond their own immediate wants, and labored directly for the welfare of those who were to come after them. They saw the hand of God before them leading the way, and they followed his directions. The whole history of this church is replete with the evidence that ministers and people sought the immediate guidance of God. We might speak of the deficiencies in their character, and it would be no difficult matter to discover points in which they failed; but we will leave this ungracious task for those whose taste prefers to look at their infirmities and infelicities rather than upon those traits which bear the evidence of a sterling character. We prefer to think of these men as trained under the ministry of that fearless herald of the Gospel who always felt that he was sent to this field by a most direct interposition of Providence, and who would adhere to his purpose of preaching the doctrines of grace though there rose up the clamor of great opposition against the truth. We would think of them as pitching their habitations in this then unbroken wilderness, opening for themselves a path through the forest; worshiping God in the first sanctuary erected in the interior of our State by the church of our order; having in their house the ordinance of family worship, that first care of the Christian parent; planting the seminary of learning by the side of the Christian sanctuary; and we will find in all these things much that we can admire in our New-Brunswick ancestors.

And the piety of these men was sincere, a serious joy in God lighting up their countenances, and inspiring within them, amid all their hardships, the blessedness of hope. Rev. Gilbert Tennent, who was on terms of special intimacy with his co-laborer in this city, Rev. Mr. Frelinghuysen, has left the record that his ministry was eminently blessed here, and that those who were in membership with the church "appeared to be converted persons, by their soundness of principles, Christian experience, and pious example." He describes, in one of his letters, the work of grace which was here enjoyed, and he says, "I may further observe that frequently, at sacramental seasons in New-Brunswick, there have been signal displays of the divine power and presence. Divers have been convinced of sin by the sermons there preached, some converted, and many affected by the love of God in Jesus Christ. Oh! the sweet meltings that I have seen on such occasions among many. New-Brunswick did then look like a field that the Lord had blessed. It was like a little Jerusalem, to which the scattered tribes with eager haste repaired on sacramental solemnities, and there they fed on the fatness of God's house, and drank of the rivers of his pleasure."

There are many other inviting pages in the history of the fathers, every one rich in instructive lessons. We could speak of their *patriotism*, and show you that these men *loved their country and hated oppression*. The teachings of history in the land from whence they came, while it exhibited the doctrine of toleration in all civil and ecclesiastical matters, at the same time furnished precedents which have been wrought out in the struggles through which our own nation has passed. The United Provinces of the Netherlands had a Declaration of Independence long before that more renowned instrument which bound into one nation the United States of America. They had a constitutional government in opposition to hereditary power. They had a motto—"Unity makes might"—which is hardly inferior to that of our own country, which is intended to express the union of these States. It is not surprising that such men gave themselves to the cause of their country, and suffered for this heritage which they have transmitted unto us.

We could speak of the *intellectual character* of the fathers; and, while not claiming for them any considerable degree of culture and learning, yet it might be shown that, for the times and poverty of advantages which they enjoyed, they were not devoid of intelligence, and had an eye to the prospective wants of the church. Coming from that Dutch republic which had its system of free schools, which so caught the attention of the Puritans in their exile, as they saw it in successful operation, that they made it their model on the settlement of New-England, it is not surprising that the first minister brought with him to this field of labor the "well-educated schoolmaster," Jacobus Schureman, a "gentleman who was respectable for his literary acquirements as well as for his piety," and planted the school-house by the side of the church. First of all, they made provision for the permanent establishment of religious institutions, and then, at great sacrifice, they furnished facilities for the highest forms of education, establishing the fifth College in the North-American colonies, and planting the first Theological Seminary in our land. These points, with others, are inviting. But the evidence is sufficient that the Lord Jehovah was with the fathers. He sent them to this field, and bestowed on them His blessing. And we have that in their record which is to us a ground of thanksgiving.

It seems to us, as we study the history of the church, that it is a special providence of God in giving to our American Zion, in the various branches of her organization, a fatherland, from which they have received the peculiar type of their theology and order. The Scotch Presbyterians hail from the hills and valleys of that land of martyrs, which is redolent with the piety of those suffering heroes who so long resisted the tyranny of a court that knew not God nor the best interests of the state. And is it any wonder that they think to-day with joyful pride how their ancestors, of a noble faith and a simple form of worship, made the forests and glens of Scotland vocal with their psalms of praise. And how often are we pointed to that exhibition of faith and devotion in the history of the pilgrims of New-England, who, after a long and boisterous passage, disembarked from the storm-beaten Mayflower in the midst of a northern winter, waded through the surf to the icy shore, bowed in worship on the snow-covered rock of Plymouth, and there, finding what they had sought in this new world—liberty and a home—made that December sky echo with their songs of praise and voice of prayer.

Grand as are these associations—and we acknowledge it all—is it not also worthy of remembrance that the church of our faith and order had its origin in that Dutch republic whose territory was rescued from the ocean by artificial embankments; a republic that gave shelter to the persecuted of all other nations, receiving the Pilgrims and Huguenots when hunted by civil and ecclesiastical intolerance from their own land ; a republic, whose noble constitution gave origin to our own form of government, and which stood so long as a rock against the in-rolling tide of Catholic dominion and prelatical and intolerant usurpation? Our history, as a branch of the American church, is worthy of preservation, and I trust that God will make me thankful that I have a home, by birth and education and ministerial life, in a church which hails from sturdy Holland.

Let me now suggest, as an appropriate close to my discourse, some lessons which the prayer of our text teaches.

1. *Our gratitude is due to God for the gift of the fathers.*

A noble ancestry is a ground of gratitude unto God, and no one can tell how much he is indebted for the bestowment of such an inheritance. The exhibition of their virtues and the power of their example has been sending down through successive generations the most healthful and beneficent influence. God selected these agents as the pioneers of his Gospel in this region, and they have been made by Providence the instruments of conferring upon us and upon the world countless blessings. These patriarchal men have stood before us during our exercises strong in faith, fervent in prayer, earnest in work for Christ, and exemplary in life. And on the divine faithfulness in the fulfillment of his precious promises we also will rely. "Know, therefore, that the Lord thy God, he is God, the faithful God, which keepeth covenant and mercy with them that love him and keep his commandments to a thousand generations."

2. *We should foster and strengthen all those institutions which the fathers established.*

The policy and wisdom of the fathers was to establish, first, the church with all its necessary appointments—the outward edifice very simple and unadorned in its construction, but, for the times, convenient and ample, and not contrasting in an unfavorable way with their own private dwellings. The original house of worship, in Burnet street, was erected from the scanty means which the first settlers, in their poverty, consecrated to the Lord. The second, built on this very site, of the more enduring stone, was a clear expression of the advancing spirit and liberal views of the congregation. This noble edifice, which has now stood in its massive proportions for more than half a century, on a still broader scale displayed the large-hearted liberality of those men who saw the need of such an edifice as this to adorn our city and invite generations to crowd its gates. The sad scene connected with its erection adds interest to this place of worship. The beloved pastor, who had ministered here for seventeen years, saw the importance of this enterprise, and upon the threshold of the work God took him. It was a day of mourning when the congregation gathered around his grave, beneath the walls of the old building now in process of demolition. Yonder is his monument, and around this venerable church are resting hundreds to whom he preached, and the record of the sainted Condict is still precious to the people of the Lord.

We shall show our appreciation of the work of the fathers by cherishing the institutions which they established. Are increased facilities demanded? let us arise and build. Have we schools and colleges and seminaries? let us see that these are maintained with vigor in our midst, and learn wisdom, by occupying important posts in the growing West, that we may do our part in providing means of intellectual, moral, and religious culture for the whole land.

3. *Let us imitate the excellences of the fathers.*

I have not represented them as perfect characters. They had their faults. But they were the faults of the age. And while we spread the mantle of charity over their failings, let us walk in the footsteps of their piety. It will be well for us to remember that the whole benefit of the past will be lost upon us if we so rely upon it as to make it a ground of repose, as if no further exertion was demanded. Do not let us, then, so rest upon the works of the fathers that we shall attempt no further progress. Let us arise and work for God, and pray, labor, toil for that gracious baptism of the Holy Ghost which would be such a crown of glory to our anniversary, and fill heaven with joy. We will prove ourselves worthy of our history if we do the great work to which the providence of God surely points us.

Let us, then, most fervently offer unto God the prayer of Solomon at the dedication of the Temple, "The Lord our God be with us as he was with our fathers." Was God graciously present with the former pastors of this church, rendering them faithful in labors and successful in winning souls to Christ? So may He be with him who now serves his Master and this church of Christ in the ministry of the Gospel. May He make me a faithful ambassador for God, a diligent worker in the vineyard, and a true leader of the people. Was God with the officers of the church, teaching them to rule well in the house of the Lord? So may He be with these elders and deacons, rendering them efficient co-laborers with the pastor, and watchful over the interests of Zion. Was God with the young men of this church, giving them wisdom to consecrate themselves to Him in the work of the ministry? So may He raise up and send forth from this communion many who shall devote their talents to the blessed work of the ministry of reconciliation. We remember the fathers, and how God was with them. But where are they? They have all passed away. Man dies, but God lives. Ministers, elders, members of this church are gone. Their bodies rest in hope in the adjoining churchyard, while their spirits have long been with the Saviour in the land of the blessed.

One hundred years ago, the spot on which we worship was

consecrated to the God of Bethel. When the next one hundred years are added, what changes shall then have taken place! It will, without doubt, be observed. But not one of us will be living to share in the succeeding anniversary. Long before that time, we will all have passed away. The church will be here, worshiping in this or in some future sanctuary. This beautiful river, with a name so redolent of the tribes who darted their swift canoes along its tide, will still flow onward to the ocean. These fields, so verdant, will still slope down to the river margin, yielding the finest of the wheat. All these institutions of religion and learning which give honor to our city will abide, we trust, more vigorous with the increase of years. But we will not be of the number who make up the great congregation on that occasion.

"Who'll pass along our city street
 A hundred years to come?
Who'll tread this church with willing feet
 A hundred years to come?
Pale, trembling age, and fiery youth,
And childhood, with its brow of truth;
The rich and poor, on land and sea—
Where will the mighty millions be
 A hundred years to come?

"We all within our graves will sleep
 A hundred years to come;
No willing soul for us will weep
 A hundred years to come.
But other men our lands will till,
And others then our streets will fill,
And others words will sing as gay,
And bright the sun shine as to-day,
 A hundred years to come."

Part Third.

APPENDIX.

OFFICERS OF THE CHURCH, 1867.

Pastor.
Rev. RICHARD H. STEELE.

Elders.

ISAAC VOORHEES,
JESSE F. HAGEMAN,
JOHN BEEKMAN,

FERDINAND S. CORTELYOU,
LEWIS APPLEGATE,
GEORGE BUTTLER.

Deacons.

HENRY K. HOW,
GILBERT S. VAN PELT,
V. M. W. SUYDAM,

NICHOLAS W. PARSELL,
JOHN V. H. VAN CLEEF,
JOHN STEWART.

Treasurer.
IRA CONDICT VOORHEES.

APPENDIX.

I.

The lands west of the Raritan lots, extending back to the Millstone river, and as far up said river as Rocky Hill, (taking in nearly all of Franklin township, and a strip in addition on the south of the Six Mile Run Turnpike,) were originally divided into four large plots, which may be in general thus described: The plot of Daniel Cox began at the north-west corner of Inians's two plots, near the Two Mile Run Tavern; thence in a straight line south-west five miles, to a point a mile and a quarter south of Six Mile Run church; thence west-south-west three and one tenth miles to the road leading from Ten Mile Run to Little Rocky Hill, being to a point on said road about one mile directly south of Ten Mile Run; thence in a straight line north-north-east eight miles and thirty chains, striking and following what is known as the Middlebush road, (which is a remnant of this eight-mile line,) to a point on the Raritan lots, (either Jones's or Clement's lot, and now the farm of J. V. L. Van Doren,) and thence along the rear of the Raritan lots two and a half miles, plus ten chains, to the point of beginning, containing 7540 acres. (Amboy Records, Lib. G, p. 314; also, Lib. E, p. 365.) The proprietors sold this tract to one of their fellow proprietors, Daniel Cox, of London, September 1st, 1694. Signed Andrew Hamilton, David Mudie, Andrew Bowne, James Dundas, L. Morris, John Inians, Thomas Warne, George Willocks, Thomas Gordon, John Reid, John Barclay.

The second plot begins at a point on Millstone River, opposite Rocky Hill, and runs east-south-east two miles, minus twelve chains, to the southern end of the eight-mile line before alluded to; thence along said line three miles, minus six chains, and thence west-north-west two miles, to the Millstone River, where the Ten Mile Run brook empties into the same; thence up the Millstone to the place of beginning, containing 5000 acres. John Harrison and George Willocks bought this tract, as well as the adjoining tract, of Daniel Cox, already described, in the year 1700. (Amboy Records, Lib. E, p. 365.)

The third plot, bought by the same parties, begins at the mouth of Ten Mile Run brook, and runs two miles south-easterly to the eight-mile line (or the Middlebush road;) thence along said line four miles and a half, minus six chains, to a point half a mile north-east of Middlebush church, and thence west-north-west three miles and eight chains to the Millstone river, at the mouth of a little brook called Ledging brook, (this is one or other of the small streams within a mile south of East-Millstone;) the fourth plot lying north of the last, and between it and the Raritan lots, (now known as the Cedar Grove District,) appears to have been taken possession of by William Dockwra, who owned neighboring lands on the Raritan and Millstone. At any rate, a portion of this land, sold by Richard Salter (Dockwra's agent) to Christian Van Doren, in 1723, had to be repurchased as late as 1760, upon the representation that Salter had no right to sell it. There were several conflicting claims to this portion of Franklin township. (See Millstone Centennial, pp. 13, 14, 16, 19, and 21.)

II.

LIST OF FAMILIES IN THE CONGREGATION—1732-35.

Jan Acten,
Jan Acten, Jr.,
Thomas Acten,

Gerardus Banker,
Jacob Buys,
James Bennet,
Jan Bennet,
Elias Barger,
Andrew Blaew,
Cornelius Bennet,
Hendrick Blaew,
Acrie Bennet,
John Buys,

Francis Costigin,
Cornelius Cornell,
Peter Cochran,
Jacobus Cornell,
Gerrit De Graw,
John De Witt,

G. De Peyster,
Frans Dilden,
Hendrick Dally,
Gideon De Camp,

Philip French,
Charles Fontyn,
Hendrick Fisher,
Abraham Fontyn,
Folkert Folkers,
Jacob Fontyn,
Jaques Fontyn,
Johannes Folkers,
Isack Fontyn,

Johannes Fontyn,
Reyner Fontyn,

John Guest,
Gerrit Gerritsen,
John Gedeman,

James Hude,
Abraham Heyer,
Daniel Hendrickson,

Isaac Jansen,

Peter Kemble,

Paul Le Boyton,
Cornelius Low,

Teunis Montague,
Johannes Messeler,
Paul Miller,
Johannes Meyer,
Peter Metselaer,
Peter Moon,
Samuel Mulford,
Paul Miller,

Andrew Norwood,
Roelof Nevius,

Frederick Outgelt,
Jacob Ouke,
Abraham Ouke,
William Ouke,

Jan Probasco,

Christofel Probasco,

Dirck Schuyler,
Jacobus Schureman,
Cornelius Suydam,
Hendrick Schenck,
Roelof Seebring,
Petrus Sleght,
Abraham Schuyler,
Gerrit Stoothof,
Johannes Seebring,
Lucas Smack,
Aaron Sutfin,

John Ten Broeck,

Isaac Van Noordstrand,
Dirck Van Arsdalen,
Hendrick Van Deursen,
Folkert Van Noorstrand,
Jeremiah Van Derbilt,
Hendrick Van Derbilt,
Aris Van Arsdalen,
Jan Van Buren,
Dirck Van Veghten,
Dirck Van Allen,
Johannes Martinus Van
Harlingen,
Benjamin Van Cleef
Aris Van Derbilt,
Abraham Van Deursen,
Abraham Van Doren,
Aris Van Cleef,
Minnie Van Voorhees,
Peter Voorhees,
Lucas Voorhees,

APPENDIX. 199

Johannes Van Norden, Jan Van Nuys, Gerrit Voorhees,
Christofel Van Doren, Roelef Voorhees, Frederick Van Lieuwen,
Frans Van Dyck, Dirck Van Norstrand, Hendrick Van Derbilt,
Nicolas Van Dyck, William Van Der Rype, William Williamson,
Court Van Voorhees, Jacob Van End, Lawrence Williamson,
Christian Van Doren, Matys Van Der Rype, Leffert Waldron,
Hendrick Van Lieuwen, Johannes Voorhees, Philip Young.

III.

CHARTER OF THE FIVE CHURCHES, NEW-BRUNSWICK, RARITAN, SIX MILE RUN, MILLSTONE, AND NORTH BRANCH, GRANTED JUNE 7TH, 1753:

GEORGE THE SECOND, By the grace of God, of Great Britain, France, and Ireland, King, Defender of the Faith, etc., To all to whom these presents shall come, greeting: Whereas, diverse and sundries of our loving subjects inhabiting within the several counties of Somerset, Hunterdon, and Middlesex, in our Province of New-Jersey, in behalf of themselves and others, being of the Dutch Protestant Reformed Church, by their humble petition presented to our trusty and well-beloved Jonathan Belcher, Esq., Captain-General and Governor-in-Chief in and over our Province of New-Jersey and territories thereon depending in America, Chancellor and Vice-Admiral in the same etc., setting forth that the petitioners are very numerous and daily increasing, and consist of five Churches and Congregations, to wit, The Church and Congregation of Raritan, the Church and Congregation of North-Branch, the Church and Congregation of New-Brunswick, the Church and Congregation of Six Mile Run, the Church and Congregation of Millstone; That the most advantageous support of religion among them, requires that some persons among them should be incorporated as trustees for the community, that they may take grants of lands and chattels, thereby to enable the petitioners to erect and repair public buildings, for the worship of God, school-houses and alms-houses, and for the maintenance of the ministry and poor, and that the same trustees may plead and may be impleaded in any suit touching the promises, and have perpetual succession; and we having nothing more at heart than to see the Protestant Religion in a flourishing condition throughout all our dominions, and being graciously pleased to give all due encouragement to such of our loving subjects, who are zealously attached to our person, government and the Protestant succession, in our royal house, and to grant the request of the petitioners in this behalf: Know ye, that we of our special grace, certain knowledge, and mere motion, have willed, ordained, constituted, and granted, and by these presents for us, our heirs and successors, do will, ordain, constitute, and appoint, that the Rev. John Light, John Frelinghouse, Ministers, John Van Middlesworth, Peter Williams, Peter Van Ess, Andrew Ten Eyck, Daniel Ceybyrn, Peter Mountfort, Hendrick Fisher, Cornelius Bennet, William Williams, Luke Voorhees, David

Nevius, Simon Van Arsdalen, John Stricker, Reynior Vechten, Elders, and Frans Cusart, Andrew Monton, John Broca, Harman Lean, Cornelius Wyckoff, Peter Schamp, Hendrick Van Deursen, John Messelaer, Abraham Hize, Christopher Hoglan, Rem Garretsen, Cornelius Van Arsdalen, Andrew Hagaman, Abraham Hagaman, and James Van Arsdalen, Deacons of the Dutch Reformed Congregations above-named, and the counties aforesaid, and their successors hereafter, the minister or ministers, Elders and Deacons of the respective Churches or Congregations, which at or any time hereafter, be duly chosen or appointed, shall be and remain one body politick and corporate in deed and fact, by the name of the trustees of the Dutch Reformed Church of Raritan, North-Branch, New-Brunswick, Six Mile Run, and Millstone in the counties aforesaid, and that all and every one, the ministers, Elders and Deacons before herein expressed, shall be the first trustees of the said churches and congregations now by these presents constituted and made one body politick by the name of the trustees of the Protestant Dutch Reformed Church, and shall so remain until others are duly called, chosen, and put into their respective place or places, and that they, the said body politick and corporate shall have perpetual succession in deed, fact, and name, to be known and distinguished by the name of The Trustees of the Dutch Reformed Church; and all deeds, grants, bargains, sales, leases, evidences, or otherwise, whatsoever which may anywise relate or concern the corporation, and also that they and their successors, by the name of The Trustees of the Dutch Reformed Church of Raritan, North-Branch, New-Brunswick, Six Mile Run, and Millstone, in the counties aforesaid, be and forever hereafter shall be, persons able in law to purchase, take, hold, or enjoy, any messuages, houses, buildings, lands, tenements, rents, or whatsoever in fee and forever, or for time of life, or lives, or in any other manner, so as the same exceed not at any time in the yearly value of seven hundred pounds sterling, per annum, beyond and above all charges, and reprizes, the statute of mortmain, or any other law to the contrary notwithstanding, and also goods, chattels, and all other things to what kind soever, and also that they and their successors, by the name of The Trustees of the Dutch Reformed Church, shall and may give, grant, demise, or otherwise dispose of all or any of the messuages, houses, buildings, lands, tenements, rents and all other things as to them shall seem meet, at their own will and pleasure; and also that they and their successors, be and forever hereafter shall be, persons able in law to sue and be sued, plea and be impleaded, answer and be answered unto, defend and be defended in all Courts and places, before us our heirs and successors, and before us, or any of the judges, officers, or ministers of us our heirs and successors, in all and all manner of actions, suits, complaints, pleas, causes matters, and demands, whatsoever; and also that the same trustees of the Dutch Reformed Churches, above-named for the time being, and their successors shall and may forever hereafter have and use a common seal with such device or devices, as they shall think proper for sealing all and singular deeds, grants, conveyances, contracts, bonds, articles of agreement, and all and singular their affairs touching or concerning the said corporation. And we do further ordain, will, or grant, that all and every such lands, tenements, and hereditaments corporeal or incorporeal, money, goods, and chattels, which at any time before or after the date of these our letters patent, have been, or shall be, devised, given, or granted, to all or any of the particular churches above-named, within the said several counties of Hunterdon, Somerset, and Middlesex, or to any person or persons, in trust for them, shall be and remain in the peaceable and quiet possession of the corporation, according to the true intent or meaning of such devise or devises, gift or gifts, grant or grants: We do further will, ordain, give, and grant, that the trustees by these presents appointed, shall continue and remain the trustees of the Dutch Reformed Churches of Raritan, North-Branch, New-Brunswick, Six Mile Run, and Millstone, in the counties aforesaid, until others shall be called and chosen according to the manner, customs and methods now in use among the said Protestant Dutch Reformed Churches, which persons so called, elected, and chosen, shall have all the powers and authorities of the above-named trustees, and all and every such person or persons so newly called, elected, and chosen, as aforesaid, shall remain until other fit persons in like manner be called, elected, and chosen, in their respective rooms and places, and so *toties quoties*. And we do further ordain, give, and grant, that there be a meeting of the several trustees of the churches aforesaid, at the Raritan public place of worship, in the County of Somerset, on the first Tuesday of August next, after the date of these our letters patent, and thereafter at such time or times, place or places, within the said counties as to them or the major part of them, shall seem meet and convenient, and then and there by plurality of votes choose a president out of them, for the time being, who shall have the custody of the seal or seals of the said corporation, and all books, charters, deeds, and writings, any way relating to the said corporation, and shall have power from time to time, and all times hereafter, as occasion shall require, to call a meeting of the said trustees, at such place within the said counties as he shall think convenient, for the execution of all or any of the powers hereby given and granted, and in case of sickness, removal, or death of the president, all the powers by these presents granted to the president shall remain on the senior trustee upon record, until the recovery of the president or until a new president be chosen as aforesaid: And we do further will, ordain, give, or grant, that every act and order of the major part of the said trustees, consented or agreed to, at such meeting as aforesaid, shall be good, valid, and effectual to all intent and purposes, as if the said number of the whole trustees had consented and agreed thereto: And we do further will and ordain, that all the acts of the said trustees, or any of them, shall from time to time be fairly entered in a book or books to be kept for that purpose by the president of the trustees, for the time being, which book or books to be kept for that purpose by the president of the trustees, together with the seal of the said corporation, and all charters, deeds, and writings whatsoever, any way belonging to the said corporation, shall be delivered over by the former president, to the president of the said trustees newly elected, as such president shall hereafter successively from time to time be chosen: And we do further of our special grace, certain knowledge, and mere motion, for us, our heirs and successors, by these presents give and grant unto the said trustees of the Dutch Reformed Church, the ministers, elders, and deacons above-named, and their successors forever, that they and their successors all and singular, the rights, privileges, powers, benefits, emoluments, and advantages, to be hereby granted, shall and may forever hereafter, have, hold, enjoy, and use without hindrance or impediment of us, our heirs or successors, or of any of the justices, sheriffs, escheators, coroners, bailiffs, or other officers and ministers, whatsoever, of us, our heirs or successors, and that these our letters, being entered upon record in our secretary's office of New-Jersey, and the record and the enrollment thereof and either of them, and all and every thing therein contained from time to time and at all times hereafter be and shall be firm, valid, good, sufficient, and effectual in law towards and against us, our heirs and successors, according to the true intent and meaning hereof, and in and through all things, shall be construed and taken and expounded most benignly and in favor for the greatest advantage and profit of the trustees of the said Dutch Reformed Church of Raritan, North-Branch, New-Brunswick, Six Mile Run, and Millstone, in the counties aforesaid, and their successors forever, notwithstanding any defect, default, or imperfection may be found therein, or any other cause or thing whatsoever. In testimony whereof we have caused these our letters to be made patent, and the great seal of our Province to be hereunto affixed, and the same to be entered of record in our Secretary's office of said Province of New-Jersey, in one of the books of record therein remaining, witness our well-beloved and trusty Jonathan Belcher, Esq., our Captain-General and Governor-in-Chief, in and over our said Province of New-Jersey, Chancellor and Vice-Admiral of the same, by and with the advice and consent of our council of our said Province, at Burlington, the seventh day of June, and in the twenty-sixth year of our reign.

IV.

LIST OF MEMBERS IN FULL COMMUNION MAY 1st, 1794.

1. Jacobus Van Nuis.
2. John Schureman, } *
3. Ann Deremer.
4. Peter Vredenburgh.
5. Johannah Van Harlingen, widow of Garret Voorhees.
6. William Van Deursen, }
7. Ann Stryker.
8. Treytje Van Wicklen, widow of Fransis Van Dyke.
9. Mary Young, w. of Abraham Ouke.
10. Magdelina Vantine, widow of Thomas Douty.
11. Edward Van Harlingen.
12. John Outgelt.

* These braces indicate husband and wife.

APPENDIX. 203

13. Ephraim Vantine, }
14. Johannah Stoothoff. }
15. John Thomson, }
16. Jane Stryker. }
17. Elizabeth Fisher, w. of Peter Vredenbergh.
18. Margaret Standley, widow of Frederick Outgelt.
19. Barent Stryker, }
20. Elizabeth Bennet. }
21. Peter Vredenbergh, Jr.
22. Frederick Outgelt.
23. Abraham Schuyler, }
24. Aleche Voorhees. }
25. Elizabeth Van Dyke, widow of Frederick Van Liew.
26. Catalina Voorhees, w. of Matthew Egerton.
27. Neltje Voorhees, widow of Ferdinand Schureman.
28. Neltje Schureman, w. of John Van Harlingen.
29. Ann Schureman, w. of Isaac Vantine.
30. John Van Este.
31. Cornelius Rapleje.
32. Janetje Cornell.
33. Garret Voorhees, }
34. Maretje ———. }
35. Dina Ditmars, w. of Benjamin Vantine.
36. Susana Van Este, w. of Jeromus Rapelje.
37. Elizabeth Campbell, widow of Charles Vantine.
38. Acrientje Nevius.
39. Denice Van Liew, }
40. Dinah Durye. }
41. Peter Voorhees, }
42. Mary Buys. }
43. Elizabeth Deremer, w. of Joseph Sillcox.
44. Mary Snoterly, w. of Leonard Nighmaster.
45. Ariantje Croesen, w. of William Nevius.
46. Catelina, wid. of Lucas Voorhees.
47. John Wykoff.
48. Frederick Van Liew, }
49. Ann Rappelje. }
50. Mary Van Arsdalen, w. of Abraham Lott.
51. Cornelius Suydam, }
52. Rachel Collens, }
53. William Van Duyn, }
54. Lena Voorhees, }

55. Mary Stolts, w. of Frederick Outgelt.
56. Ariantje Van Este.
57. Catelina Cornell.
58. Rachel Totten.
59. Mary Ryder, w of Roelef Cornel.
60. Elizabeth Stevenson, w. of Peter Voorhees.
61. Martha Mount, widow of James Voorhees.
62. Anetje Cornell, w. of Cornelius Van Derbilt.
63. Arientje Cortelyou, w. of Roelef Cornell.
64. Jane Nevius, widow of Ryck Van Derbilt.
65. Maria Melleger, w. of Isaac Bennet.
66. Ida Van Derbilt.
67. Christina Pietersen, widow of Joris Rappelje.
68. Neeltje Nevius.
69. Aaltje Rappelje, w. of Hendrick Suydam.
70. Simon Probasco.
71. John Buys.
72. Catherina Collier.
73. John Whitlock, }
74. Eleanor Voorhees, }
75. Geertje Vantine, w. of David Nevius.
76. Jane Williamson, w. of Cornelius Van Duyn.
77. Machteltje Peterson, w. of Jeremias Rappelje.
78. Doretta Lott, w. of John Van Liew.
79. Ann Hance, w of Dirck Van Arsdalen.
80. Ann French.
81. Nicolas Bordine.
82. Philip Ouke.
83. Peter Ten Eyck.
84. Magdalena Messerole.
85. Margareta Vredenberg, w. of Andrew Powers.
86. Lenah Van Devoort, widow of John Messerole.
87. Abraham Ackerman, }
88. Jane Romeyn. }
89. Altje Tunison, w. of John Van Est.
90. Bernardus Garretsen.
91. Abraham Lott.
92. Martha Striker, widow of Albert Collins.

93. Martha Collier, w. of Garret Gerritsen.
94. Dinah Hardenbergh, widow of Rev. J. R. Hardenbergh.
95. Eleanor Hendrickson, w. of John Buys.
96. Frances Covenhoven.
97. Nicolas Van Brunt,
98. Catherine Covenhoven.

V.

MEMBERS OF THIS CHURCH WHO HAVE ENTERED THE GOSPEL MINISTRY.

The following members who united with this church by profession of their faith, have gone forth to preach the Gospel. I include the names of the five sons of Mr. Frelinghuysen and the two sons of Mr. Leydt, though they do not appear among our members. But they stand on our register of baptisms, and as this was their home, it is a natural inference that they here united with the church by profession. I omit a list of about the same number who were members by certificate:

	RECEIVED.	LICENSED.
Rev. Theodore Frelinghuysen............	....	1745
" John Frelinghuysen..................	....	1750
" Jacobus Frelinghuysen...............	....	1753
" Ferdinandus Frelinghuysen...........	....	1753
" Hendricus Frelinghuysen.............	....	1755
" Samuel Verbryck....................	1744	1748
" Matthew Leydt......................	....	1778
" Peter Leydt........................	....	1788
" Abraham Van Horn...................	1786	1788
" John S. Vredenbergh.................	1796	1800
" John Schureman, D.D.................	1797	1801
" Robert Bronk.......................	1811	1813
" Nicholas J. Marsellus, D.D...........	1812	1815
" Abraham D. Wilson..................	1812	1815
" Jacob D. Fonda.....................	1817	1819
" James B. Ten Eyck..................	1818	1821
" David Abeel, D.D...................	1821	1826
" Jefferson Wynkoop..................	1821	1824
" Robert J. Blair.....................	1822	1823
" John G. Tarbell....................	1822	1825
" Samuel Centre......................	1822	18—
" Ira Condict Boice...................	1823	1826
" Cornelius C. Van Arsdale, D.D........	1824	18—
" Frederick B. Thompson..............	1827	1834
" John Manley........................	1828	1831
" Richard L. Schoonmaker.............	1828	1832
" John Forsyth, D.D..................	1828	1832
" John C. Van Liew,..................	1829	1832
" Peter D. Oakey.....................	1830	1844
" James A. H. Cornell.................	1837	1841
" Martin L. Schenck..................	1837	1840
" Charles S. Hageman, ...D.D.........	1837	1843
" Paul D. Van Cleef, D.D..............	1837	1846
" John A. Staats.....................	1837	1840

APPENDIX.   205

	RECEIVED.	LICENSED.
Rev. John L. Janeway	1837	1840
" David D. Demarest, D.D.	1837	1840
" William H. Steele	1837	1840
" John De Witt, D.D.	1837	1842
" William A. Cornell	1838	1844
" Abel T. Stewart	1838	1846
" Cornelius E. Crispell, D.D.	1838	1842
" Charles R. Von Romondt	1841	1844
" William D. Buckelew	1841	1851
" Abraham V. Wyckoff	1842	1845
" James B. Wilson	1842	1851
" John N. Jansen	1848	1851
" Philip Furbeck	1848	1851
" William W. Letson	1850	1854
" Robert R. Proudfit	1855	18—
" Alexander Proudfit	1855	18—
" Nathaniel H. Van Arsdale	1856	1867
" Richard M. Whitbeck	1858	1862

INSCRIPTION ON THE MONUMENT ERECTED TO THE MEMORY OF REV. JOHN H. LIVINGSTON, D.D.

SACRED to the memory of the Rev. John H. Livingston, D.D., S.T.P. Born at Poughkeepsie, State of New-York, May 30th, 1746; educated for the ministry at the University of Utrecht, in Holland; called to the pastoral office of the Reformed Dutch Church, in New-York, in 1770; appointed by the General Synod of the Reformed Dutch Church in America, their professor in didactic and polemic theology, in 1781, and elected to the presidency of Queen's College, New-Jersey, in 1810. There, in performance of the duties of his office, and blessed in the enjoyment of mental energy, high reputation, and distinguished usefulness, he suddenly but sweetly fell asleep in Jesus, January 20th, 1825, in the seventy-ninth year of his age, the fifty-fifth of his ministry, and the forty-first of his professional labors. In him, with dignified appearance, extensive erudition, almost unrivaled talents, as a sacred orator and professor, were blended manners polished, candid, and attractive, all ennobled by that entire devotion to his Saviour which became such a servant to yield to such a Master. In token of their gratitude for his services, and veneration for his memory, the General Synod have ordered this monumental stone to be erected.

INSCRIPTION ON THE MONUMENT ERECTED TO THE MEMORY OF REV. JOHN SCHUREMAN, D.D.

BENEATH this stone are deposited the remains of Rev. John Schureman, D.D., professor of pastoral theology, ecclesiastical history, and church government, in the Theological Seminary of the Reformed Dutch Church, at New-Brunswick; who, while engaged in a course of active and highly useful labors, enjoying the confidence of the churches and the affections of his brethren, departed this life, May 15th 1818, in the fortieth year of his age.

206   APPENDIX.

VI.

CHURCH OFFICERS.

	ELDERS.	DEACONS.		ELDERS.	DEACONS.
April, 1717	Roelef Seebring	Hendrick Bries Roelf Lucas (Van Voorhees)	1765	Hendrick Fisher Fernand Schureman Derrick V'n Veghte Johannes Schureman John M. Van Harlinger	Cornelius Seebring Ernestus Van Harlingen Jacobus Van Nuise Hendrick Van Derbilt John Thompson James Stryker William Van Deursen
1718	Aart Aartsen Isack Van Dyck Roelf Seebring;	Johannes Folkers Hendrick Brics Roelef Lucas			
1719	Jan Aten Laurens Willems	Jacob Ouke	1789	Peter Vredenburg William Van Deursen	John Thomson Peter Vredenburg, Jr.
1720	Charles Fontein	Hans Stoothoff Hendrick Bries			
1721	Roelef Nevius Johannes Folkersen	Laurens Willimse Minne Van Voorhees	1790	Adrian Hageman Abraham Schuyler Rynear Snock	Jacobus Stryker Johannes Van Neste Frederick Van Leuwen
1722	Thomas Bowman	William Moor Hendrick Fisher	1793	John Schureman John Van Neste William Van Deursen Garret Voorhees	Frederick Outcalt John Thomson Denice Van Liew John Bice
1724	Johannes Stoothof Roelph Nevius;	Abraham Ouke			
1725	Thomas Bowman Minne Van Voorhees	Hendrick Fisher Albert Voorhees	MARCH 12, 1794.		
			*Denice Van Llew Peter Vredenburgh, Jr.	Peter V. Voorhees, son of Garret Francis Covenhoven	
1727	Johannes Stoothof Minne Van Voorhees Hendrick Fisher	Albert Voorhees Abraham Ouke	APRIL 5, 1795.		
			Peter Vredenburgh, Sr. Nicholas Van Brunt	Nicholas Bordine Cornelius Rappleyea	
1732	Hendrick Fisher Abraham Ouke Roelef Nevius	Cornelius Bennet Jeremias Van Derbilt Peter Wilmsen	APRIL 25, 1796.		
			James Striker Garret Voorhees	Philip Oke John Wyckoff	
1733	Roelef Seebring Roelef Van Voorhees	Jakobus Buys	APRIL 20, 1797.		
1734	Albert Voorhees Petrus Slegt	Dirck Van Arsdalen	John Thompson, Sr. Frederick Outgelt	Cornelius Van Debilt Simon Anderson	
1735	Hendrick Fisher		APRIL 20, 1798.		
1736	Hendrick Fisher Roelef Nevius Abraham Ouke	Derrick Van Arsdalen Gerrit Fabryck Jan Aten, Jr	Denice Van Liew Abram Schuyler	Francis Covenhoven Henry Cock	
1740	Gerrit Gerritsen	Nicolas Van Dyck William Davids	MAY 14, 1799.		
			Nicholas Bordine William Van Deursen	Benjamin Taylor Abram A. Voorhees	
1741	Jeremiah Van Derbilt	William Willmsen Abraham Van Dooram	MAY 13, 1800.		
1742	Hendrick Fisher Gerrit Gerritsen	Nicolas Van Dyck Christian Van Dooram	Peter Vredenburgh, Jr. Peter Voorhees, of Middlebush	John Van Liew Peter Tenike	
1743	Hendrick Van Leuwen Roelef Voorhees	Peter Slegt	MAY 19, 1800.		
			*†Abram Schuyler		
1749	Cornelius Bennett	Hendrick Van Deusen Johannes Meselar	JUNE 15, 1801.		
1750	William Williamson Gerrit Gerritson	Abraham Heyr	Frederick Outcalt *William Van Deursen	Ruliff Cornell Jerome C. Rappelyee	
			MARCH 30, 1802.		
1752	Hendrick Fisher Chris'n Van Doorn	Derrick Van Veghte Abraham Van Doorn	Phillip Oake Garret Voorhees ‡	Abm. Lott Cornelius Cornell	
1753	Petrus Sleght	Andrew Meyr	APRIL 17, 1803.		
1754	Johannes Messelaer	Johannes Schureman Archibald Tomson	Cornelius Meflar Nicholas Bordine	Benjamin Taylor Simon Anderson	
1756	Cornelius Bennett William Van Duyn	Peter Vredenburg	MAY 19, 1804.		
1757	Hendrick Fisher	Albert Voorhees Abraham Van Doorn	Denice Van Llew Alexander Rosegrants	Frederick Outcalt, Jr. John Van Harlingen	

* Reëlected.   † To fill vacancy.   ‡ Died in office.

APPENDIX.

ELDERS.	DEACONS.
\multicolumn{2}{c}{MAY 5, 1805.}	
William Van Deursen	Peter Voorhees
Frederick Outcalt	Philip Pierson

MAY 10, 1806.
John Wyckoff — Peter S. Wyckoff
Philip Oake — Henry Cock

MAY 3, 1807.
Abram Schuyler — Benjamin Taylor
Nicholas Bordine — John Boice

MAY 14, 1808.
John Van Harlingen — Richard Lupardus
Jeromus C. Rappleyee — John Van Liew

MAY 15, 1809.
Frederick Outcalt — Abraham Voorhees
William Van Deursen — Bernardus Rider

MAY 12, 1810.
Philip Okey — Henry Van Arsdalen
Peter Voorhees (Middle- David Fine
bush)

MAY 1, 1811.
Benjamin Taylor — *Abraham Voorhees
Peter Wyckoff — Jacob Bergen

JULY 15, 1812.
William Van Deursen — Dennis F. Van Liew
Garret Voorhees — Frederick Outcalt, Jr.

MAY 14, 1813.
Nicholas Bordine — John Boice
Abm. Brower — Peter P. Voorhees

APRIL 30, 1814.
Richard Lupardus — Abm. Van Arsdalen
John Wyckoff — Peter Gordon
†Henry Van Arsdalen
†John D. Van Liew

APRIL 3, 1815.
*Henry Van Arsdalen — *John Boice
*John D. Van Liew — Garret Van Arsdalen

MARCH 11, 1816.
Peter Voorhees — Henry Outcalt
Peter Vredenburgh, Jr. — Jacob J. Bergen
Abraham Voorhees — †Uriah Lott
John F. Van Liew (one — Henry Johnson
year) — William French (one year)

MARCH 18, 1816.
†Francis Covenhoven
†Bernardus Ryder

MARCH 17, 1817.
Henry Cock — George G. Nevius
Peter Gordon — William Hageman
Philip Okey — *‡Uriah Lott

SEPTEMBER 15, 1817.
†James Schureman — Richard Manley

MARCH 17, 1818.
John D. Sutphin — Frederick Van Liew
John Boice — Henry Hoagland
Garret Voorhees — †Abm. Van Arsdalen

APRIL 20, 1819.
Dennis F. Van Liew — Thomas Letson
Frederick Outcalt — Henry Outcalt
Henry Van Arsdalen — Garret Van Arsdalen

ELDERS.	DEACONS.

APRIL 28, 1819.
†James Schureman

APRIL 18, 1820.
Garret Van Arsdalen — *Richard Manley
John C. Wyckoff — Denice Van Liew
Jeromus Rappleyea — Cornelius I. Wyckoff
 — †Jacob J. Bergen

MAY 3, 1821.
Peter Voorhees — Nicholas Booraem
David Fine — Abm. O. Voorhees
George G. Nevius — John Van Nortwick

MAY 16, 1822.
John D. Sutphin — Jacob Wyckoff
William French — Henry H. Schenck
Henry Hoagland — John Stothoff

APRIL 7, 1823.
Francis Covenhoven — Adrien Manley
Henry Outcalt — Robert Lyle
Frederick Outcalt — Rulif Van Nostrand

APRIL 5, 1824.
Peter Gordon — *Henry H. Schenck
Peter Voorhees — David Nevius
Henry Van Arsdalen — David D. Nevius (Middlebush)
†Philip Okey
†Frederick Van Liew

MAY 20, 1825.
George G. Nevius — Jacob Wyckoff
Thomas Letson — Abm. O. Voorhees
Abraham Voorhees — Isaac S. Brower
 — †Henry V. Demott

APRIL 1, 1826.
Richard Manley — Abraham Suydam
Cornelius I. Wyckoff — Henry Vroom
Jacob I. Bergen — *Henry V. Demott

MARCH 26, 1827.
Frederick Outcalt — George Boice, Jr.
*Thomas Letson — Abm. V. Thompson
Henry H. Schenck — Isaac G. Sillcocks

MARCH 24, 1828.
Henry Van Arsdalen — Richard Duryea, Jr.
John Stothoff — Powell Dehart
Nicholas Booraem — Ralph Voorhees

MARCH 23, 1829.
George G. Nevius — William Mann
Jacob Wyckoff — David Nevius
David Fine — James Garretson

MARCH 31, 1830.
Richard Manley — Abraham Suydam
Henry Outcalt — Henry Dehart
Frederick F. Van Liew — Cornelius Van Doren

FEBRUARY 22, 1831.
Henry H. Schenck — Henry Vroom
Isaac G. Sillcocks — Lewis Carman
Isaac S. Brower — William Sunderland
*†David Fine

FEBRUARY 21, 1832.
Nicholas Booraem — Powell Dehart
Richard Duryea, Jr. — Henry V. Demott
John Stothoff — William W. Van Duyn

FEBRUARY 18, 1833.
Thomas Letson — Lewis D. Hardenbergh
George G. Nevius — Henry Van Liew
Jacob Wyckoff — George Boice, Jr.
†David Fine

APPENDIX.

ELDERS.	DEACONS.	ELDERS.	DEACONS.

FEBRUARY 14, 1834.

*John Stothoff	Henry Schenck	Peter Wyckoff	Ralph Van Nostrand
Henry H. Schenck	John Doty	David Voorhees	Peter O. Buckelew
Abraham Suydam	Nicholas E. Baynon	Lewis Carman	James Egerton

JUNE 7, 1834.

†George Boice

FEBRUARY 9, 1835.

Powell Dehart	John W. Brunson
Lewis Carman	James Garretson
Richard Duryea, Jr.	Cornelius L. Hardenbergh

FEBRUARY 1, 1836.

*George Boice	Jacob T. B. Skillman
David Fine	David Voorhes, Jr.
Nicholas Booraem	John Degraw
	†Peter Buckelew

FEBRUARY 13, 1837.

Henry H. Schenck	Jacob H. Outcalt
Cornelius L. Hardenbergh	James I. Garretson
William Mann	Jacob A. Van Deventer

FEBRUARY 5, 1838.

Henry Van Liew	*David Voorhees
George Boice, Jr.	John Doty
Henry Van Arsdale	Abraham J. Voorhees

FEBRUARY 4, 1839.

David Fine	Johnson Letson
Richard Manley	John W. Bergen
Lewis Carman	John H. Stothoff

FEBRUARY 3, 1840.

James Garretson	Richard Outcalt
Peter Wyckoff	Nich. R. Cowenhoven
Nicholas Booraem	William McDonald

FEBRUARY 9, 1841.

Jacob Wyckoff	*John H. Stothoff
John Doty	James H. Newell
Henry Hoagland	John W. Brunson

FEBRUARY 7, 1842.

Powell Dehart	Jacob Dehart
George G. Nevius	John Johnson
*James Garretson	Henry Vroom

FEBRUARY 15, 1843.

Henry H. Schenck	James Van Nuise
Richard Manley	Johnson Letson
David Fine	George Eldridge
*†Jacob Wyckoff	

FEBRUARY 7, 1844.

Richard Outcalt	Peter Wyckoff, Jr.
Peter Buckalew	Francis C. Manley
Jacob T. B. Skillman	John M. Hagaman

FEBRUARY 5, 1845.

James Garretson	William Waldron
Abraham J. Voorhees	John S. Letson
Author B. Sullivan	Lewis Applegate

FEBRUARY 4, 1846.

Powell Dehart	Robert Van Nuise
Henry Vroom	Benjamin V. Ackerman
John Doty	Stephen Voorhees

FEBRUARY 10, 1847.

Henry H. Schenck	William G. Dehart
John Johnson	James Van Nuise, Jr.
John W. Brunson	Isaac Voorhees

FEBRUARY 2, 1848.

FEBRUARY 7, 1849.

Nicholas Booraem	Cornelius Van Neste
David Fine	John A. Manley
William Waldron	David Cole

FEBRUARY 5, 1850.

James Garretson	Jacob Outcalt
Henry Van Liew	Jesse F. Hagaman
George Eldridge	Alfred W. Mayo

FEBRUARY 5, 1851.

John Doty	James Wyckoff
‡Henry H. Schenck	Isaac Voorhees
Peter Buckelew	Lewis Applegate

MAY 7, 1851.

*‡Peter Z. Elmendorf

FEBRUARY 11, 1852.

James Conover	Martin Nevius
Johnson Letson	Peter V. Wyckoff
John W. Brunson	Stephen Voorhees

FEBRUARY 9, 1853.

John Doty	James Van Nuise, Jr.
Richard Outcalt	William G. Dehart
Cornelius Van Neste	George Ackerman

FEBRUARY 16, 1853.

†William McDonald   †Jesse F. Hagaman

FEBRUARY 4, 1854.

Abraham J. Voorhees	Ira C. Voorhees
William Waldron	Peter Wyckoff, Jr.
James Garretson	John Clark, Jr.

FEBRUARY 15, 1855.

Nicholas Booraem	John Bergen
George Eldridge	Ralph Voorhees
Henry Van Liew	Jonathan B. Connett

JANUARY 31, 1856.

John Johnson	Robert Van Nuis
Jacob Outcalt	R. V. V. Bailey
Ralph Van Nostrand	Krozen T. B. Spader

JANUARY 29, 1857.

David Voorhees	Rich'd A. Van Arsdale
Jacob H. Outcalt	Alfred B. Van Derhoef
Johnson Letson	Benjamin V. Ackerman
	*†John Bergen

FEBRUARY 11, 1858.

William McDonald	Isaac Voorhees
William Waldron	Lewis Applegate
John W. Brunson	Charles Dunham
	†John A. Manley

FEBRUARY 10, 1859.

Jacob Dehart	James H. Sillcocks
Ira C. Voorhees	George Butler
Martin Nevius	James Garretson, Jr.
	*†John A. Manley

FEBRUARY 19, 1860.

William G. Dehart	Peter V. Wyckoff
James Egerton	Abraham A. Voorhees
Peter Buckelew	Jesse F. Hagaman

APPENDIX.

ELDERS.	DEACONS.
FEBRUARY 7, 1861.	
James Garretson	Lewis Applegate
Johnson Letson	Jonathan B. Connett
David Voorhees	George V. Smith
FEBRUARY 6, 1862.	
John Bergen	Henry H. Booraem
John W. Brunson	John H. Tapping
Isaac Voorhees	John S. Dehart
FEBRUARY 5, 1863.	
John Johnson	George Buttler
John M. Hagaman	Adam Lutz
Benjamin V. Ackerman	‡John Clark, Jr.
FEBRUARY 4, 1864.	
Nicholas Booraem	Richard A. Van Arsdale
Henry Van Liew	Krozer T. B. Spader
John V. M. Wyckoff	Abm. A. Voorhees

ELDERS.	DEACONS.
FEBRUARY 2, 1865.	
Johnson Letson	David Coddington
Martin Nevius	John Brunson
Ira C. Voorhees	Henry V. D. Schenck
FEBRUARY 8, 1866.	
Isaac Voorhees	Van Marter W. Suydam
John Beekman	Gilbert S. Van Pelt
Jesse F. Hagaman	Henry K. How
	†John S. Dehart
FEBRUARY 9, 1867.	
Ferdinand S. Cortelyou	John S. Stewart
Lewis Applegate	John V. H. Van Cleef
George Buttler	Nicholas W. Parsell

VII.

MEMBERS OF THE FIRST REFORMED DUTCH CHURCH OF NEW-BRUNSWICK, N. J.

(*c* for certificate; *m* for living members; names inclosed in braces indicate husband and wife; names of ministers in small capitals.)

"THE CHURCH MEMBERS OF THE RIVER AND LAWRENCE BROOK, 1717."

Adriaen Bennet }
Angenietie }
Aart Aartsen }
Elisabit }
Isack Van Dyck }
Barbera }
Roelof Seebring }
Christyn }
Johannes Folkersen }
Angenietie }
Hendrick Bries }
Henne }
Roelof Van Voorhees }
Helena }
Laurens Wilimsic }
Saara }
Roelof Nevius }
Katalyna }

Jan Van Voorhees }
Neeltje }
Minne Van Voorhees }
Antie }
Samuel Molfort }
Maria Frelanth }
Jakobus Oukee }
Henne }
Johannes Stoothof }
Neeltje }
Abraham Bennet }
Jannitie }
Elisabit Bries }
Jakis Fontyn }
Annike }
Sluarls (Charles) Fontyn }
Helena }
Annatie Folkersen }

Jakobus Buys }
Marrietie }
Jan Aten }
Thomas Aten }
Elsie }
Thomas Davidts }
Annatie }
Heelena Hogelandt }
Willim Klaasen }
Marija }
Maregeretle Reynierse }
Thomas Bouwman }
Neeltie }
Marten Van Der Hoeve }
William Moor }
Andries Woortman }
Jannitie }
Johannes Koevert }
Jannitie }

Barbara Janse }
Niccklas Bason }
Hendrick Meesch }
Annamadeline }
Bernardus Kuetor }
Elizabeth }
Johannis Metsolaer }
Geurtie Smock }
Elizabit Smock }
Christofel Van Arsdalen }
Madaleentie }
Jakop Corse }
Adriaantie }
Katrina Boyd }
Cornelius Sudam }
Maritie }
Joris Anderse }
Jacomendie }

The above list comprises the original membership of the church, and was completed probably about August 1st, 1717. There are seventy-three names, embracing that portion of the Three Mile Run church living in the neighborhood of New-Brunswick, and favoring this enterprise.

APRIL 5, 1720.

Jacobus Schurerman
Staetje Staats, w. of
Hendrick Blauw *c*
Gillesje Van Esp, w. of
Andries Bouwman *c*

Albert Van Voorhies *c*
Arrlaentie *c*
William Tysen Van
De Rype *c*
Aaunetje

AUGUST 11, 1721.

Abraham Ouke   Cornelis Bennet
HendrickVisser(Fisher)

SEPTEMBER 20, 1728.

Peter Slegt   Roelef Voorhees, Jr.
Peter Willimsen

MAY 17, 1734.

Jan Aeten, Jr.   Catharintja Slegt
Saertie, wid. of ——
Voorhees

SEPTEMBER 20, 1736.

Jacobus Garritsen   Isaac Jansen *c*
Lemetje Volkers   Jannetje *c*

SEPTEMBER 10, 1738.

Anna Baum, wid. of Nicolas Daily
Jan De Peyster   Jannetje Wilmsen
Nicolas Groesheck   Willem Wilmsen
Johanna Corlear   Abraham Haeir
Catharina Van Emburg, Lea Range
w. of Richard Gibbs

1740.

Aeltje Van Norden, wid. Nicolas Van Dyck
of Jan La Montes *c* Josina Van Norden

APPENDIX.

August 10, 1741.

Elizabeth Daeyli — Gerhardus Baucher c
Catherina Schuyler — Maria De Peyster c
John M. Van Harlingen c — Ida Hendrickson
— Dirck Schuyler
Maria Bussing c — Isaac Van Noordstran
Hendrick Van Deursen c — Archibald Tompson - Hannah Meier
Arrientje Stants c — Susanna French
Dirck Van Vegten c — Rebecca Montangue
Maria Bedlo, wid. of Joseph Smith c — Anna Clarinson Marrietje Van Der Bilt
Anna Smith, w. of Hendrick Langeveld c — Antje Van Aersdalen Aeltje Van Aersdalen

March 29, 1744.

Jacobus Van Nuis — Elisabeth Ten Broecke,
Samuel Verbryck — w. of Dirck Van
Philip Yong — Vegten
Eva Tys

October 27, 1749.

Jan Voorhees — Elizabeth Meyer, w. of
Neeltje — Petrus Slegt
Catelzyntje, w. of Hendrick Blauw

November 9, 1750.

Peter Voorhees — Antje Deremer, w. of
Sophia Van De Boogard — Peter Stryker - Andrew Meyer
Coba Scheurman, w. of Archibald Thompson.

November 2, 1752.

Fredrick Berge c — Johannes Martinus
Gerretje c — Van Harlingen
Albert Voorhees c — Arnoldus Van Harlingen
Adrianna Van Dervoort c — Johanna Van Harlingen, w. of Gerret Voorhees
Margaritje Terhune, wid. of Henricus Van Dyck,
Marritje Van Arsdalen c — Elizabeth Deremer, w. of Abraham Vanteyn
Petrus Vredenberg
Francois Van Dyck — Trenmetje Voorhees
Johannes Schureman

April 1, 1753.

William Van Duyn — Ealtje, w. of Cornelus
His wife — Piterson
George Anderson — Antje, wid. of Hendrick Snock
Denys Van Duyn
Lena — Derrick Volkersen
Simon Van Wicklen — Lidia, w. of Cornelius
His wife — Buys
Derck Rappleyea — Peter Cowenhoven
His wife — Elizabeth
Eelje, w. of Evert Duyckin — Johanna Daely, wid. of Bernardus Begardus
Marrytje, w. of Jan Noordwyk

October 25, 1754.

Hendrick Onderdonk c — Elizabeth Oathout, w.
Antje Van Gelder, w. of Johannes Folkerse c — of Jan Ten Broek c

May 15, 1755.

Aasje Erickson, w. of Jan Van Orden c — Marytje Wyckoff, wid. of G. Garretsen

May 27, 1757.

Hendrick Van Derbilt — Lena Denyse, wid. of
Cornelius Sebering — Fredrick Van Lieuwen
Reyk Van Derbilt
Maria La Fever, w. of Johannes Vanteyn — Lebytje Bries, w. of Hendrick Fisher
William Van Deursen — Maria Ouke. w. of Abraham Heyr.
Angenitje Bennet
Catherina Tenbroek, w. of Derrick Van Alen

December 23, 1758.

Jan Misserol
Lena Vander voort

November 2, 1759.

Johannes Van Schalck c — Genietje Vredenburg, w. of Laurens Van Kamp
Aleha Bogart c
Treytje Van Wickle, w. of Francis Van Dyck — Maria Oothout
Elizabeth Van Deursen

May 14, 1763.

Gertruid Schuyler, w. of John Cochran c — Ernestus Van Harlingen.
Jannetje Stryker, wid. of Jacobus Stryker c

November 4, 1763.

John Philip Herbit c

May 8, 1764.

Cornelius Clapper

June 13, 1766.

Lucas Voorhees — Denys Van Leuwen
Neeltje Van Derbilt — Ida Wykhoff
Abraham Van Leuwen — Engelje, w. of John
Eva Ouke — Sleight

April 17, 1767.

Samuel Molfort

November, 1769.

Catlyntje Westervelt, w. of Johannes Ryder

June 28, 1770.

Jacobus Van Deventer — Magdalen, w. of Thomas Doughty
Elizabeth Springstein — Antje Van Cleef, wid. of John Wilson
Catrina Stryker, w. of William Van Deursen.
Maria Young, w. of Abraham Ouke — John Voorhees
Fredrick Oudgelt c

October 2, 1772.

Jacobus Cornel — Geertruy Schuyler, w.
Edward Van Harlingen — of Peter Voorhees
Leffert Waldron — Maria Van Derbilt, w.
Abraham Ouke — of Johannes Voorhees.
Johannes Oudgelt
Ephraim Vanteyn — Elizabeth Fisher, w. of
Johanna Stoothoff — Petrus Vredenburg
Johannes Thomson — Margaret Standley, w.
Jannetje Stryker — of Fredrick Oudgelt.
Jacobus Hassert

September 16, 1773.

Abraham Freland c — George Anderson
Lenah Ackerman c — Metje Van Wickelen
Abraham G. Ackerman c — Barent Stryker
— Elizabeth Bennet
Jannetje Romeyn c — Jannetje Voorhees, w.
— Meyer, wid. of Frans Brait — of Jacobus Cornell
John Sleght

May 8, 1779.

Peter Low — Altje Tunison, w. of Johannis Van Nest c
Janitje Van Deursen
Aaron Gilbert — Peter Vredenburgh, Jr. c
Jacobus Stryker
Maria Smyth, wid. — Margaret Schureman c
Maria Lefevre, wid. — Bernardus Gerritsen

APPENDIX.   211

JUNE 28, 1782.
Dirck Deremer   Neltje Schureman, w.
Fredrick Outgelt   of John Van Harlin-
Abraham Schuyler   gen
Aelchi Voorhees   Antje Schureman, w.
Fredrick Van Lieuw-   of Isaac Van Tyn
  nen   Neltje Schureman, wid.
Elizabeth Van Dyck   of Ferdinand Schure-
Catelyna Voorhees, w.   man
  of Matthew Egerton

            NOVEMBER 9, 1786.
Abraham Lott c   Cornelius Rappelje
Martha Stryker, wid. of   Jannetja Cornel
Albert Collyer c   Garret Voorhees
Martha Collyer c   Marretja Ditmas
Dina Hardenbergh, w.   Dina Ditmas
  of Rev. J. R. Harden-   Susanna Van Neste, w.
  bergh c   of Jeromus Rappleje
Johannes Van Neste   Elizabeth Cammel, wid.
ABRAHAM VAN HORNE,   of Charles Fonteyn
  Jr.   Arriantje Nevius

              JUNE, 1787.
Adriaen Hegemen c   Margaret Snotterly, w.
Barbara M. Teison, wid.   of Leonard Nighmas-
  of Richard Gibbs c   ter
Nela Hendrickson, w.   Ariantje Croesen, w. of
  of Johannes Buys c   William Nevius
Dennice Van Lieuw   Margareta Nevius, w.
Dina Durye   of James Renten
Peter Voorhees   Catalina, wid of Lucas
Marya Buys   Voorhees
Elizabeth Deremer, w.
  of Joseph Cilcox

            NOVEMBER 2, 1787.
John Wyckoff   Mary Van Arsdalen, w.
Fredrick Van Leuwen   of Abraham Lott
Antje Rappeljee

              JUNE 7, 1788.
Cornelius Suydam   Elizabeth Stephenson,
Rachel Collens   w. of Peter Voorhees
William Van Duyn   Martha Mount, w. of
Lena Voorhees   Jacobus Voorhees
Maria Low, w. of Peter   Annaetje Cornel, w. of
  Dumont   Cornelius Van Der-
Maria Stolts, w. of Fred-   bilt
  rick Outgelt   Rachel Collens
Ariantje Van Neste   Elizabeth Stephenson
Catalina Cornel   Martha Mount
Rachel Totten
Maria Ryder, wid. of
  Roelf Cornel

           NOVEMBER 8, 1788.
Peter Crolius c   Marya Mellger, w. of
Mary Lock c   Isaac Bennet
Tennis Rappeljee   Ida Van Derbilt
Antje Dorlants   Christeyntje Pietersen,
Ariantje Cateljou, w. of   wid. of Joris Rap-
  Roelf Cornel   peljee
Janetje Nevius, wid. of   Aaltje Rappeljee, w. of
  Ryck Van Derbilt   Hendrick Suydam

              JUNE 6, 1789.
Frances Covenhoven c   Jennetje Williamson,
Simon Probasco   w. of Cornelius Van
John Buis   Duyn
John Whitlock   Marchteltje Pieterse,
Neely Voorhees   w. of Jeromus Rap-
Peter V. Dumont   peljee
Geertje Fonteyn, w. of   Doretta Lott, w. of Jan
  David Nevius   Van Leuwen

            OCTOBER 23, 1789.
Jacobus Stryker c   Anne Hans, w. of Dirck
Sara Messelaer c   Van Arsdalen
                             Anne French

              JULY 7, 1792.
Nicolas Van Brunt c   Philip Ouke
Catherine Covenho-   Peter Ten Eyck
  ven c   Maria Suydam
Nicolas Berdine   Magdalene Messerole
Cornelus R. Wyckoff

              JULY 20, 1793.
Margarite Vredenburgh,
  w. of Andrew Powers

              MAY 3, 1794.
Jacob Rappleyee   Elizabeth, wid. of Jaco-
Joseph Silcocks   bus Gulick c
Marin, Voorhees w. of   Abraham Slover
  Jaquish Van Liew   Maria Van Liew
Ann, w. of Jacobus De-   Ann Colcher, w. of
  hart   Nich's Berdine
Elsey Van Dervoort, w.   Sarah Dehart, w. of Ru-
  of Abram Voorhees   lif Voorhees
Sarah Perine, w. of   Sarah Van Tine, w. of
  Rev. Ira Condict c   Jacobus Hegeland c
Elizabeth Trimbach c   Helena, wid. of Lucas
  w. of Stephen Van   Voorhees
  Sielen

            OCTOBER 5, 1795.
Johannah Voorhees   Mary Covenhoven, w. of
Phebe Tenike, w. of Si-   Hendrick Bergen
  mon Probasco

              MAY 2, 1795.
Simon Anderson   Catharine Van Derbilt,
Mary Van Angler   w. of Jacob Meserole
James Striker c   Benjamin Taylor c
Sarah Mesler c   Catharine ——— c

            OCTOBER 3, 1795.
George Rappleyee   Mary Covert, w. of
Jane Bergen   Abram Van Doren
Phebe Van Deveer, w.   Johannah Bennett, w.
  of John M. Voorhees   of James Perine
Mary Van Tine, w. of   Maria Farmer, w. of
  Jerome Van Este   Matthias Van Der-
Henry Outgelt   veer c
Margaret ———   Nellie, serv't of James
Henry Cock   Schureman c
Jane Gulick

              APRIL 23, 1796.
Cornelius Van Derbilt   Jacob Meserole
Cornelius Van Doren   Sarah Loop
Polly Lott   Getty Wyckoff c
Jane Van Nortwick, w.   Hilleje Van Debilt, w. of
  of John Bice c   Dennis Stryker c

            OCTOBER 22, 1796.
John Van Harlingen   Cornelius Cornel
Gertring ———   JOHN S. VREDENBURGH

            OCTOBER 22, 1796.
Sarah Taylor, w. of   Christiana, w. of Peter
  John Voorhees   Thompson
Catherine Van Deursen   Ann Thompson
Sarah Whitlock, w. of
  Daniel Brinson

              APRIL 29, 1797.
JOHN SCHUREMAN   Abraham Voorhees
Catharine, wid. of Jas.   Catharine Brown, w.
  Brown   of Phillip Oky
Mary Mount, w. of   Nancy Farmer, w. of
  John Voorhees   Jacob Berdine
Sarah Johnson, w. of   Eve Johnson, w. of Wil-
  Abram Buckeliew   liam Van Sichlen
Cornelia, serv't of Jas.
  Schureman

APPENDIX.

October 21, 1797.

John Van Devender — Benjamin Woodward
Alche Rappleyea, w. of Maria Vredenburgh, w.
John Bergen — of Matthew Sleght
Ann Spader, w. of Frederick Van Liew — Ann Van Arsdelen, wid. of Hendrick Hulick
Eve, serv't of Abram Voorhees c

April 15, 1798.

Rulif Cornel — Catharine Haviland, w. of Abram Van Tine
Frederick Outgelt } Samuel, serv't of Abm.
Abigal Voorhees } A. Voorhees
Adrien Van Nostrand }
Helena Meserol { Maria Meslar c
Ann Voorhees, wid. of Rem Garrison
Jacob Hazard Elizabeth Vacter m }
Catharine Sroby, w. of now the wid. of }
Abraham Voorhees John Williamson }
Cornelius Meslar c }
Andriantha —— c }
Christiana Giddiman, wid. of Gideon Van Campen

October 26, 1798.

Frederick Van Liew — John Nevius
Jane Striker, w. of Jane Schureman, w. of
Francis Covenhoven — Abraham Van Arsdalen
Mary Hofmer
Ceasar, serv't of Jeromus Rappleye — Sarah Nevius

May 10, 1799.

Peter Voorhees — Bernardus Rider
John Van Liew — Auttie Van Doren
Anna Voorhees, w. of Ann Smork, wid. of
Peter Vredenburgh — John Outer
Ellen Schuyler, w. of Margaret Ellis, w. of
John Clark — Wm. Van Horn

October 19, 1799.

Garret Nevius — John Demott

April 25, 1800.

John Manley } Elenor Williamson, w.
Charity Addis } of James Schureman
Lanah Van Tine, w. of Elenor Schureman
John Dunham Catharine Hude, wid.
Elizabeth Nevius of Cornelius Low
Oke Van Hanglen c
Lanah Schureman, w. of Jonathan Combs

October 10, 1800.

John Bergen — Anna, w. of John Van Liew
Lanah Voorhees, w. of
Peter Voorhees — Mary Cock, w. of Caleb
Betsey Garretson — Haviland

May 8, 1801.

Philip Pierson — Sarah Garrison, w. of
Mary Rowlin, w. of Dirck Demutt
John Nevius Temperance Tallmage,
Peter Wyckoff c } w. of Abram Ackerman
Gertrude Nevius c }
Alexand'r Rosecrans c } Scitje Nevius c
Mary Wortman c }

July 12, 1801.

Mary Baldwin, w. of Philip Pierson c

October 2, 1801.

Dinah Van Wicklen, Jane Van Van Middleswarth,
wid. of John Probasco w. of John Bennet c
Catharine Van Arsdalen, w. of John Van Nostrand
Elizabeth, w. of Martin Cozine c — Barbara Garrison, wid. of John Voorhees
Idah Garrison
Catharine Garrison

April 30, 1802.

William Nevius — Elizabeth Voorhees
Luke Knight — Hannah Hoagland, w.
Catharine, w. of Jno. of Joakim Van Arsdalen
Van Arsdalen
Abraham Van Arsdalen

October 16, 1802.

Daniel Pierson
Elizabeth Covenhoven, w. of George Rappleyea

April 29, 1803.

Mary McNeil, wid. of Creshe Van Derripe, w. of John Van Nuise
John Bennet

October 15, 1803.

Jerome Rappleyea, Jr. Cornelius Dehart
Elise Underdunck, w. of John Stotoff

May 19, 1804.

William Dehart Elizabeth Jaqnish, w.
Sarah Voorhees, w. of of Nich. Van Brunt
John Perine Johannah Striker, w. of
Anna Reynolds, w. of Martinus Stephison
Christian Van Nortwick c — Sarah Smock, w. of
Abram Voorhees

October 20, 1804.

Idah Omerman, w. of Jane Covenhoven, w.
Cornelius Dehart of Garet Nevius
Nancy Service, w. of Catharine Silcocks, w.
Isaac Hulick of Aaron Ross c

May 5, 1805.

Peter Wortman c

October 27, 1805.

Anne Houten, w. of Agnes Ackerman, w. of
Hendrick Van Dyke Daniel Pierson
Joseph and Phebe, servants of Henry Vacte c

May 10, 1806.

Richard Lupardus David Fine c }
John D. Striker c Ann Cortelyou c }

May 3, 1807.

Henry Van Arsdalen Dennis Van Liew
Willard Preston Hannah, servant of
Lidia Carle c Staats Van Deursen

October 3, 1807.

Margaret Schureman
Elenor Rue, w. of John Gordon c

May 14, 1808.

William French } George Lott
Catharine Stothoff } Jane Voorhees, w. of
Martha Vacte, wid. of Richard Manley
Jacobus Garretson

October 29, 1808.

Cornelius Bordine Garret Van Arsdalen }
Abigal Denton, w. of Alche Dehart }
Obadiah Buckelew William Hagaman c
Robert Watts c }
Ann Bell c }

May 6, 1809.

Nicolas Borum } Elizabeth Montania
Mercy Rolf } wid. of Ambrose Appleby
John H. Caile
Patience Williamson, Sarah, serv't of Samuel
w. of Joshua Martin Dunham

APPENDIX. 213

October 14, 1809.
Harriet Suydam, w. of Mary Schuyler, wid. of
 Michael Garrish *m*   Matthew Rue
Anna Voorhees, w, of Anna Breese, w. of
 Minard Wilson   Guisbert Dehart

February 5, 1810.
Henry Johnson

May 12, 1810.
Elizabeth Demott, w. Sarah Carle, w. of Wm.
 of Philip Okey   Van Doren Tunison *c*
Mary Reed, wid. of
 John Allen *c*

October 20, 1810.
Jacob J. Bergen   ⎫ Cornelius Vermule
Syche Bergen   ⎭ Elenor Van Doren
Eliza Van Harlingen, Helichy Van Arsdalen,
 w. of Uriah Lott   w. of John Nevius
Mary Thompson, w. of Jacob E. Tunison *c*
 Peter Bennett

May 1, 1811.
Robert Bronck   Peter Gordon   ⎫
Helena Van Liew, w. of Caroline Van Liew ⎬ *m*
Garret Van Liew   Mahala Everett   ⎭
Mary Kenon, w.of John Harriet Van Arsdalen,
 Williamson   widow of Rynear
Elizabeth Hulick,wid. *c* Smock *c*
Gertrude, wid. of Mar- Tone, freedman of Ry-
 tin Nevius *c*   near Smock *c*

May 16, 1812.
Thomas Letson   Lewis Carman
Garrett Parsells   George G. Nevius
Zilpah Allen, w. of Hen- Elizabeth Manley, w.
 ry Van Arsdalen   of Daniel Ellison
Richard Sluyter *c*   Harry, a person of color *c*

November 21, 1812.
Nicholas Booraem *m*   Abraham Blauvelt
Nicholas J. Marselus   Frederick Ver Mullen
Adm. D. Willon   James Ogilvie
Ann Dunn, w. of Hen-
 ry Van Nortwick

May 14, 1813.
Abigal Perrine   Abm. Brower, M.D. *c* ⎫
Ann Schureman   Elizabeth   Stouten- ⎬
                       burgh *c*   ⎭

October 2, 1813.
Peter Buckelew   Mary Outcalt
Catharine Voorhees, w.
 of Lewis Carman *m*

April 30, 1814.
Richard Manley   Elizabeth Van Liew, w.
Susan Silcocks, w. of of Joseph Van Doren
 Richard Milnes   Joseph, serv't of Thos.
Patience Ryall, wid. of Letson
 Wm. Churchward   Susan, w. of Rev. Jesse
Henry Hougland *c* ⎫ Fonda *c*
Gertrude Van Liew *c* ⎬ Margaret Johnson *c*
John Voorhees

November 9, 1814.
Jacob R. Hardenburgh Ellen Voorhees
Ellen Perrine, w. of Peter Van Liew *c*
 Guisbert Dehart   Syche Van Liew *c*
John Van Liew *c*   ⎫ Jane Probasco, w. of
Magdalena Wyckoff *c* ⎭ —— Frazee *c*
John Swartwout *c*
Hannah Solomon, w. of
 Wm. Schanck

November 11, 1814.
Ellen Emley, w. of Jo- Betty, a woman of color
 seph Silcocks   John Ludlow *c*
Mary Ann Clarkson, w. Sarah Van Derhoven,
 of Geo. G. Nevius *c* w. of William Post

April 26, 1815.
John A. Burtis   Helen Voorhees, w. of
Dowe D. Williamson ⎫ Nicholas Wyckoff
Mary Ann Abeel   ⎭ Ellen Huyler, w. of Hen-
Jane Hassart, w. of Da- ry V. Low
 vid Abeel   Mary Lawrence, w. of
Syche Boice, w. of Jon- Nathaniel McChesney
 athan Rue   Mary Buckelew, w. of
Elizabeth Meserole, w.   Peter Buckelew
 of Elijah Hunt   Sarah Manley, w. of
Rebecca Jenkins, w. of   Henry Hagaman *m*
 Wm. Low   Maria Silcocks, w. of
Elizabeth Van Horn, w.   Christian Van Doren
 of Wm. Williamson   Margaret and Hannah,
Sarah Allen   persons of color
Amos Cornell *c* ⎫   Ava Neal *c*
Mary Totten *c* ⎭   Sarah Van Doren *c*
Mary Voorhees, w. of Elizabeth Carson, w. of
 William Phillips *c* James Denton
William Schanck   Susan Evertson
Henry H. Schenck, ⎫ Alida Gansbergh *c*
 M.D. *c*   ⎭
Ellen Hardenburgh *c*

May 8, 1816.
Peter Skinkle   Frederick Van Liew ⎫
Deborah Voorhees, wid. Maria Voorhees   ⎬
 of Garret Van Der-   Ann Suydam, w. of ⎭
 veer   Stephen Mundy
Catharine Striker, w. of Ida Van Liew
 Andrew Craig   Sarah Thompson, w. of
Sarah, Mark, Dinah,   Wm. Hall *m c*
 Phebe and Caty, per- Elizabeth Thompson, w.
 sons of color   of Abm. Pittenger *c*
Cornelius Bogardus *c* Mindart Wilson *c* ⎫
John D. Sutphin *c* ⎫ Ann Voorhees *c*   ⎬
Alletta Van Doren *c* ⎭

October 25, 1816.
Cornelius Wyckoff   ⎫ Gitty Ellison, w. of Jon-
Elizabeth Van Nest   ⎭ athan Dunn *m*
Mary Dumont, w. of   Elizabeth Van Deventer,
 Samuel King   w. of Jacob Wyckoff *m*
Hannah Dunham   Sarah Van Doren
Elenor Van Liew   Rachel Baldwin, a per-
Margaret Bergen, w. of son of color
 Nathaniel Compton *c* Mary Brown,w.of Benj.
Elizabeth Arrowsmith, Taylor
 wid. of John Kells

April 25, 1817.
James Schureman   John Brown
William Benton   John Van Liew
Jacob D. Fonda   Ida Van Arsdalen, w of
Lydia Cheeseman, w.   Henry P. Van Arsda-
 of Jas. Ackerman   len
Ann Britton, w. of John Eve Voorhees, w.of Hen-
 Thorp   ry H. Schenck *m*
Eleanor Hendrickson, Lydia Freeman, w. of
 w. of Wm. Van Deur-   David Schureman
 sen   Margaret Harris, w. of
Ralph Van Nostrand   Abm. O. Voorhees
Julia Ann, w. of Caleb John C. Van Dervoort *c*
 Peckham   Maria Van Liew
Ann Stanley   Mary Oakey
Ellen Nevius   Sarah Ann Potts
Rebecca Appleby   Martha Jenkins, colored

APRIL 15, 1818.

Adrien Manley } Letitia Schenck, wid. of
Cath'rine Coverhoven } Israel Harris
John Ditmars Charity Manley, wid. of
Mary Hogeland, wid. of John Reed
John Silcox Mary Vroom, w. of Ja-
Catharine Schureman cob D. Wyckoff
Catharine Van Liew Arietta Van Arsdalen
Caroline M. Hankinson Sarah Sutphin
GABRIEL LUDLOW c Hannah, Dinah and Di-
Eleanor Schureman, w. nah, Persons of color
of C. Johnston JARED DEWING c
Abraham P. Voorhees

NOVEMBER 7, 1818.

Abraham Van Tine Jane Voorhees, w. of
Richard Van Arsdalen John H. Speer
Joanna Schuyler, w. of Hannah Lyle, w. of Ja-
Staats Van Deursen cob Richmond
Ann Degraw, w. of Nancy Hart, w. of Cor-
Amos Flagg m nelius Bergen
Mary Griggs, w. of Catharine Voorhees
Abm. Lott Susan, w. of Cæsar Rap-
Elizabeth Compton pleyen, colored
Sarah Probasco Catalina V. S. Ryley, w.
John Rawls c of Rev. John Ludlow c
JAMES B. TEN EYCK
Mary Van Brunt, w. of
Peter Garritson

APRIL 28, 1819.

Henry H. Schenck Robert Lyle
Mary Sutphin, w. of Rebecca Remer, w. of
Henry Taylor Henry Oram
Mary D. Combs, w. of Mary Marsh, w. of Dan-
William Oram iel Van Arsdalen
Sarah Taylor, w. of Jas. Ida Van Liew, w. of Hen-
Underdunck ry Demot
Eleanor Ten Eyck Eve Wedsell
Betty and Caty Smock, Ann Hopper, w. of John
persons of color Van Nortwick c
Elizabeth Monconcha,
w. of Miles Smith c

OCTOBER 29, 1819.

George Rappleyea Richard Wynkoop
Cataline Voorhees Ann Hulick, w. of Angle-
Hannah and Julia, per- burt Hartough
sons of color ISAAC M. FISHER c
SEYMOUR I. FUNCK c HERMAN B. STRYKER c
JOSEPH WILSON c CHARLES WHITEHEAD c

MAY 13, 1820.

Mary Hillyer, wid. of John Van Nortwick
Martin Nevius

NOVEMBER 25, 1820.

Eve Finley, w. of John Mary Conover, w. of Jo-
Van Horn seph Van Doren c
ABRAHAM FORT c FERDINAND VAN DER-
DOW VAN OLINDA c VEER c
SAMUEL VAN VECHTEN c William Ferry c

MAY 26, 1821.

John Stothoff } ROBERT J. BLAIR
Ida Garretson } MAURICE W. DWIGHT c
Robert Clark and Jane, Catharine Burchan, w.
his wife c of Rev. Isaac Ferris c
Elizabeth Vechte, w. of
John Williamson

NOVEMBER 10, 1821.

Phebe Bennett DAVID ABFEL, Jr
Jacob Wyckoff Sarah Conover
Nancy Seguine, wid. of Dorothy Van Liew, w. of
Cornelius Wyckoff m H. Traphagen
Susan Rowland ABRAHAM MESSLER c
JEFFERSON WYNKOOP GUSTAVUS ABEEL c
WILLIAM CRUIKSHANK c Wm. S. Dillingham c
Gertrude Harris c
Catharine L. Harden-
burgh m

APRIL 27, 1822.

Letitia Brunson, w. of Harry Quick, person of
John S. Leeson color m
Sarah Mount, w. of Gar- Catharine Moor, w. of
ret D. Stryker John Fine
Maria Jenkins

OCTOBER 20, 1822.

SAMUEL CENTER Abraham J. Voorhees }
JOHN G. TARBELL Letitia Rappleyea }
Isaac Langstaff Susan Bennett
Ann Van Nuis, w. of Elizabeth Bennett
Peter Wyckoff Maria Bergen, w. of
Maria Bordine, w. of Matthew Egerton
Archibald Thompson Ann Hassart m
Maria Ann Denton Catharine Stoothoff
Catharine S'anley Mary Van Derveer
Eliza Hutchings Mary Taylor, w. of Geo.
Rachel Voorhees A. Jenkins
Ann Oakey George Boice
Sarah Van Liew Gertrude Gordon, wid.
David Nevius, Jr of John Cox c
Isaac Fisher c }
Maria c }
Elizabeth Booraem,
wid. of Abram Van
Nostrand m

APRIL 26, 1823.

Ephraim Marcellus David Nevius, Jr.
David Nevius } Joseph Brewer
Jane Van Derveer } Garret Nevius
Ann Martin Isaac S. Brower }
Margaret Thompson, Ann Bennett }
w. of William W. Van Mary, wid. of James
Duyn Wilson
Sarah Nevius, w. of Catharine Lyle
Isaac Voorhees Henry V. De Mott
Catharine French BENJ. VAN KEUREN c

OCTOBER 19, 1823.

IRA CONDICT BOICE Caroline Hapart
Maria Van Liew m Mary Schanck, w. of
Catharine Outcalt, w. Henry Solomon
of John Voorhees Peter R. Voorhees }
Wm. W. Van Duyn Sarah Garretson }
Lanah Voorhees, w. of Caty, person of color
Dennis Van Derbilt Hannah Van Arsdalen c
ELBERT SLINGERLAND c
Hannah, Eve and Sa-
rah, colored c

JANUARY 4, 1824.

CORNELIUS C. VAN ARS- John A. Voorhees
DALEN Lanah Voorhees
Susan Boice
Margaret Cook, w. of
Abm. V. Schenck

APRIL 3, 1824.

Mary Stanbury, w. of Elizabeth, w. of William
John Hutchings Mann c
Flora, a person of color Charlotte, daughter of
Mrs.Cath'rine Herder c William Mann c
Joanna B. Abeel c Maria Conover, w. of
Joanna Hardenberg Jos. Van Doren c

JULY 3, 1824.

Elizabeth Nevius Peter Voorhees c
Mary Packer c m Cornelius Messler c }
James Stevenson c Jemima Ten Eyck c }

SEPTEMBER 28, 1824.

Lanah Van Arsdale, w. Henry V. L. Dehart
of J. Stillwell Maria Reisner
Flora, a person of color Sarah Minor, w. of Jo-
CHRIST'S Z. PAULISON c seph Hall c

APPENDIX. 215

JULY 2, 1825.

Harriet Van Vranken, Stephen Rider w. of Rev. John S. Mabon
Charlotte Andre, wid. of Wm. Suydam
Catharine S. Conover Ellen Thompson c —
Frances R. Cook, w. of Miriam, person of col. c
Rev. Jas. B. Hardenbergh c

OCTOBER 9, 1825.

Catharine R. Tice
Matilda Voorhees
Dominicus J. Stryker c
Henrietta A. Vethake m
Jane Metlar, w. of Jas. A. Van Deventer m
Ann M. Bridgen, w. of Rev. John De Witt, D.D. c

JANUARY 16, 1826.

Powell Dehart
Elizabeth Fisher
Elizabeth Bunce, w. of Stephen Strong
Ann Fisher, w. of Lawrence Fisher m
Elizabeth Stephens, wid. of Jacob E. Tunison
BENJ. B. WESTFALL C
Cornelia, w. of Rev. Dr. Woodhull c
Margaret Steele, w. of Rev. Philip Milldollar, D.D. c
Mrs. Davis c
William Mann
Susan Ann Taylor
Charity Martin, w. of David Lisk
Mercy Dunn, w. of Fred. H. Outenle
HENRY HERMANCE c
William Sunderland c
Leah Powelson c

APRIL 16, 1826.

Abm. V. Thompson
Nelly, wid. of Jerome Van Derbilt
Elizabeth Stanley, w. of Peter Obert
Thomas, svt. of Henry Veghte
Maria Broach, w. of Samuel Thomas c
ALEXANDER M. MANN c
Isaac G. Sillcocks c
Nancy Sebring c
Henry Vroom c
Mary Pierson, wid. of Ephm. P. Dunn
Letitia Rowland, wid. of John Whitlock
Providence Runyon, w. of George Boice
Jacob Davies c
Mary Holford c
John J. Powelson c
Maria Dehart c
Abraham Suydam c
Hager Calder, person of color c

JULY 29, 1826.

Catharine Van Nordstrand, w. of A. V. Thompson m
Catharine, w. of Jasper Provost
James J. Garretsen c
Elsie Wortman c
Dinah, svt. of Henry Veghte
JAMES DEMAREST c
Mary Schoonmaker c
Elizabeth French, wid. of J. Van Vleet c

OCTOBER 21, 1826.

Ann Blakeney
Christina Lyle, w. of John Van Nuis m
Julia Norman, w. of Wm. V. Hardenbrook
Jane Bergen, w. of Wm. Wilson c
Harry, a man of color
Helen Snydam, w. of Aaron Bennet
Sarah Mundy, w. of Ralph Voorhees m
Mary Ann C. Wilson, w. of Rich. Duryee, Jr
Maria Arrowsmith, wid. of John Chlvis c

JANUARY 20, 1827.

Richard Duryee, Jr
Peter Serviss
Julia Ann Low
Esther Ten Brook
Sarah Ann Elberson, w. of John Pratt
Mary H. Warren, w. of Cornelius L. Hardenburgh c
Peter Backelew c
Mary Buckelew c
Sarah Van Derveer, w. of Elias Conover c
Richard Van Brunt
FREDERICK B. THOMPSON
Jane Garretson
Margaret Baird, w. of Jeremiah Van Liew
Jane Ten Brook, w. of Isaac Voorhees m
Phebe Lewis, w. of Griffeth Harriott c
Affee Harriott, woman of color c
Harry, person of color
GARRET C. SCHANCK c

APRIL 14, 1827.

John M. Hagaman m
Eliza Thompson m
Mary Ackerman
Susan Maria Griffeth, w. of Thos. B. Bell
Catharine Van Dine, wid of John Ranken
Louisa Gregory, w. of Rev. J. G. Tarbell
Dinah Voorhees, m
William Wilson c
Mary Ann, w. of Rev. John Mulligan c
Sarah Britton c
Martina Talmage c
Ann Vredenburgh c
Ralph Voorhees
Maria Harriet Stanley
Abigal Van Deventer m
Maria Van Harlingen, wid. of Abm. Dittmars
Margaret Henderson, w. of Cornelius Dehart
Sarah Willett, w. of Nicholas Booraem
Jane Van Doren, m
Cornelius Van Doren, Sen. c
Cornelius Van Doren, Jr c
Mary Brokaw c
Maria C. Vredenburgh c
Harriet Vredenburgh c

JULY 14, 1827.

Martha Hall, w. of Isaac Sillcocks
Frances Green, w. of Thos. H. Dunn
Maria Messler, w. of Peter Blew

OCTOBER 14, 1827.

Garret Van Riper
Margaret Moore, wid. of Abm. Hutchings
Magdalena Bell c
Gilbert D. Van Arsdalen
Ellen Davis, w. of Mahlon Carel
Lena Van Duyne c

JANUARY 19, 1828.

JOHN MANLEY
Catharine Van Zandt, w. of Clark Smith
Mrs. Mary Smith c
Ann Van Neste, w. of James Harriott c
Mary Ann Manley, w. of Zebulon Mount
Caty Baldwin, colored person
WILLIAM H. COOPER c

APRIL 12, 1828.

Isabella Hull, w. of Henry Sillcocks m
Abigal Sturges, w. of Corn lius Dehart m
Letitia Hassart
Magdalen Terhune, wid. of George Talmage c
Ann Maria Caldwell c
Mary Riley, col. c
Ann Bennett, w. of Wm. W. Schureman m
Phebe Hassart, wid. of Dr. Montgomery
Catharine Wyckoff
Mrs. Ann Caldwell c
Harriet Caldwell c
Elizabeth, col. c

JULY 7, 1828.

Mary Loyd, wid. of Jno. Hendrickson
JACOB ENNIS c
Alletta Wyckoff, w. of Jeremiah Voorhees
Betty Polhemus, col. c

OCTOBER 18, 1828.

RICHARD L. SCHOONMAKER
JOHN FORSYTH
Thomas Vail
Stephen Ryder c
Elizabeth English, w. of Abm. Suydam c
Henry Wyckoff
John Y. Robbins
Elizabeth G. Bell
Mrs. Mary Hampton c
Sarah Schenck, w. of Joseph Van Doren c
Frank, man of color c

JANUARY 16, 1829.

Jacob Van Arsdalen
Ann Coddington, w. of Geo. Bole, Jr. m
Henry H. Dehart c
Amelia Lott c
Francis Hampton
Jemima Barkelew, w. of John King c

APRIL 6, 1829.

Hannah Blanchard, w. of Abm. H. Meyers
Charlotte Dehart, colored person

JULY 6, 1829.

James C. Zabriskie
Mrs. Theodosia Sutphin c
Abraham Bennett c
Catharine c
JOHN CANNON VAN LIEW
Mary Hagaman c
Ralph Van Norstrand c m
Barent Voorhees c
Mary Johnson, colored person c

APPENDIX.

October 12, 1829.

Abraham V. Schenck — Henry Schenck
Cynthia Stauley, w. of ABRAHAM H. MEYERS c
Peter Packer — Rachel Mundy, w. of
Adrianna Vethake c — Daniel C. Grue
Ann Dumont, w. of Cor- Catharine S. Denice, w.
nelius Emmons — of Lewis Conover

January 12, 1830.

Betsey and Julia, co- Alletta Beekman c
lored persons — Mrs. Amy Scott c

May 30, 1830.

Mrs. Ruth Van Tine — Martha G., w. of Rev.
Matilda Manley m — J. J. Janeway. D.D. c
Samuel Crane c — William Sunderland c
Frances Richardson c — Leah Powelson c
Sarah Conover c — Joseph Quick and Nel-
Susan Fisher, w. of Pe- lie, persons of color c
ter P. Van Doren

September, 1830.

PETER DAVIS OAKEY — LEONARD RODGERS c
OSCAR H. GREGORY c — Eliza Fletcher c
Johannah Freeman,
person of color

December, 1830.

Rachel Wooden, w. of Sarah Farmer, w. of Pe-
Thomas Vail — ter O. Buckelew
Susan Cloyd, w. of Julia Henry, w. of John
James Fisher — G. Fisher
Gisbert Dehart — Joseph Breese
JOHN H. BEVIER c — ELIHU DOTY c
Catharine, wid. of Hen- PETER J. QUICK c
ry Plum c m — BENJAMIN BASSLER c

February, 1831.

Elizabeth Dehart, w. of Eliza Maria Hall, wid.
Abram Van Arsdalen — of Chas. A. Stewart
Sarah Estler, w. of John
V. N. Waycoff

September 10, 1831.

Gertrude Aberl — Sarah, wid. of Peter R.
Mary Adeline Van Wag- Voorhees
ner. w. of Rev. John Jacob A. Van Deventer
C. Van Liew — John W. Brunson
ohn Thompson — Sarah Van Tine

December 24, 1831.

Catharine Parker, w. of Cornelius Loyd
Abm. P. Provost — John C. Baldwin c
ALEXANDER H. WAR-
NER c

March 9, 1832.

Peter H. Blew — Garret V. Manley
John H. Stothoff — Sarah Ann Wyckoff, w.
John Doty — of David S. Garrigues
Rebecca Wyckoff — Deborah Van Derveer,
Eliza Williamson — w. of David Codding-
Harriet Plum — ton m
Margaret Post m — Catharine Thompson m
Eleanor V. Manley — Delilah Dunn
Margaret H. Buckalew — Margaret G. Harriott
Helen Maria Wyckoff — Sarah E. Manley
ROBERT O. CURRIE c — Eleanor Wyckoff
Wm. J. Van Arsdalen — Abigal Van Derveer

June 16, 1832.

Ann Graham c — Mary Snowdan, w. of
Rebecca Parker c — Rev. S. B. How, D.D.
William W. Perrine c — c
Sarah Voorhees c

September 8, 1832.

John Degraw — Peter V. Degraw
Cornelius L. Harden- Elizabeth J. Conover
bergh — William E. Conover
Jacob Dehart m — Henry Van Liew m
Nathan F. Denton — Ann Eliza White m
Mary Cheesman, wid. Jane Fletcher
of Rich. White — Mary Voorhees, wid. of
Elizabeth Degraw — Garret Thompson
Jane Cox, wid. of Peter Dominicus J. Stryker c
Suydam — CHARLES E. FORD c
Lewis D. Harden-
bergh c
Ellen Voorhees c

December 8, 1832.

David Voorhees, Jr — Abraham Bergen
Ann Eliza Clarkson m — Nicholas F. Baynon
George Boice — Emma L. Hapart
Jane Van Sickell, w. of Julia A. McKnight, w.
Wm. Goodhart — of Rev. A. H. Du-
J. T. B. Skillman, M.D. — mont c
c — Alexander Gulick c
Rachael Ayres c m — WILLIAM J. POHLMAN c
Jane Tisen, wid. of Susannah Stuats c
Abm. Staats c

March 9, 1833.

John Moule — Eliza Fletcher, w. of
Fanny Jane Van Liew — — Rodgers
Mrs. Elizabeth Degraw Eliza Gulick
c — James H. Newell c
Lewis H. Terrill c — Eliza D. Hankinson c
ROBERT A. QUIN c — WILLIAM RELLEY c
Mercy Ann Manning — Caroline Green, wid. of
Anthony Voorhees, per- Samuel Degraw
son of color — JOHN F. MESICK c
James Garretson c m — HARRISON HEERMANCE c
Catharine Wortman c

September 7, 1833.

Elizabeth Harriott m — John A. Voorhees c
Joseph B. Beekman c — Catharine Outcalt c
Sarah Burniston c — Maria Buckelew c
John P. Van Arsdalen c Amanda Buckelew c
Maria Dumont, w. of June Van Doren c
Wm. Elmendorf c
Eliza Webb, w. of John
D. Hager

December 7, 1833.

Samuel O. Crane — HART E. WARING c
Ferdinand Y. Cortel- Sarah Williamson, w.
you c — of John Creed
Margaret G. Harriott c Mrs. Catharine Van
Margaret Smith Ewing, Middlesworth
wid. of Dr. Morris c Hannah M. Morris c
Ann H. Ayres, w. of JOHN WHITBECK c
Henry Van Liew c m

March 8, 1834.

Henry Solomon — Arrietta Hoagland c
Maria Voorhees m — John Pearman
Mary Ann Richmond, Ida Van Arsdalen
wid. of Dr. J. Boyd — Maria Ten Eyck m

June 7, 1834.

Ida Van Liew, w. of Rosannah Rappleyea,
Abraham J. Voorhees — person of color
Elizabeth Ann Voor- Mrs. Nancy Davis c
hees, w. of Jacob Hannah Davis c
Outcalt m — Dinah Perrine, colored
Henry Hoagland c — person c
Gertrude Van Lieu c
Jane Jackson

APPENDIX. 217

SEPTEMBER 20, 1834.
Eliza Lawrence, w. of James Van Nuise m
Phebe Musherole, wid. of Fred. Buckelew
Abraham J. Voorhees m
William McDonald
Sarah Dehart, w. of Matthew E. Bergen
Sarah Hoagland
Archibald M. Gordon m
John Voorhees, person of color

DECEMBER 13, 1834.
Eliza Williams, w. of Garret Nafey m
Alice Conover, wid. of Richd. Rappleyea
Nancy Dunham
John W. Cortelyou c }
Mary Ann Beasley c }
Anna L. Stewart, w. of John H. Stothoff
Elizabeth Gordon c m
Juliet Smith, w. of Lewis Carman, Jr
Jane Kelley, wid. of Henry Hoagland m
Mrs. Maria Hoagland
Ida Bensley c
Elmira Howard c
John Lillie c
Eve, a person of color

MARCH 7, 1835.
Jacob H. Outcalt m }
Prudence Runyon }
Syche Boice, w. of Thos. Clark c p
Mary Ann Rappleyea, w. of Nich. Lefferts
John Pray Knox c

JUNE 26, 1835.
Catharine A. Schenck
Mary Voorhees, w. of Peter Stevenson
Mrs. Mary Rightmire c
Sarah B. Egerton m
Mary Jane Tunison, w. of Jacob Dehart m
Abraham Voorhees c
Wm. Green c p

SEPTEMBER 5, 1835.
Simon H. Bergen m
Matthew E. Bergen
Eliza Degraw
Jane Hordine
Jane White, w. of John Jackson, persons of color m
Sarah Stelle, person of color
John W. Bergen
Eliza Conover, w. of Joseph Rappleyea
Hannah Ten Eyck m
Garret Van Liew
Elizabeth Van Liew c m
Aaron Van Pelt

DECEMBER 5, 1835.
Catharine Cortelyou, w. of Henry Sillcocks
Lydia Buckelew, w. of Cornelius Van Sickell m
Jane Van Arsdale c
Joanna Voorhees, w. of Voorhees Cortelyou c
CORNELIUS S. VAN SANTVOORD c
John J. Van Antwerp c
Ellen Voorhees, wid. of Eleazer Losey
Rachael Van Zandt, w. of Jonathan Provost
William H. Smith c
Gertrude Jane Voorhees c m
ISAAC P. STRYKER c
Elizabeth Van Dyke, wid. of Isaac Terhune c

MARCH 5, 1836.
Lucas H. Hoagland m
Eliza Shaddle, w. of Johnson Letson m
Susan Voorhees, person of color m
PHILLIP MILLDOLLAR BRETT c
Lydia Mount, wid. of John Buckelew
Frances Tilton
Matthew Brown c }
Garretta Quick c }

JUNE 18, 1836.
James C. Van Derbilt m
Eliza Wendover, w. of Evert Egerton
Helena Hutchinson, w. of Cornelius Provost
Cornelius Van Neste c }
Susannah L. Van Derveer c m }
Ellen Voorhees, wid. of Isaac Miller c
James Egerton m }
Phebe Conover m }
Margaret Van Norstrand m
Abraham Bergen c
Cornelia Boice
Catharine Hamilton

SEPTEMBER 3, 1836.
John M. Hoagland
Jeremiah Whitenack c }
Alletta —— c }
Martha Garretson
Henrietta Van Derveer

DECEMBER 4, 1836.
John A. Manley m
Ellen Cox, w. of Stephen Voorhees
John Johnson c
Elizabeth Vredenburgh
Ann Makel, w. of John Connelly m
Rosanna Voorhees c

MARCH 4, 1837.
Jane Voorhees, wid. of John H. Speer
Eliza Provost c

JUNE 3, 1837.
James Fisher
Richard Outcalt m
Ralph N. Perlee
Jonathan B. Stewart
William Blakeney }
Ida Ann Dehart }
George Eldridge m
Peter Vroom
John F. Cornell
Maria Fulkerson, w. of Edwd. Cunningham
Catharine Perry, w. of Dr. John Cool
Mary Voorhees Losey
Adeline Fisher
Margaret V. D. Hagaman
Lucretia Ann Van Nuis
Mary Ann Van Nuis
CHAS. S. HAGAMAN
WILLIAM S. MOORE c }
Mary Ann c }
Christopher Gifling c }
Catharine c }
Frederick Outcalt
William G. Dehart m }
Maria Schenck m }
Ezekial Miller
Henry V. Dehart
Isaiah Rolfe }
Charlotte Mead }
JAMES A. H. CORNELL
MARTIN L. SCHENCK
Mary Augusta Harris
Eliza Appleby, w. of Wm. Rhodes
Abigal Voorhees, w. of Nich. B. Dehart
Sophia Fisher
Catharine Flagg
Eliza Haviland, w. of Barent Voorhees m
Catharine Voorhees, w. of Anthony Farmer, m
Esther Baldwin, w. of Harry Freeman
Isabella Stelle
Lemmetie Lott, wid. of John Remsen c
Catharine Thompson c m
Thomas, Dinah Conover, m, and Dlow, persons of color

SEPTEMBER 1, 1837.
Adriana Nevius, w. of Lewis F. Runyon m
Ann Lappleyea, w. of Nich. R. Cowenhoven
Catharine E. Oakey
Sarah Mann
Margaret McNair, w. cf Henry V. Dehart
Catharine Meseroll
Louisa Booraem
Catharine O. Nevius
Anna Maria Garretson
Adeline Bergen, w. of Nicholas Hoagland m
Emmeline Booraem
Eveline Oakey
Johnson Letson m
PAUL D. VAN CLEEF
Peter P. Wyckoff m }
Jane Howell }
James Wyckoff }
Sarah Outcalt }
Elizabeth Parsells
Mary Ann Heard
Sarah Ann Dehart
Ida Voorhees
Elizabeth Boice
Lewis Applegate m
Theodore Dehart m
Luke Hassert
Abraham Oakey m
JOHN L. JANEWAY
Abigal Slover c v
Joanna Van Derbilt m
Joanna Van Deusen m
Getty Ann Voorhees m
Alletta Dehart m
Jane Alletta Degraw
Catharine Degraw
Amelia Miller
Eliza Jane Garret
Eliza Luce, w. of Isaac B. Van Dyke
Abigal Voorhees m
James Van Nuise, Jr
Robert Van Nuls m
Richard A. Van Arsdalen m
JOHN A. STAATS
Abraham Powelson
William R. Janeway
Elizabeth Van Norstrand m
Catharine Vleet, w. of Peter B. Meserole
Theodosia Atkinson, w. of John Nafey m
Margeret Buckelew, w. of John Connet m
Mary Ann Gifling
John S. Letson m
Jesse F. Hagaman m
Henry Van Arsdalen, Jr
William Messeroll
Louisa Runyon, w. of Nelson Boice

APPENDIX.

Eliza Freeman *c p*
Mary Eliza Reasoner *c p*
Betsey Bergen *c p*
William Hartough *c*
John Henry Ackerson *c*
Hester Bailey, wid. of
  Isaac Vredenburgh

Alice Thompson *c p*
Flora Lupardus *c p m*
Jane Ditmars *c p*
Henry Freeman *c p*
Anthony Farmer *c p m*
Peter P. Staats *c*
Catharine Voorhees *c*

September 25, 1837.

David D. Demerest   William H. Steele

December 3, 1837.

Robert Mann
Eliza Van Deursen *m*
Isabella Mann
John Outcalt
Harriet McClelland
Ann McClelland
Harriet V. Nafey
Ann Eliza Hedden
Cheesman Ackerman
Maria Bergen *c p m*
Nicholas B. Dehart

John De Witt
Rebecca Hall
Getty Hall
Nicholas R. Cowenhoven *m*
Amanda Fisher
Francis C. Manley *m*
Mary Ann Meyers *m*
Phebe Ann Voorhees
Squire Thompson *c p m*

March 3, 1838.

Sarah Sillcocks, w. of
  James Sutphin
Alletta Hall
Nicholas Booraem, Jr
William Augustus Cornell.
Abel T. Stewart
Hannah Conover *c p*

William L. Crawford
Cornelius E. Chispell
Joseph A. Cross
Maria Nevius, w. of
  Ditmars Duryea
David Neefus *c*
Lacomia Lant *c*

June 2, 1838.

Magdaline Terhune, w.
  of Isaac Boice *m*
Jane Cornell, wid. of
  Cornelius Tenbrook
Lavinia Scott, wid. of
Rev. Richd. V. Day
Abraham A. Dumont *c*
Judith Davis *c*
Hector S. Van Buren *c*
Jane —— *c*

Abraham Staats Van
  Neste
Mary Van Sickell
Peter Wyckoff *c p*
Mrs. Judith Johnson *c*
Jane Dumont *c m*
Phebe Dumont *c*
Mrs. Mary A. Van Arsdale, w. of Paul Lewis *m*

September 1, 1838.

Ann Van Sickell
William Thompson *c*

Sarah Cory, wid. of
  Enos Ayres *c*

November 24, 1838.

Betty Tunison *c p c*

March 2, 1839.

Stephen Voorhees *m*
Mary Ann Kirkpatrick,
  w. of Rev. S. B. How,
  D.D. *c m*

June 1, 1839.

Mary Ann McNair, w.
  of John Johnson *m*
Jane Voorhees
Anthony Elmendorf *c*
Maria Walker, w. of
  Cornelius Tunison *m*

Samuel Hopper
Rachel Peack, w. of
  James Esler *c*
Mrs. Harriet Plum, w.
  of Edwd. Miller *c m*

August 31, 1839.

John Johnson *m*
Elizabeth Van Middlesworth, w. of Lewis
  Applegate *m*

Jane Alletta Degraw *c*
Henry Sodon
John Newton Schultz
Eliza Degraw *c*

November 30, 1839.

Gertrude Ann Mercereau *m*

Catharine A. Degraw, w.
  of Joseph S. Suydam *c*

February 29, 1840.

Mary Booraem *m*   Matilda Rappleyea *m*

June 6, 1840.

Peter O. Buckelew
Mary Ann Thompson *c p*
Ephraim E. De Puy *c*

Cornelia C. How
Samuel Naylor *c*

September 5, 1840.

Abigal Eliza Post *m*
Philip Van Arsdalen

Sarah Booraem

December, 1840.

Ida, w. of Henry Van
  Arsdalen
Ann Duryea, w. of Jas.
  Barcalow
Abigal D. Wyckoff
Jacob Outcalt *m*
Margaret Cassiday

John Compton *c*
Syche Van Liew *c*
Wm. E. Turner *c*
Sarah Van Arsdalen,
  wid. of Richd. Van
  Nostrand *c m*

March 6, 1841.

Garret S. Wycoff *m*
Ellenor Outcalt
Lucy Miller *c p*
Robert Cleland

Huldah Matilda Carman *m*
Samuel W. Mills *c*

June 5, 1841.

Chas. R. Von Romondt
James H. Fonda
Dianah Johnson *c p*

Ruth Compton
Abigal Vroom, w. of
  Cor. Suydam *c*

September 4, 1841.

John Pierman
Ida Van Arsdalen
Mrs. Zilpah Van Arsdalen *c*
Catharine Wycoff *c p c*

Joanna Memory *c p*
Rosana Wyckoff *c p*
Mary W. Van Arsdalen *c*

December 4, 1841.

Cornelius Suydam
William Sunderland *c*
Leah Powelson *c*

William H. Van Nortwick

March 5, 1842.

William Van Horne
Sarah Johs
Sarah Mercereau *m*
Lavinia Sutphin, wid.
  of Garret Breese
Johnson Owens

William D. Buckelew
Elizabeth Gibson, w. of
  Thos. Hopper
Rebecca Van Nortwick,
  w. of Abm. Oakey
Mrs. Nighmaster *c*

May 28, 1842.

Anna Beekman
Mary Jane Dunn *m*
Catharine Van Derbilt,
  w. of John W. Bergen
Nelly Van Liew, wid. of
  Jonathan Smith *c*
James M. Compton *c*
Bergen H. Van Fleet *c*

Matthew E. Bergen *c*
Mary Parsells
Catharine Henry, w. of
  Jas. Fisher, Jr
Mary Morfit *c p m*
Mary Skillman *c p c*
A. Bruyn Hasbrouck *c*
Julia F. Ludlam *c*

September 3, 1842.

William Nelson
Mary Conover *c p*
William T. Runk *c*
Adaline S. Nelson *m*

Jane Ann Nelson *m*
John Henry Stagg
Sarah Stryker

December 3, 1842.

Abraham V. Wyckoff
Mary B. Dodd *c*

Arthur B. Sullivan *c*
Ann B. Hoagland *c m*

March 11, 1843.

Paulus Ellen, wid. of
  Dr. Launy
Isaac Voorhees *m*
Catharine Stothoff, w.
  of Powell Dehart *c*

Jane Eliza Sillcocks
Nancy Stevens *c p m*
Margaret Sullivan *c*

APPENDIX.   219

JUNE 3, 1843.
John G. Fisher   Cornelius Van Sickle
JAMES B. WILSON   Edward M. Voorhees
Eliza Bowne, w. of C.   John Van Nuis, Jr
  J. Waker *m*   Eliza Harriot, w. of Cor-
Maria Voorhees, wid.   nelius Powelson *m*
  of Frederick Outcalt.   Matilda Montfort
Susan Voorhees   Margaretta Van Dyke
Jane Voorhees   Catharine Jane Manley
Sarah C. Ackerman *m*}   Catharine Ann Manley
Virginia Plum   Peter V. Wyckoff *c m* }
Mrs. Sarah Paynter   Eliza Williamson *c m* }
Catharine Maria Payn-   *d*
  ter
           SEPTEMBER 2, 1843.
William Waldron   Benjamin V. Ackeman
Martha Dell, w. of John   *m*
  Van Nostrand *c m*

           DECEMBER 2, 1843.
Hannah Van Sickell,   Lucy Van Dyke *c p*
  w. of Joseph Brower   Catharine Maria Payn-
Sarah Paynter *c*   ter *c*

           MARCH 2, 1844.
Gertrude Solomon   Louisa Johnson
Mary Elizabeth Solo-   Catharine Van Arsdalen
  mon   Margaret S. Elmendorf
Peter Z. Elmendorf *c* } Elizabeth Elmendorf
Maria Van Vechten *c* }

           MAY 31, 1844.
Garretta Cowenhoven   Catharine Ann Powel-
  m   son
Catharine Cowenhoven   Hannah C. Corwin, w. of
Margaret McDougal, w.   Stephen Voorhees *m*
  of John Powelson   Sarah Hartough, wid. of
John C. Elmendorf   John P. Hall
Gareta Vroom, wid. of   Mrs Margaret Nevius *c*
  Peter Nevius   Ellen Nevius *c*

           AUGUST 31, 1844.
Lydia Van Dyke

           NOVEMBER 30, 1844.
Sarah Marsh *c p*   Sophia Fisher, w. of Jo-
Martha Beekman, w.   seph A. Beaver
  of John Van Dyke

           MARCH 1, 1845.
Henry H. Booraem *m* }   Betsey Simpson *c p m*
Maria Van Liew *m*   }
Margaret   Elizabeth
  Eichman, w. of Peter
  A. Van Deventer *m*

           SEPTEMBER 6, 1845.
Douglas Smith   Sarah Wyckoff Day *m*
Joanna Voorhees, w. of Jane Buice
William Nelson *m*   Grace Hudson, wid. of
Isaac Van Arsdale *c*   Horace Riley

           DECEMBER 6, 1845.
Ebenezer Poor   Elizabeth Cortelyou, w.
Jane Helena Manley   of John Ackerman *c m*
Joanna Dehart, w. of
  John Meserole *m*

           FEBRUARY 20, 1846.
Clarissa M. Gray *m*   Sarah Ford, w. of Staats
                            Clark
           JUNE 6, 1846.
James S. Taylor *c* }   Hannah Voorhees *o*
Ellen ——— *c*   }
Ann Eliza Danberry, w
  of John Nafey *c m*

           SEPTEMBER 5, 1846.
Stephen J. Voorhees   Elizabeth Harriott, w. of
                            Lewis H. Terrill *c m*.

           DECEMBER 5, 1846.
James Conover   Lavinia Jackson, w. of
                            Joseph Zabriskie *m*

           MARCH 6, 1847.
Ann Van Nostrand   Elizabeth V. N. Van
Margart Fisher, w. of   Derripe
  Squire Thompson *c m*   Afe Brown *c p c*

           OCTOBER 2, 1847.
Susan Mary Provost   Mary Cowenhoven
Maria Buckelew, w. of   DAVID COLE *c*   }
  Peter W. Van Liew *m*   Abigal D. Wyckoff *c* }
Cornelia Polhemus *c*   Abigal Davison, w. of
Ellen Polhemus *c*   Jacob Sillcocks *c*
Joseph Francis *c*   }
Sarah Ann ——— *c*   }

           DECEMBER 4, 1847.
Azariah D. Hall   Henrietta Thompson
Nancy, w. of John H.
  Hooker *c*

           MARCH 3, 1848.
Thomas McCarty   Martha V. Wilson *c*
Sarah Garretson, wid.
  of ——— Polhemus *c*

           JUNE 3, 1848.
JOHN N. JANSEN   Ralph G. Voorhees
Margaret Denton Cor-   WM. H. TEN EYCK *c*
  nell, w. of John Bor-   Catharine Ten Broeck,
  dine *m*   wid. of David Gulick
Alfred W. Mayo *c*   } Nancy Gulick
Matilda Errickson *c* }

           SEPTEMBER 2, 1848.
Ellabeth Van Sickel,   Hannah Hunt, w. of
  w. of Ralph Van Nos-   Thomas Bergen *c p*
  strand

           DECEMBER 2, 1848.
Jane Combs Ackerman   Henry K. How *c m*
Mary Smith Ackerman   Emma C., w. of J. V.
Peter Elmendorf *c*   Spader *c m*
Judith Johnson *c*   Krosen T. B. Spader *c m*
Louisa Jackson *c*   Jane Metlar, wid. of
Henry V. D. Voorhees *c*   James Van Deventer *c*
Amelia A. Letson

           MARCH 3, 1849.
Mary Ann Collins   Emma Schenck
Catharine Brown Oak-   James Waldron *c p c*
  ey

           JUNE 2, 1849.
Ann R. Holbert, w. of   Pheb: Pearsall, w. of
  Ira C, Voorhees *m*   Jarvis Wanser *m*

           SEPTEMBER 1, 1849.
Mrs. Hannah Schanck *c*   Theresa Schanck *c m*

           DECEMBER 1, 1849.
Samuel R. Walker   Caroline H. Hasbrouck
Jane G. Gulick   David Julian *c*

           MARCH 2, 1850.
Garrendeanah French,   John V. A. Parsell
  w. of Peter S. Voor-   Mrs. Shadruck
  hees *m*   Ann Wyckoff, wid. of
Henrietta Suydam, w.   Abel Sammis
  of Robert Van Nuis   George Neefus
  m   John Roberts

           JUNE 1, 1850.
Mary Ann Rappleyea,   Abby Ann Coddington
  wid. of Nicholas Lef-   PHILIP FURRECK
  ferts   Abraham B. Perlee
Matilda Rappleyea

APPENDIX.

August 31, 1850.

Martin Nevius *m* } Rovine Moore Dehart *m*
Sarah Ann Van Do- } Peter Wortman *c*
ren *m* } Maria Cortelyou *c*

November 30, 1850.

Sarah Voorhees   Eliza Schenck
Sarah Conover, w. of George Ackerman
Jacob Van Dyke   Matilda Van Liew, wid.
William W. Letson   of Daniel Disborough *c*
Mary S. Hillyer *c m*   Cath. Disborough *c m*

March 1, 1851.

John Clark, Jr.   Sylia B. Hooker, w. of
Sarah A. Hooker *n*   Joseph A. Beavers *m*
Catharine V. Thomp- Mary Ann Hooker
son *c r*

May 31, 1851.

Cornelia J. Stults   Cornelius Cornell *c*
Louisa Booraem, wid. Mrs. Margaret Smith *c*
of Rev. Jacob Book- Abraham B. Perlee *c*
staver *c m*   Diana Voorhees *c p c*

September 6, 1851.

Jane E. Parsell *m*   Frederick Van Dyke
Rosina Neefus, w. of Reusellear Bailey }
Henry Lyle *c*   Eliza Westervelt *c* }

December 6, 1851.

David Coddington *m*   Hannah Kershow *c p*
Jeholakim Hartough

March 6, 1852.

Henry Sodon   Enos A. Skillman *m*
Cornelius Van Der- } Sarah Ann Morren, w.
bilt } of James Conover *m*
Rosanna Elizabeth } Sarah Jane Smith, w. of
Tunison *m* } George Neefus
Abby Eliza Buckelew   Catharine Egerton *m*
Harriet Ann Voorhees *m*

May 28, 1852.

Abby Ann Bush, w. of Alletta Jane Flagg, wid
Henry Smith *m*   of Isaac V. Van Doren
Delilah Dunn, w. of *m*
John Anderson *c m*   Myndert W. Wilson *c* }
Cornelia Polhemus *c*   Elizabeth W. —— *c* }

September 3, 1852.

Sophia Van Doren, wid. Mrs. Nancy Jennings *c*
of Staats Van Deur- Maria Reeves, w. of T.
sen   R. Thompson *c p*

December 3, 1852.

Augustus Voorhees *m*   Charles C. Guldin *c*
Sarah F. Voorhees   Ann Elizabeth Letson
Elizabeth B. Codding- Alice S. French *m*
ton   Mary B. Eichman *m*
Ann Letson, w. of John Fannie A. Price, w. of
Van Deventer *m*   J. V. A. Parsell *m*

March 4, 1853.

Ira C. Voorhees *m*   Mary Ann Boyd
Catharine L. McDo- Mary Elizabeth Hoag-
well, w. of Israel H. land *m*
Voorhees *m*   Catharine Mary Cast-
Jane Ann Ackerman   ner, w. of J. V. L.
Mary Louisa Bergen *m*   Hoagland *c m*
John Bergen *m*

June 3, 1853.

Sarah Hoagland   Jane Ditmars *c p c*
Maria Voorhees, w. of James Garretson, Jr. *m*
Augustus Voorhees Anna E. Wortman
m   Susan Veghte *c*

September 3, 1853.

Margaret Miller, w. of William G. Schultz *c* }
William Timmons *c* Margaret Voorhees *c* }
m

December 3, 1853.

Isaac Sillcocks *m* } James P. Sillcocks *m* }
Rosina Runyon *m* } Cornelia Sedam *m* }
Ellen Sedam, w. of Jo- Sarah Augusta Van Ars-
nathan Connet *m*   dale

March 3, 1854.

Almira Nevius   Moses Voorhees *c p c*
Alfred B. Van Dehoef

June 2, 1854.

Jonathan B. Connett *m* Jane Maria Powelson
Lydia A. Yates   Rosanna Randolph *c p m*
Mrs. Sarah Paynter *c*

March 9, 1855.

Robert Ralston Proud- Alexander Proudfit
fit   Christiana Voorhees, w.
Sarah Maria Outcalt   of John Van Norden
Mary Ann Outcalt, w. *m*
   of Peter J. Gulick   William Irvin *c*
Peter J. Gulick *c*   Sarah Ann Nevius *c*
Agnes McDowell, w. of Elizabeth Jane Nevius *c*
   Sam. Applegate *c m*
John D. Neefus *c* }
Mary Ann Van Do- }
ren *c* }

June 8, 1855.

Jane Connett, w. of Jane Schanck, w. of Levi
James H. Sillcocks *m*   K. Schenck

August 31, 1855.

Abraham A. Voorhees Mary Brunson
m   Sarah Lefferts, w. of
Adaline Dehart *m*   Henry L. Stebbins *c*

November 30, 1855.

Letitia Brunson   Jane Boice *c m*
Anna Coddington, wid.
   of George Boice *c m*

February 29, 1856.

David Nevius, Sen.   Emma Candice *c p*

May 30, 1856.

Nathaniel H. Van Catharine Ann Berrian,
Arsdale   w. of John Conover
Dinah Conover *c p*   Sarah Garretson, wid. of
Sarah Hoagland, wid.   Isaac Polhemus *c m*
   of E. Johnson *c m*   Magdalene Boice *c*

September 5, 1856.

Charles Dunham   Tunis Q. Hall *c m* }
Deborah Ann King, w. Susan L. Sunderland }
   Abraham Blew *c*   *c m* }
Sarah Elizabeth Sill-
cocks

December 5, 1856.

Catharine Cortelyou, Ellen Polhemus, wid.
   wid. of Thomas Dell   of Thomas Skillman,
Jane Powelson, w. of   M.D. *c m*
   Edward Christopher

February 27, 1857.

Eleanor Nelson *m*   Harriet M. Messler
Nancy Smith *c p c*   Dinah Smith *c*

June 5, 1857.

James H. Sillcocks *m*   Wilhelma V. Hoagland

APPENDIX. 221

September 4, 1857.

Elizabeth Rausch *m*

December 4, 1857.

John H. Hooker   Emily O. Hooker *m*
Elmira Bullman, w. of
H. C. Hooker

March 5, 1858.

Adaline Van Derbilt *m*   Sarah M. Dehart *m*
Eliza Ann Gordon *m*   Helen Thompson *m*
Abby Eliza Gordon *m*   Deborah P. Provost
Cornelia H. Gordon   Ann Matilda, w. of T.
Mary Jane Hoagland *m*   W. V. P. Mercereau
Mrs. Sarah Ann Sillcocks, w. of Benjamin Furman   Peter V. C. Suydam
Sarah A. Sperling
Margaret Lott *c m*
John S. Dehart *m*   Rachel Van Doren *c p c*
George V. Smith *m*
Peter Melvin Gordon *m*
J. Baay *c*

June 4, 1858.

Ida Maria Nelson *m*   Sarah L. Cowenhoven *m*
Anna Maria Skillman *m*   Abbie Louisa Jenkins *m*
Eliza Jane Bodine   Jane Maria Jenkins, w. of John Y. Brokaw
Margaret Ryder, w. of Lucretia Ann Wyckoff,
John Ackerman *m*   w. of Edward Tunison *m*
Mary Elizabeth Wyckoff *m*   Hannah A. Fisher *m*
Augusta McDonald *m*   Getty Ann Manley, w. of
Edward F. Randolph *m*   Matthew E. Bergen *m*
Caroline Remsen   Elizabeth Smith, w. of John Verbrycke *m*
John Van Arsdale   George Buttler *m*
Henry V. D. Schenk   Rynear V. N. Quick
Richard Garretson   Gilbert S. Van Pelt *m*
Maria Elizabeth, wid. of Henry H. Van Amburgh *m*
Dr. G. A. Van Dyke *c*
Sarah Hoagland   Morel Dunham *c*
Abby Freeman, wid. of Luciuda —— *c*
Job Wells *m*   Abby M. Miller *m*
Rachel Francis, w. of Richard M. Whitbeck
Thomas Quick *c*

September 3, 1858.

Jane Bergen, wid. of Ezekial Vunk *m*
Simon Hillyer   Ann Louisa Hoagland
Maria Hillyer, wid. of *m*
Stephen J. Emmans   Julia Alletta Van Doren *m*
Maria Louisa Van Tine *m*

December 3, 1858.

Ann Eliza Booraem, w. of John Van Arsdale   Ann Van Liew *c*
Helen Nafey *m*
m   Jane Van Nostrand, w.
William E. S. Dehart *m*   of Andrew Ten Eyck
Elloner Ten Broeck   *m*
Skillman, wid. of Peter Van Tine *m*   John H. Tapping *m*

March 4, 1859.

Andrew Ten Eyck *m*   Mary Ann Cowenhoven
Anna Matilda Bogert   *m*
John S. Outcalt *m*

June 17, 1859.

Caroline S. Van Neste   Hannah Francis *c*
m
Matthew E. Bergen *c m*

September 2, 1859.

Elizabeth Nevius
Christiana Manning,
w. of John T. Jenkins *m*

December 2, 1859.

Martha V. Wilson *c*   John Beekman *c m*
Richard M. Beekman   Sarah E. Mauley *c m*
c m
Nathaniel Scudder *c p*

March 3, 1860.

Charles A. Richmond *m*   Elizabeth Smith, w. of
James Henry Titus *c p*   Duncan McNair *m*

June 1, 1860.

Abraham P. Provost *m*   William Whyte
Eliza W., wid. of Cornelius Shaddle   Adam Lutz *c m*

August 31, 1860.

Margaret McNair *m*   Jacob D. Wyckoff
Mary A. Marshall, w.
of Henry V. D.
Schenk *c*

December 1, 1860.

Phebe, wid. of Michael Julia Smith, w. of Re
Nevius *c m*   Willlam Cornell
Matilda Nevius, *c m*
Sarah M. Nevius *c m*

March 1, 1861.

Lydia D. Shotwell, w. Maria L. Schenck, w.
of A. M. Gordon *m*   of Isaac V. D. Williamson *c m*
Mary Alletta Wortman
c p c

August 31, 1861.

Helena V. Bergen, w.
of Henry D. Bergen
c m

November 29, 1861.

V. M. Wyckoff Suydam *m*

February 28, 1862.

Runyon R. Outcalt *m*

May 30, 1862.

Ann Crooks McNair   Ann Disborough *m*
Sarah M. Disborough, William H. Van Llew
w. of David M. Bogart *m*   *c p m*

December 5, 1862.

Mary Ann Buckelew, Richard M. Plumb
w. of George W. ley *c*
Schenck   Sarah Doremus *c*
Mrs. Elnora, w. of Rev. Amelia P. Berg *c m*
J. F. Berg, D.D. *c m* Herman C. Berg *c m*
Anna F. Berg *c*

June 5, 1863.

Abigal D. Wyckoff, w. Mary Elizabeth Cole *c*
of Rev. David Cole *c*

September 4, 1863.

Jane H. Manley, wid. of Sarah Maria Clark *m*
A. S. Bevier *c*

December 11, 1863.

Josephine Nevius *m*   John V. M. Wyckoff
Fannie H., w. of Rev.   *c m*
R. H. Steele *c m*   Anna Walters *c*
Lizzie T. Kelley, w. of Margaretta F. Clark *c m*
H. H. Van Amburgh *o m*

222   APPENDIX.

MARCH 4, 1864.

Cornelius L. Emmons *m*
Charles M. Webber *m*
Sarah M. Bergen *m*
Sarah Agnes Booksta-ver
Elizabeth Miller *m*
Mary Higgins, w. of Henry Hoagland *c m*
Adaline W. Hoagland *c m*
Mary Williamson, w. of John Brunson *c m*
Annie H. Foster, w. of T. B. Booraem *c m*
Martha B. Van Nostrand, *c m*
John Brunson *m*
Mary Elizabeth Franken, w. of K. T. B. Spader *m*
Elizabeth Van Nostrand
Eliza Evans Voorhees *m*
Ann Lott, w. of John Eldert *c*
Maria Nighmaster, w. of J. G. Taylor *c*
Sarah L. Hoagland *c m*
Letitia Brunson, wid. of Abraham Suydam *c m*
Emily Barker, w. of Abraham V. Schenck *c m*

JUNE 3, 1864.

Catharine Farmer, w. of Peter Cornell *m*
Susan D. Nevius *m*
Jane A. Wyckoff *m*
Cassie Wyckoff *m*
Cornelia Voorhees *m*
Louisa Augusta Applegate *m*
Ellen S. Clark *m*
John B. Stryker *c*
Jane Van Tine *c*
Ellen Ann Nevius, w. of E. V. T. Brunson *m*
Mrs. Martha J., w. of J. S. Debart *c m*
Abraham S. Johnson *m*
Almira J. Meyer *m*
Jemima M. Manley *m*
Abigal Maria Dehart *m*
Sarah Johnson *m*
Sarah S Voorhees *m*
Abraham Blew
Isaac Covert *c m*
Rachel Ann Smith *c m*
Mrs. Harriet Wyckoff *c*
Mrs. Caroline, w. of Otis D. Stewart *c m*
Amanda Stewart *m*

SEPTEMBER 2, 1864.

Rebecca Packer, w. of William Maloy *m*
Garret Polhemus *c m*
Cords. H. Gordon *c m*
Eliza S. Schenck, wid. of Edward Manning *m*
Oscar Johnson Jr. *c m*
Margaret Timmons, w. of Cornelius Hoagland *m*
Sarah A. Van Arsdale, w. of —— Smith *m*

DECEMBER 1, 1864.

Margaret C. Sillcocks *m*
Samuel S. Van Anglen *m*
Miss Huttie A. Foster *c*
Martha F. Hanlen *m*
Peter Brunson *m*
Abigal Voorhees, w. of N. B. Dehart *c m*

MARCH 2, 1864.

Letitia Van Arsdale *m*
Sarah Hoagland *m*
Mary P. Spangler, w. of Thomas M. Letson *c*
Cornelia Smock, w. of Robert Rowland *m*
Mary Jane, w. of Edwin Stewart *c m*

JUNE 1, 1865.

Sarah S. Bergen *m*
Margaret J. Beekman *m*
Joanna Brunson *m*
Jane Elizabeth Wyckoff *m*
Amelia Brunson *m*
Ellen V. Manley, w. of Rev. Cornelius Wyckoff *c*

AUGUST 31, 1865.

Mary Connett *m*
John C. Hall *m*
Abigal M., w. of Henry M. Price *m*
Matilda S. Hall *m*
Mrs. Mary Latcher, w. of Adam Lutz *m*

NOVEMBER 30, 1865.

Catharine L. Van Nuis, w. of J. V. H. Van Cleef *m*
Mary B. Remsen
Ellen Louisa Wyckoff
Anna C. Beekman *m*

Nicholas W. Parsell *m*
Jane D. Van Arsdale *m*
James McNair *m*
Ellen Wyckoff, w. of J. V. N. Garretson *c m*
Catharine Eliza Stryker, w. of Josiah Schenck *c m*

MARCH 1, 1866.

Ruth V. Berdine *m*
John Van Nuis, Sr. *m*
O. A. Kibbey *c m*
Catharine Stryker *c m*
James W. Van Liew *c*
John R. Cortelyou *c m*
Martha Elizabeth Manley *m*
Peter R. Boice *c m*
Sarah S. Schenck *c m*
Ferdinand F. Cortelyou *c m*
Margaret G. Harriet *c m*

MAY 31, 1866.

Mrs. Elizabeth C. Warner *m*
Mattie M. Garretson *m*
John Y. H. Van Cleef *m*
Archibald Craig Voorhees *m*
Charles H. Steele *m*
Mrs. Catharine Rappleyea *c m*
Lizzie A. Van Cleef *m*
Caroline Van Arsdale, w. of James A. Bergen *m*
Ella Garretson *m*
James C. Garretson *m*
William Skillman
Isaac S. Schenck *m*
Mary Halstead, w. of James C. Van Arsdale *c m*
Joanna Stothoff, w. of John Cortelyou *m*
Ann Augusta, w. of Garret V. Wilson *c m*

AUGUST 30, 1866.

Carrie A. Coddington *m*
Jacob E. Bookstaver *m*
Susan Van Neste *m*
Jerome H. Borden *c m*
Rebecca A. —— *c m*
Maria Schenk, w. of William H. Williamson *m*
William T. Manley *m*
Levi Levy *m*
Susan M., w. of John C. Voorhees *m*
Garret Q. Brokaw *c m*
Elizabeth Cortelyou *c m*
Mary Jane McWilliams *c m*

NOVEMBER 29, 1866.

Ephraim Van Tine Brunson *m*
Adaline Horton, w. of William Flagg *c m*
Maggie E. Ackerman, w. of William H. Aldenderph *c m*
Louisa Ackerman *c m*
Sally Dehart *c m*
Matilda Ann Stephens *c p m*
Phebe Davis *c m*
Catharine Davis *c m*
Amelia Ackerman *c m*

FEBRUARY 28, 1867.

Catharine Miller, w. of Isaac Williamson *m*
Matilda Garretson *m*
Charles D. Voorhees *m*
Frances Turnbull, wid. of James W. Van Liew *m*
Edwin Stewart *c m*
Theodore Quick *c m*
Cornelia Johnson *c m*
Catharine Burhans *c m*
Elizabeth Atkinson, wid. of J. F. Hart *m*
Abbie Voorhees *m*
Robert L. Hoagland *m*
Otis D. Stewart *m*
Mary Bulman, w. of James Nicholson *m*
Mary Lenn, w. of Prof. Jacob Cooper *m*
Sarah Clark, wid. of Rev. Anthony Elmendorf *c m*
Harriet Stryker, w. of N. D. Atkinson *c m*
Jane V., w. of John Waldron *c m*
Henry L. Elmendorf *m*

MAY 30, 1867.

Susannah B. Hoagland *m*
Julia McDonald *m*
Cornelia J. Suydam *m*
Anna Ten Eick *m*
Mary Stout *m*
Abraham P. Cox *m*
J. Newton Terrill *m*
Mercy A. Hoagland *m*
Eliza A. Beavers *m*
Gertrude Eldridge *m*
Mary E. Eldridge *m*
Catharine Rausch *m*
Frederick O. Van Deursen *m*
Sylvester G. Dehart *m*

APPENDIX.   223

Benjamin Smith *m* Stewart R. Dehart *m* Annie B. Schenck *m* Eliza F. Williams, w. of
Howard M. Van Cleef *m* Silas W. Sillcocks *m* Sarah P. Manley *c m* William E. De Hart *m*
Jacob W. Schenck *m* Chauncey P. Wheeler *m* Sarah Ann Manley, w. Hannah, wid. of Wm.
Rachel F. Dunham *m* Anna Smith *c m* of Solomon Painter McDonald
Gertrude Beekman, w. Harriet Goddard, w. of *c m*
  of Benjamin Smith *c* John R. DeMott *c m* Hannah M. Byram, w.
  m Mary F. Outcalt *c p m*   of Rev. A. McKelvey
Mary Jane Van Dour-   *c m*
  sen *c m*
                                  NOVEMBER 29, 1867.
     AUGUST 29, 1867. Sarah French, w. of Clara A. Jones *m*
Catharine Ann Outcalt, Annie H. Billis, w. of   Peter J. Suydam *m* Jeremiah V. D. Stryker
  w. of Abraham P.   Richard D. Fisher *c m* Maggie H. Suydam *m*   *m*
  Provost *m* · Gertrude F. Fisher, w. Mary Jane Suydam *m* Sarah A. Schofield *c m*
Kate Suydam *m*   of J. C. Scott *c m* Henrietta Suydam *m*

www.ingramcontent.com/pod-product-compliance
Lightning Source LLC
Chambersburg PA
CBHW021833230426
43669CB00008B/960